# Radical JESUS

## A Graphic History of Faith

Paul Buhle, EDITOR

Sabrina Jones, Gary Dumm, Nick Thorkelson, ARTISTS

**Herald Press**

Harrisonburg, Virginia
Waterloo, Ontario

**Library of Congress Cataloging-in-Publication Data**
Radical Jesus : a graphic history of faith / Paul Buhle, editor.
    pages cm
  ISBN 978-0-8361-9621-4 (pbk. : alk. paper)  1.  Church history--Comic books,
strips, etc. 2.  Christian biography--Comic books, strips, etc. 3.  Jesus Christ--Comic
books, strips, etc. 4.  Graphic novels.  I. Buhle, Paul, 1944- editor of compilation.
  BR153.R33 2013
  270--dc23
                                                          2013029179

RADICAL JESUS
Copyright © 2013 by Herald Press, Harrisonburg, Virginia 22802
            Released simultaneously in Canada by Herald Press,
            Waterloo, Ontario N2L 6H7. All rights reserved.
Library of Congress Control Number: 2013029179

International Standard Book Number: 978-0-8361-9621-4
Printed in United States of America
Illustrations by Sabrina Jones, Gary Dumm, Nick Thorkelson
Cover by Sabrina Jones

Bible text is quoted, sometimes compositely, from a variety of translations—but mostly
from the New Revised Standard Version, © 1989, Division of Christian Education of the
National Council of Churches of Christ in the United States of America.

To order or request information, please call 1-800-245-7894 in the U.S. or 1-800-631-
6535 in Canada. Or visit www.HeraldPress.com.

17 16 15 14 13        10 9 8 7 6 5 4 3 2 1

To those many Christians
who have sacrificed their lives,
across two millennia,
for the causes of peace and justice.

A MOVING EXAMPLE OF HOW COMICS CAN DO MUCH MORE THAN DAZZLE READERS WITH COLORFUL FISTICUFFS. READERS OF ALL AGES WILL FIND THEMSELVES ENTHRALLED.

— Kent Worcester, professor of political theory, Marymount Manhattan College

IN EVERY GENERATION, AMONGST EVERY PEOPLE, SOME ARISE WHO BREATHE ALOUD THE TRUTH THAT COMES THROUGH THE HOLY BREATHING-SPIRIT OF ALL LIFE. RADICALS ARE THOSE WHO NOURISH THAT ROOT. WE REMEMBER THEM, AS THIS BOOK DOES, TO EMULATE THEM.

— Rabbi Arthur Waskow, author, *Godwrestling—Round 2*

WEAVES HISTORY AND FAITH INTO THE TIMELESS NEED FOR SOCIAL STRUGGLE. HALLELUJAH!

— E. Ethelbert Miller, director, African American Resource Center, Howard University

A WORK OF FAITH, HOPE, PEACE, AND REMEMBRANCE, RENDERING THE TEACHINGS OF CHRIST AND THE INSPIRING WORKS OF HIS FOLLOWERS, ESPECIALLY THE ANABAPTISTS, IN BEAUTIFUL LANGUAGE AND MEMORABLE IMAGES.

— Bill Kauffman, author of *Ain't My America* and screenwriter of *Copperhead*

BEAUTIFUL, MULTISTYLED GRAPHIC TREATMENT OF THE RADICAL NATURE OF LIFE IN CHRIST.

— Jeffry Odell Korgen, author of *The True Cost of Low Prices* and *Wage Theft Comics*

# INTRODUCTION

The life and teachings of Jesus Christ have inspired art for two millennia, drawing upon some of the finest craftspeople in recorded history. Adaptations to comic art, however, are necessarily recent. In *Radical Jesus* you will find "the greatest story ever told" narrated, illustrated, and explored afresh in comic art and yet still rooted in the centuries-old history of illuminated text. The book has been designed with a purposeful color progression: from black and white in the first section, to a color choice reminiscent of the illuminated texts of the Middle Ages, to the full color of modern times.

The vibrant productive capacity of North American society made it a natural place for comic art, arising first in the tabloid newspapers of the 1890s and then again in the comic books of the 1930s and '40s. The traditions of religious freedom prompted a variety of approaches, ranging from the two-volume *Picture Stories from the Bible* in the 1940s to the long-running series of comic art in the Catholic magazine *Treasure Chest*, for juvenile readers. More recently, we have seen the appearance of *The Book of Genesis Illustrated*. Set against these examples, *Radical Jesus* is distinctly social and very much in the present day.

Why is Jesus "radical"? At its origins, the word radical really means "root." The radicalism of Jesus has nothing to do with men hoarding guns against the imagined threat of black helicopters, or bearded fanatics burning down schools for women. Instead, Jesus goes to the roots of assorted hatreds—not only our destructive exploitation of humanity but also our plundering of creation. All of life is endangered and we cannot afford these hatreds running rampant much longer.

*Radical Jesus* carries the saga forward from biblical days to the rich and complex history of the sixteenth century Radical Reformation, and then forward to the New World and the events of the last century. Each story, each page, bears the unique stamp of the artist, but each story is part of a whole and seamless in its own fashion.

Each page is also a work of comic art. This genre, which today is much more than a juvenile distraction, is serious art indeed. We believe that what you see in this book offers new insights, new sources of inspiration, and even new hope for a better future.

PAUL BUHLE, EDITOR

# Acknowledgments

We are profoundly grateful to Sandra and Kevin Sauder for a special fund allotted to the artists of the book, and to Sandra for her significant role in initiating and helping to conceptualize and plan this project.

We are grateful to Herald Press, most especially to the kind and careful attention given to this book throughout by our editor, Amy Gingerich. Amy and her colleagues Byron Rempel-Burkholder and Josh Byler courageously and creatively scripted some of the early parts of section 2. Similarly, Dave Wagner, a writer with an abiding interest in the cultural history of Pennsylvania, provided text for the latter part of the same section.

Laura Dumm assisted Gary Dumm at every phase of his work, but especially in the conceptualization of the layout for section 2. Many thanks to her.

Many activists helped us with our final section on faith-based resistance by sharing their experiences and providing further contacts and resources. Special thanks to Father John Doyle, Janine Carreiro, the Reverend Duane Clinker, Beth Davies-Stofka, Lew Finfer, Mary Jane Rosati, Bill Tabb, Father Ray Tetrault, George Veasey, and Camilo Viveiros.

To the many nameless others who offered their thoughts and prayers along the way, we hope that our common effort has lived up to your expectations.

8

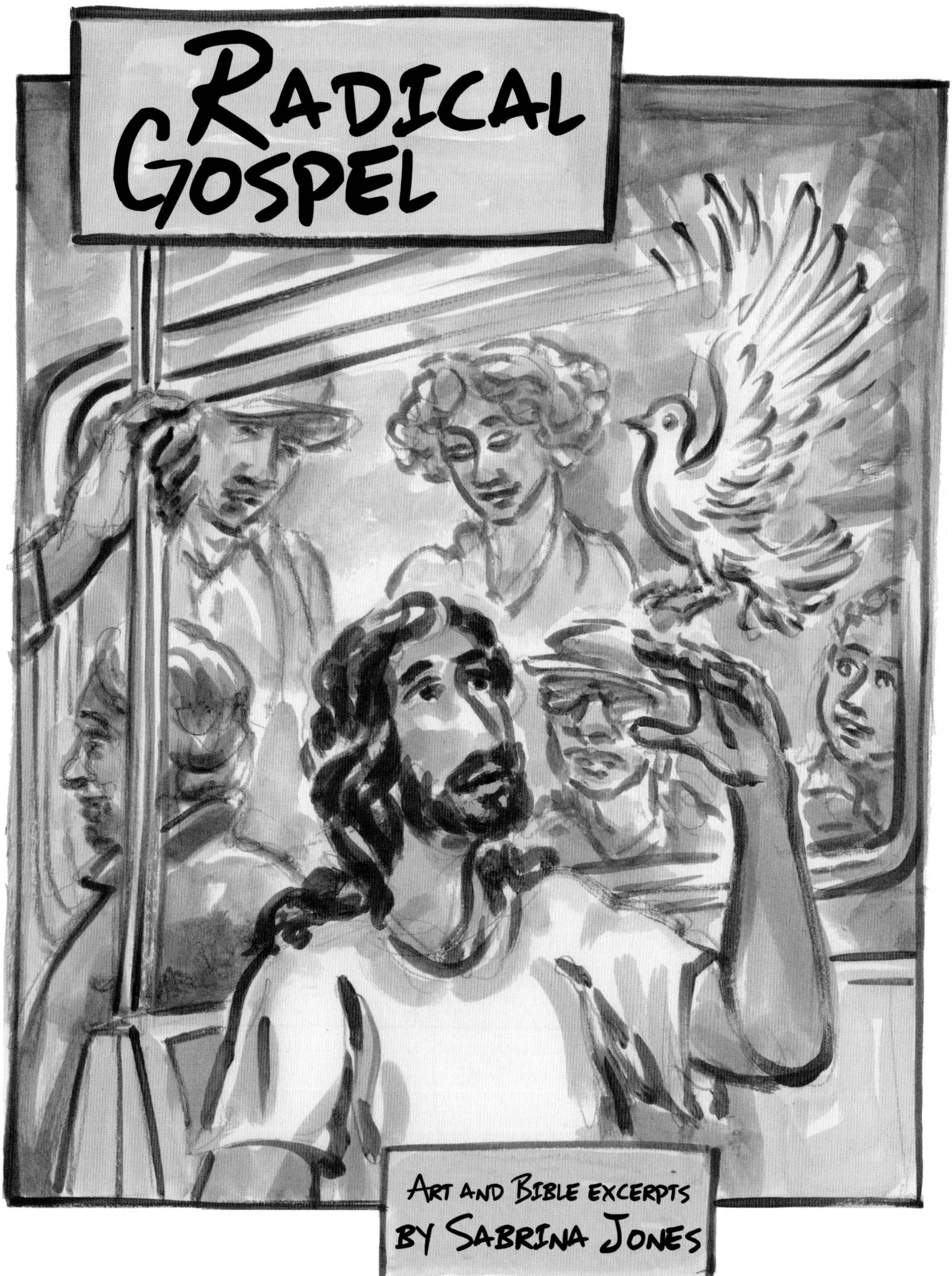
RADICAL GOSPEL
ART AND BIBLE EXCERPTS
BY SABRINA JONES

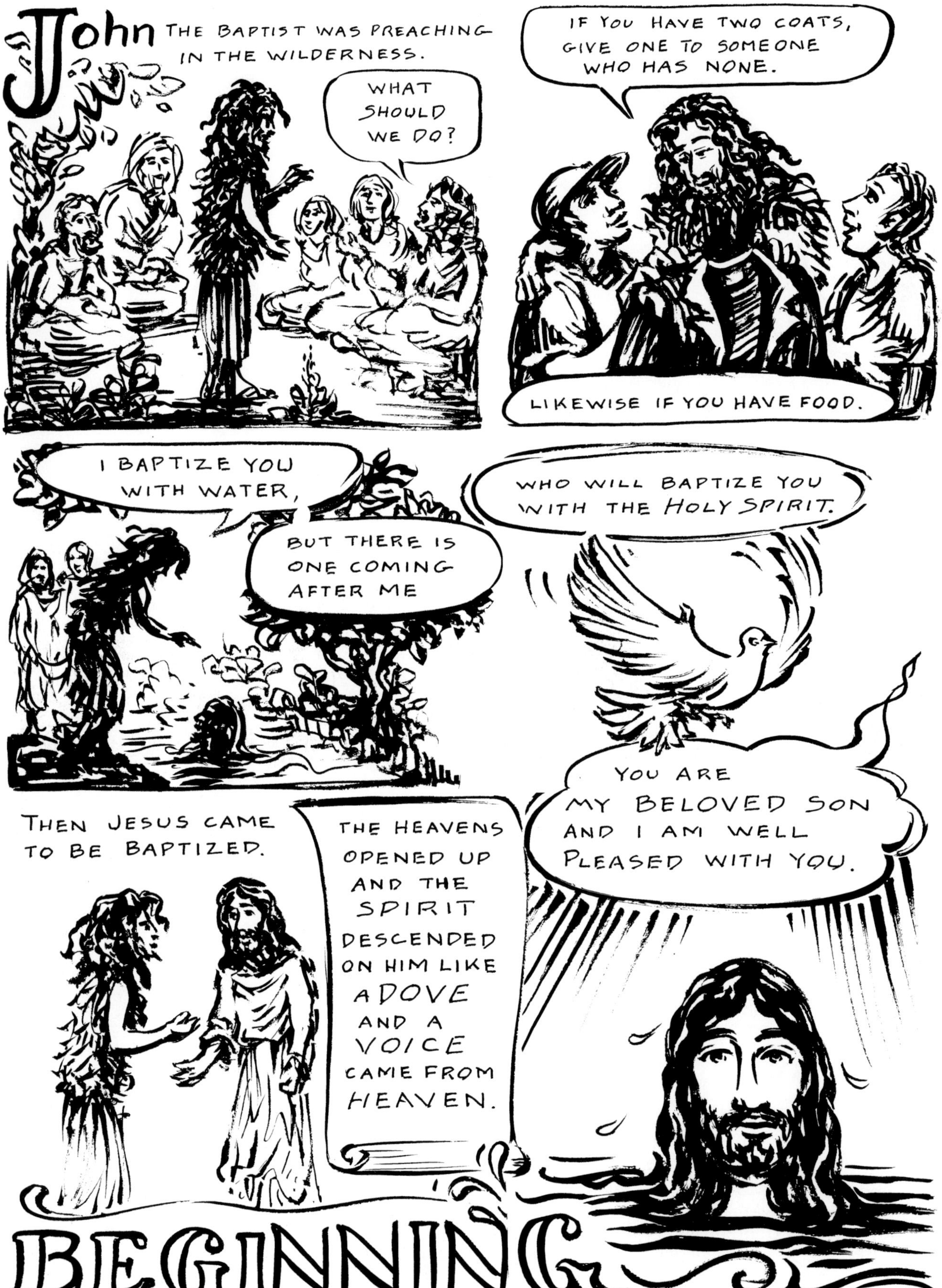
John the Baptist was preaching in the wilderness.
What should we do?
If you have two coats, give one to someone who has none.
Likewise if you have food.
I baptize you with water,
but there is one coming after me
who will baptize you with the Holy Spirit.
Then Jesus came to be baptized.
The heavens opened up and the Spirit descended on him like a dove and a voice came from heaven.
You are my beloved son and I am well pleased with you.
BEGINNING

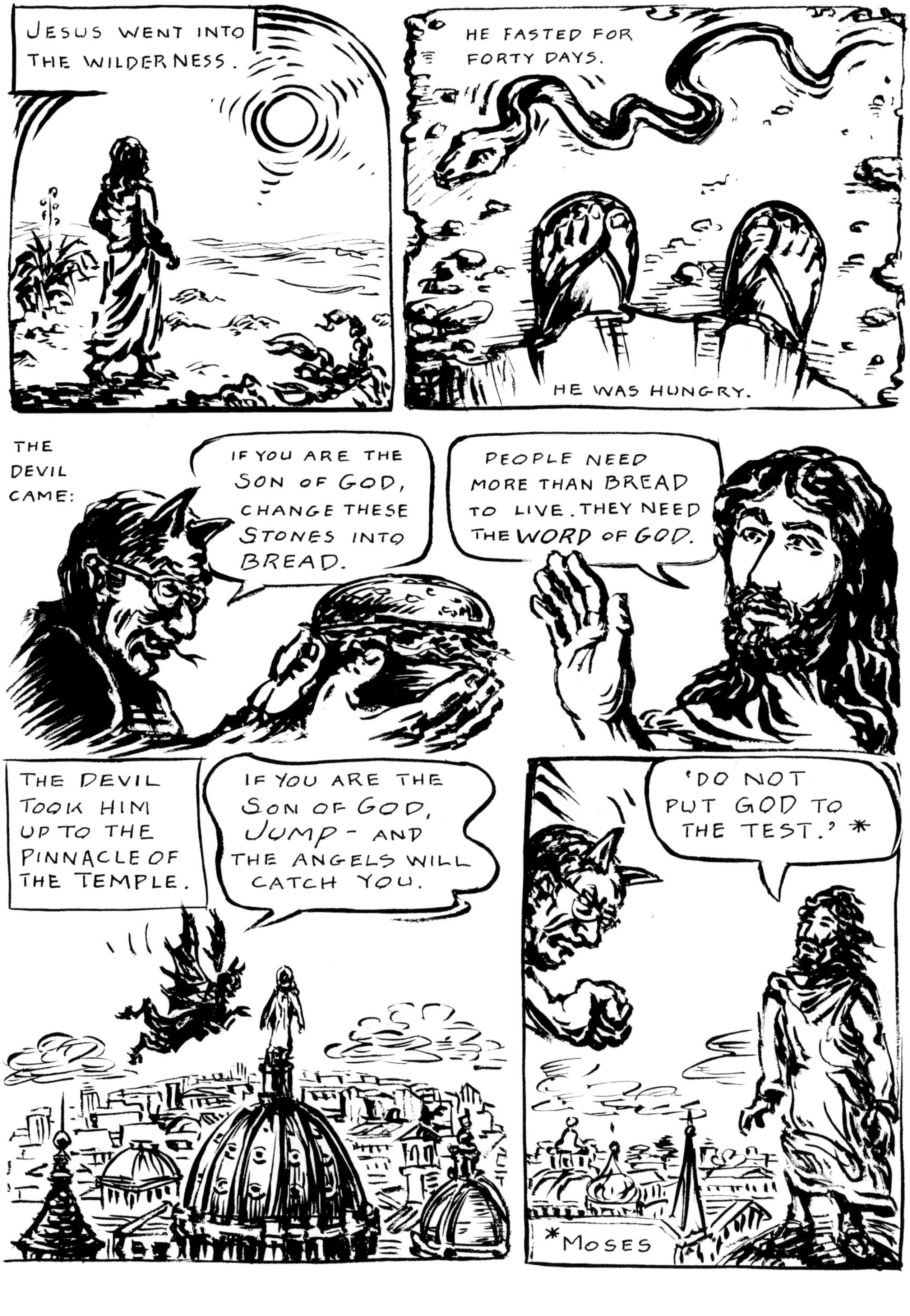
JESUS WENT INTO THE WILDERNESS.
HE FASTED FOR FORTY DAYS.
HE WAS HUNGRY.
THE DEVIL CAME:
IF YOU ARE THE SON OF GOD, CHANGE THESE STONES INTO BREAD.
PEOPLE NEED MORE THAN BREAD TO LIVE. THEY NEED THE WORD OF GOD.
THE DEVIL TOOK HIM UP TO THE PINNACLE OF THE TEMPLE.
IF YOU ARE THE SON OF GOD, JUMP - AND THE ANGELS WILL CATCH YOU.
'DO NOT PUT GOD TO THE TEST.' *
*MOSES

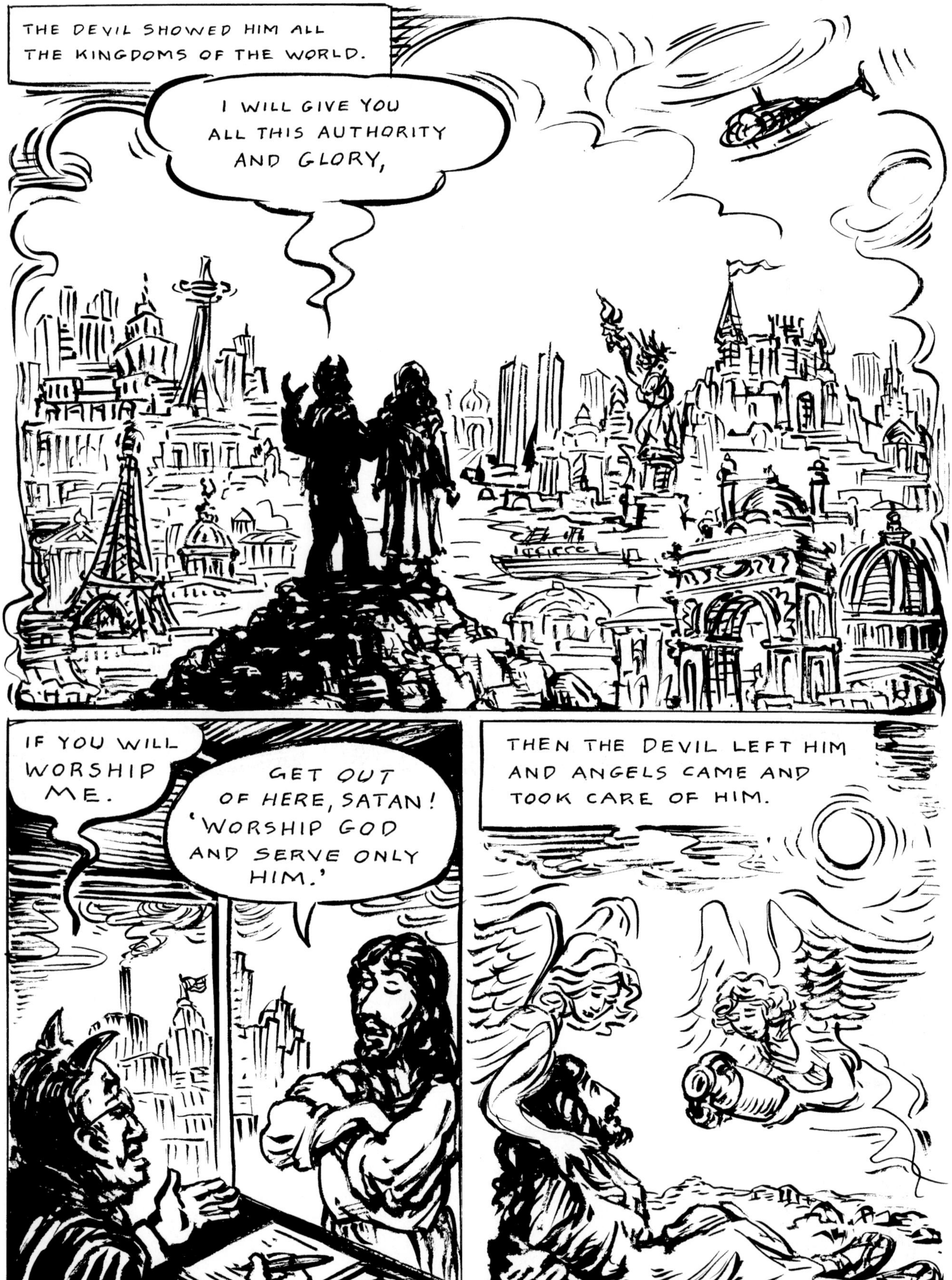
THE DEVIL SHOWED HIM ALL THE KINGDOMS OF THE WORLD.
I WILL GIVE YOU ALL THIS AUTHORITY AND GLORY,
IF YOU WILL WORSHIP ME.
GET OUT OF HERE, SATAN! 'WORSHIP GOD AND SERVE ONLY HIM.'
THEN THE DEVIL LEFT HIM AND ANGELS CAME AND TOOK CARE OF HIM.

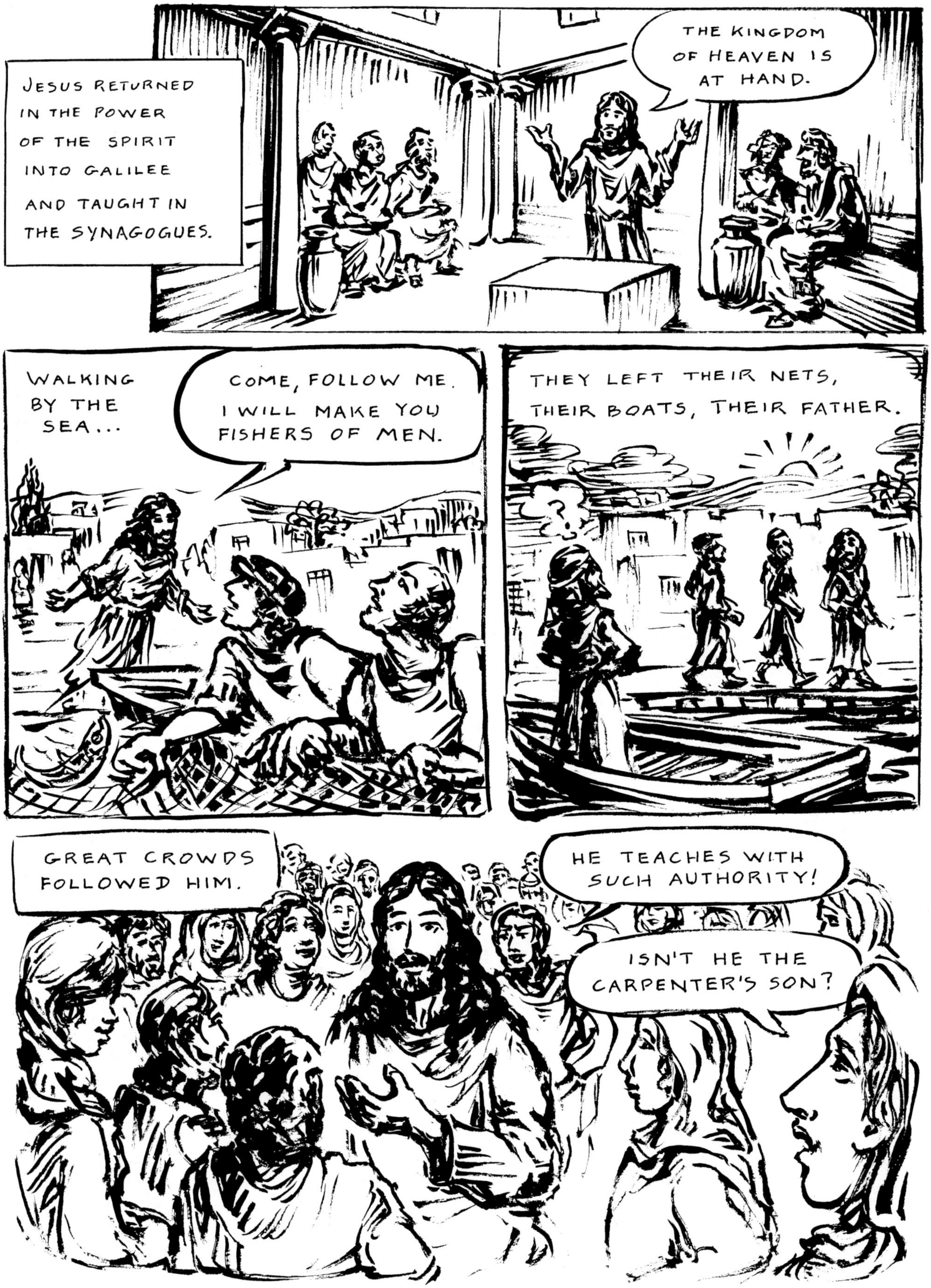
JESUS RETURNED IN THE POWER OF THE SPIRIT INTO GALILEE AND TAUGHT IN THE SYNAGOGUES.
THE KINGDOM OF HEAVEN IS AT HAND.
WALKING BY THE SEA...
COME, FOLLOW ME. I WILL MAKE YOU FISHERS OF MEN.
THEY LEFT THEIR NETS, THEIR BOATS, THEIR FATHER.
?
GREAT CROWDS FOLLOWED HIM.
HE TEACHES WITH SUCH AUTHORITY!
ISN'T HE THE CARPENTER'S SON?

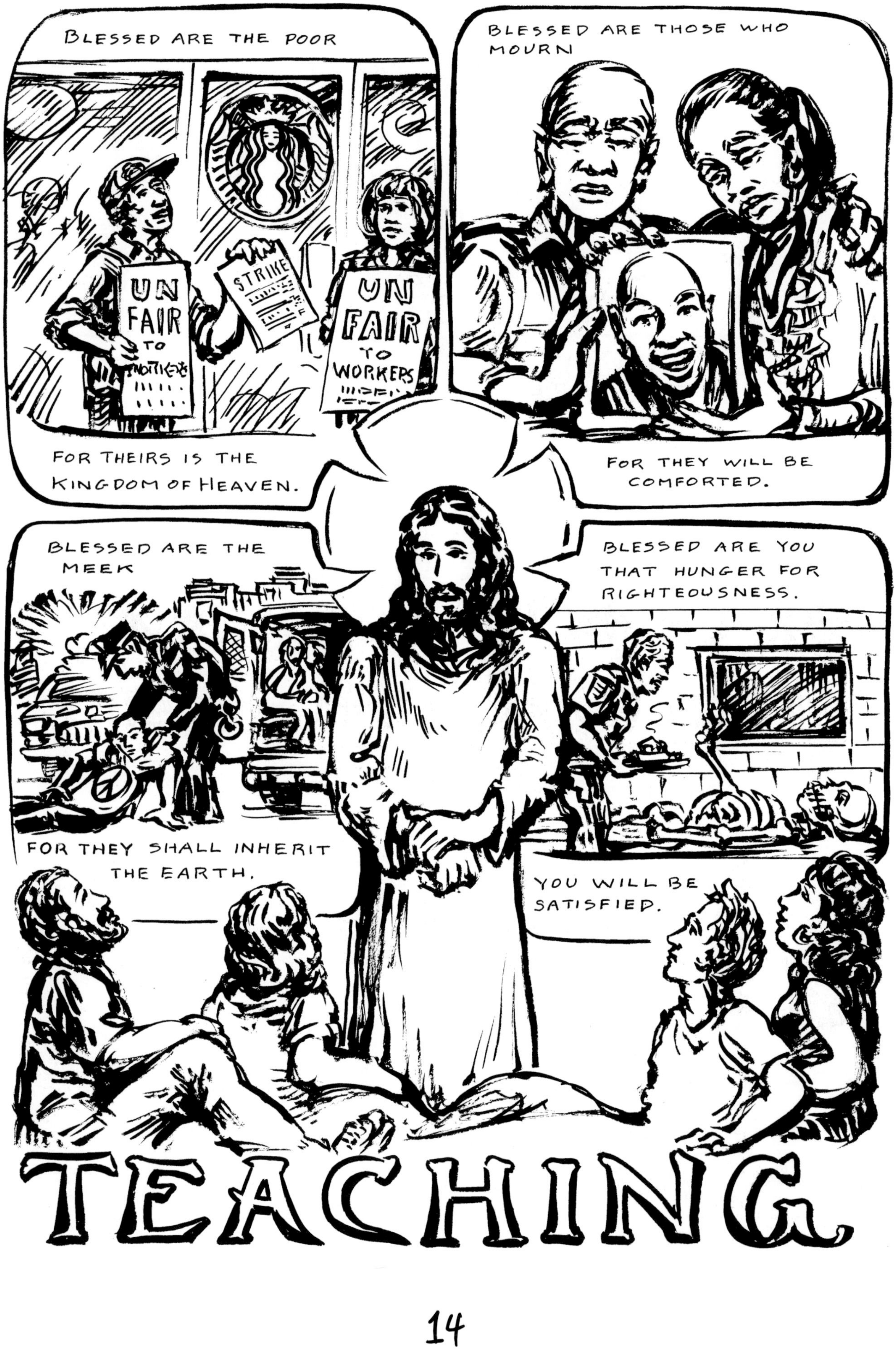
BLESSED ARE THE POOR
UN FAIR TO
STRIKE
UN FAIR TO WORKERS
FOR THEIRS IS THE KINGDOM OF HEAVEN.
BLESSED ARE THOSE WHO MOURN
FOR THEY WILL BE COMFORTED.
BLESSED ARE THE MEEK
FOR THEY SHALL INHERIT THE EARTH.
BLESSED ARE YOU THAT HUNGER FOR RIGHTEOUSNESS.
YOU WILL BE SATISFIED.

# TEACHING

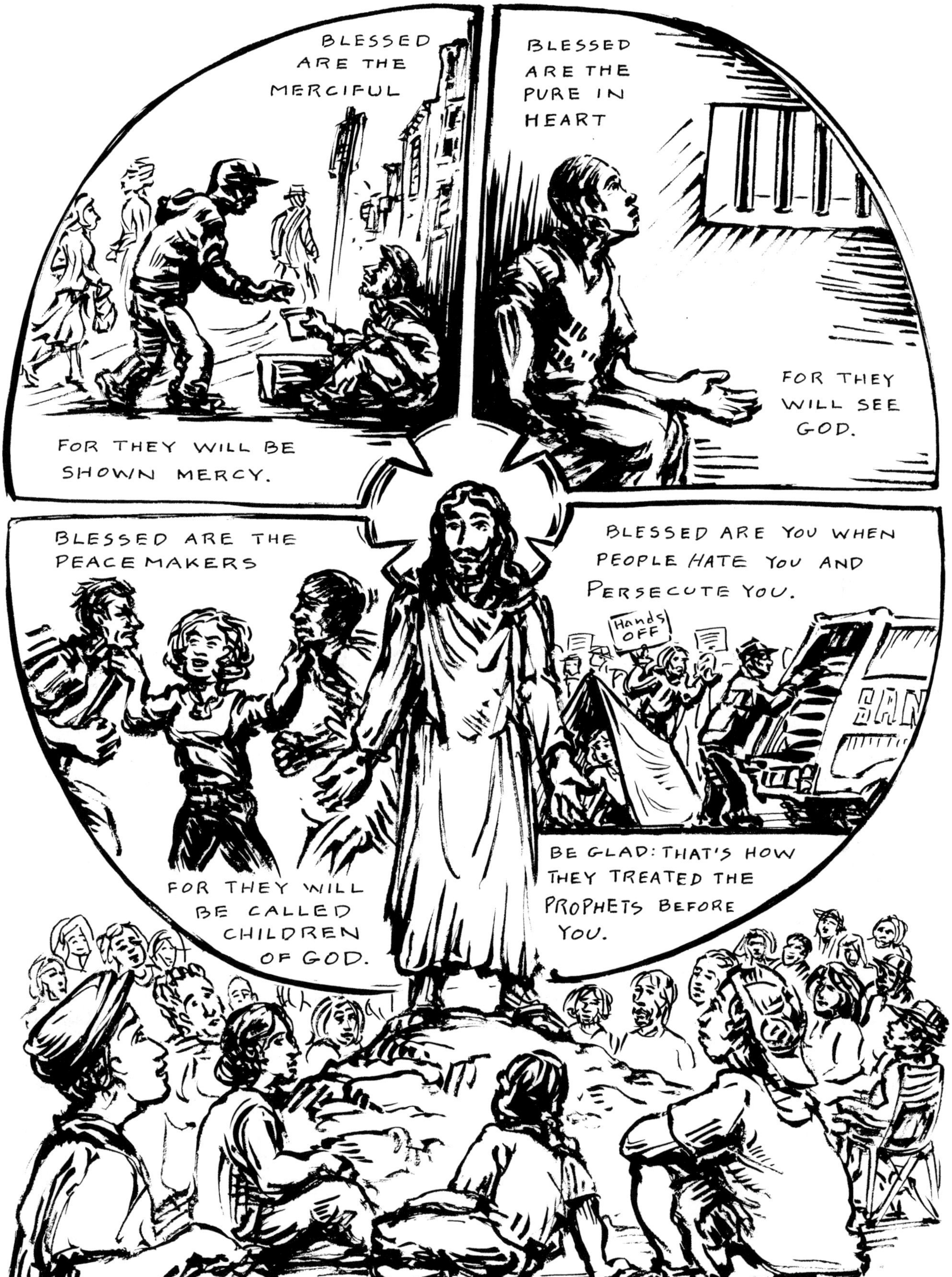
BLESSED ARE THE MERCIFUL
FOR THEY WILL BE SHOWN MERCY.
BLESSED ARE THE PURE IN HEART
FOR THEY WILL SEE GOD.
BLESSED ARE THE PEACEMAKERS
FOR THEY WILL BE CALLED CHILDREN OF GOD.
BLESSED ARE YOU WHEN PEOPLE HATE YOU AND PERSECUTE YOU.
Hands OFF
BE GLAD: THAT'S HOW THEY TREATED THE PROPHETS BEFORE YOU.

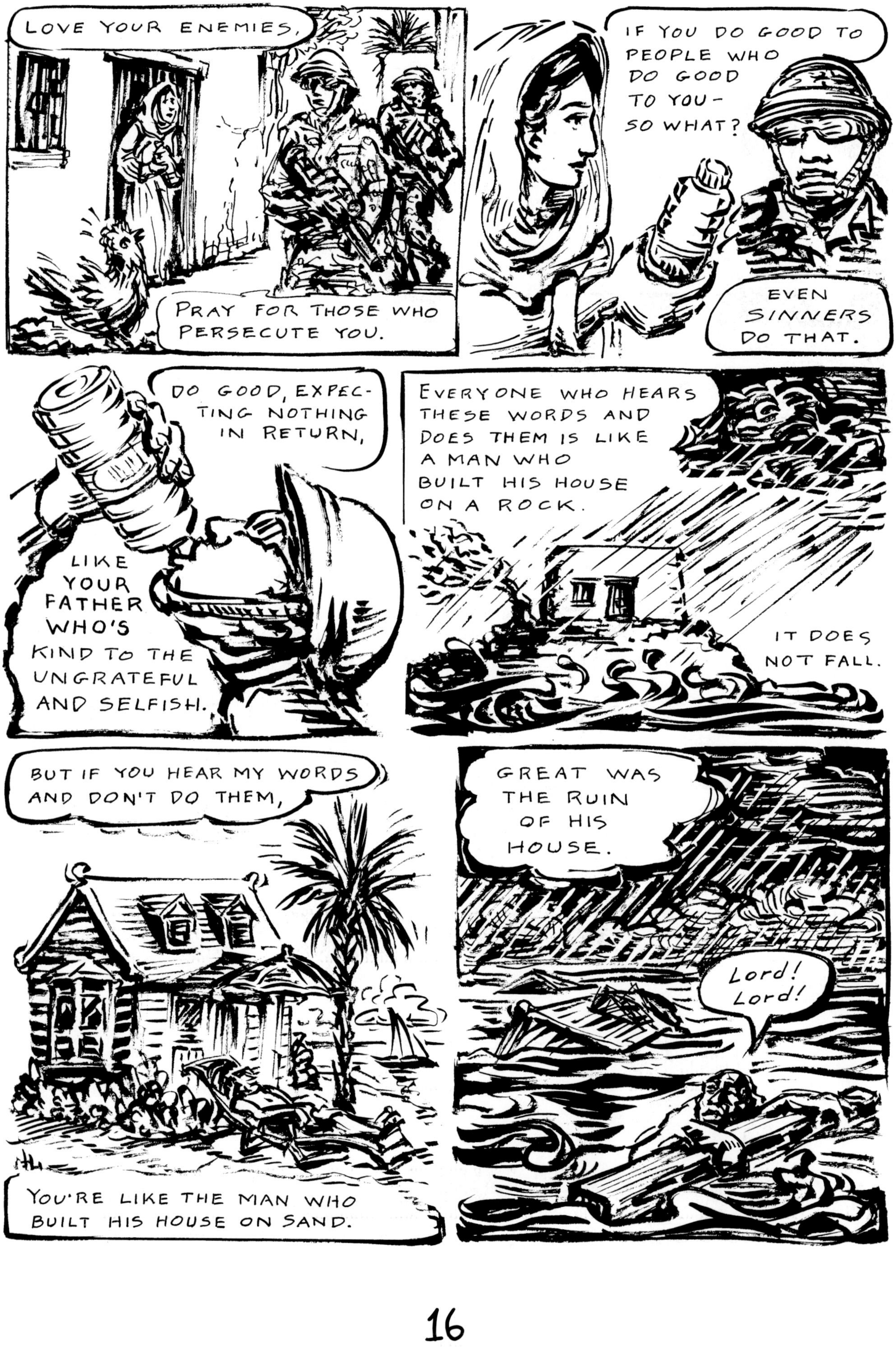
LOVE YOUR ENEMIES.
PRAY FOR THOSE WHO PERSECUTE YOU.
IF YOU DO GOOD TO PEOPLE WHO DO GOOD TO YOU- SO WHAT?
EVEN SINNERS DO THAT.
DO GOOD, EXPECTING NOTHING IN RETURN,
LIKE YOUR FATHER WHO'S KIND TO THE UNGRATEFUL AND SELFISH.
EVERYONE WHO HEARS THESE WORDS AND DOES THEM IS LIKE A MAN WHO BUILT HIS HOUSE ON A ROCK.
IT DOES NOT FALL.
BUT IF YOU HEAR MY WORDS AND DON'T DO THEM,
YOU'RE LIKE THE MAN WHO BUILT HIS HOUSE ON SAND.
GREAT WAS THE RUIN OF HIS HOUSE.
Lord! Lord!

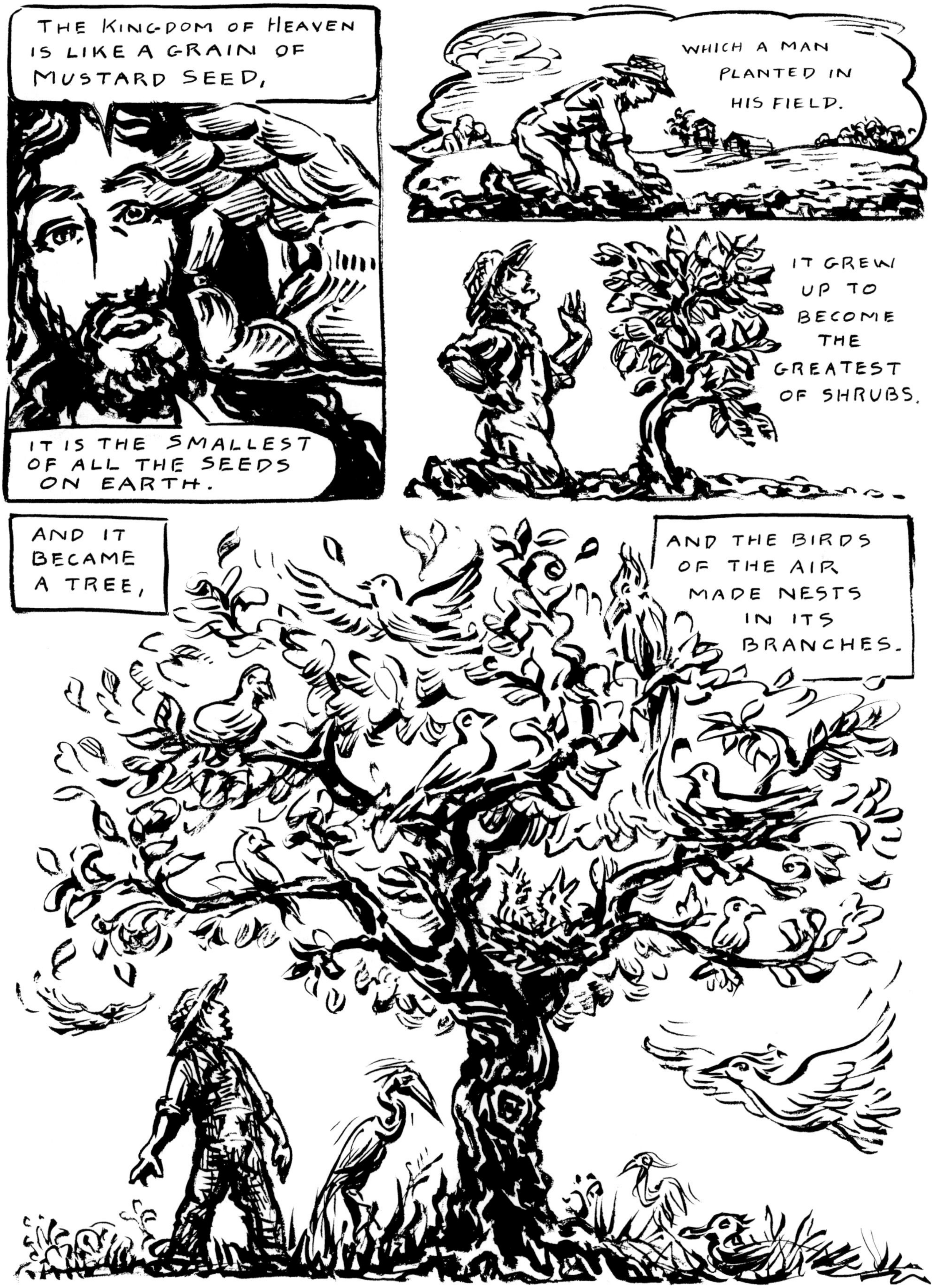
THE KINGDOM OF HEAVEN IS LIKE A GRAIN OF MUSTARD SEED,
IT IS THE SMALLEST OF ALL THE SEEDS ON EARTH.
WHICH A MAN PLANTED IN HIS FIELD.
IT GREW UP TO BECOME THE GREATEST OF SHRUBS.
AND IT BECAME A TREE,
AND THE BIRDS OF THE AIR MADE NESTS IN ITS BRANCHES.

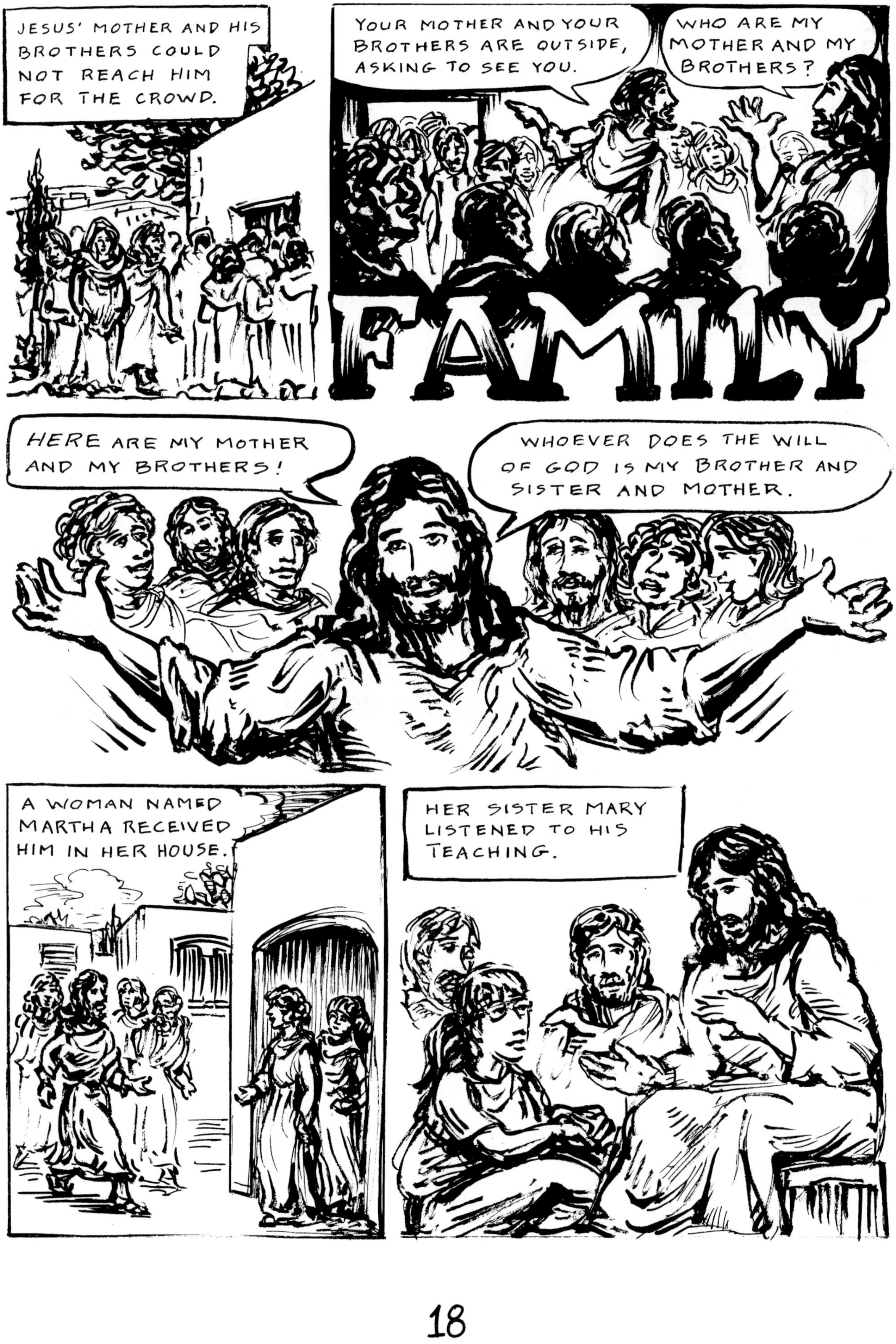
JESUS' MOTHER AND HIS BROTHERS COULD NOT REACH HIM FOR THE CROWD.
YOUR MOTHER AND YOUR BROTHERS ARE OUTSIDE, ASKING TO SEE YOU.
WHO ARE MY MOTHER AND MY BROTHERS?
FAMILY
HERE ARE MY MOTHER AND MY BROTHERS!
WHOEVER DOES THE WILL OF GOD IS MY BROTHER AND SISTER AND MOTHER.
A WOMAN NAMED MARTHA RECEIVED HIM IN HER HOUSE.
HER SISTER MARY LISTENED TO HIS TEACHING.

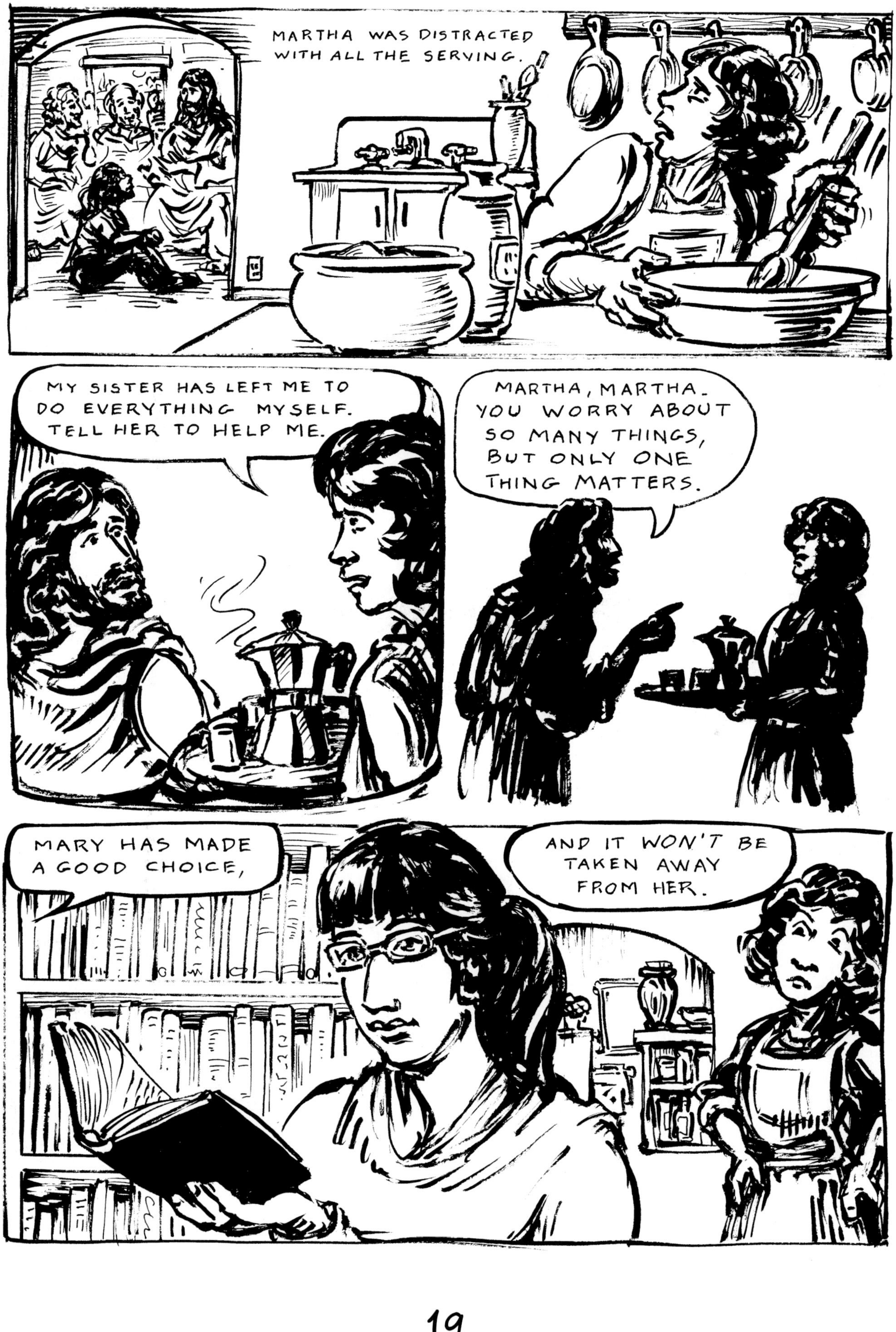
MARTHA WAS DISTRACTED WITH ALL THE SERVING.
MY SISTER HAS LEFT ME TO DO EVERYTHING MYSELF. TELL HER TO HELP ME.
MARTHA, MARTHA. YOU WORRY ABOUT SO MANY THINGS, BUT ONLY ONE THING MATTERS.
MARY HAS MADE A GOOD CHOICE,
AND IT WON'T BE TAKEN AWAY FROM HER.

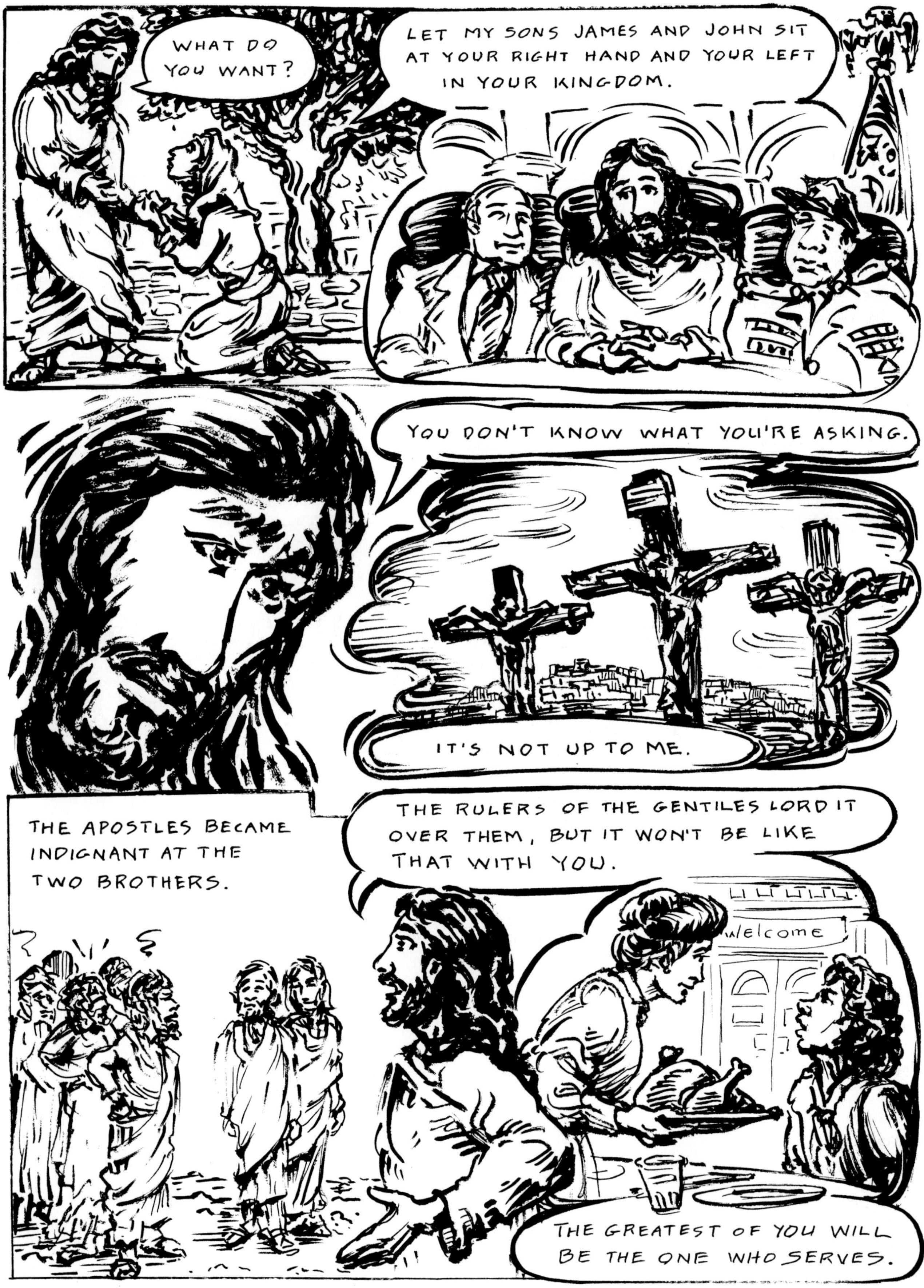
WHAT DO YOU WANT?
LET MY SONS JAMES AND JOHN SIT AT YOUR RIGHT HAND AND YOUR LEFT IN YOUR KINGDOM.
YOU DON'T KNOW WHAT YOU'RE ASKING.
IT'S NOT UP TO ME.
THE APOSTLES BECAME INDIGNANT AT THE TWO BROTHERS.
THE RULERS OF THE GENTILES LORD IT OVER THEM, BUT IT WON'T BE LIKE THAT WITH YOU.
welcome
THE GREATEST OF YOU WILL BE THE ONE WHO SERVES.

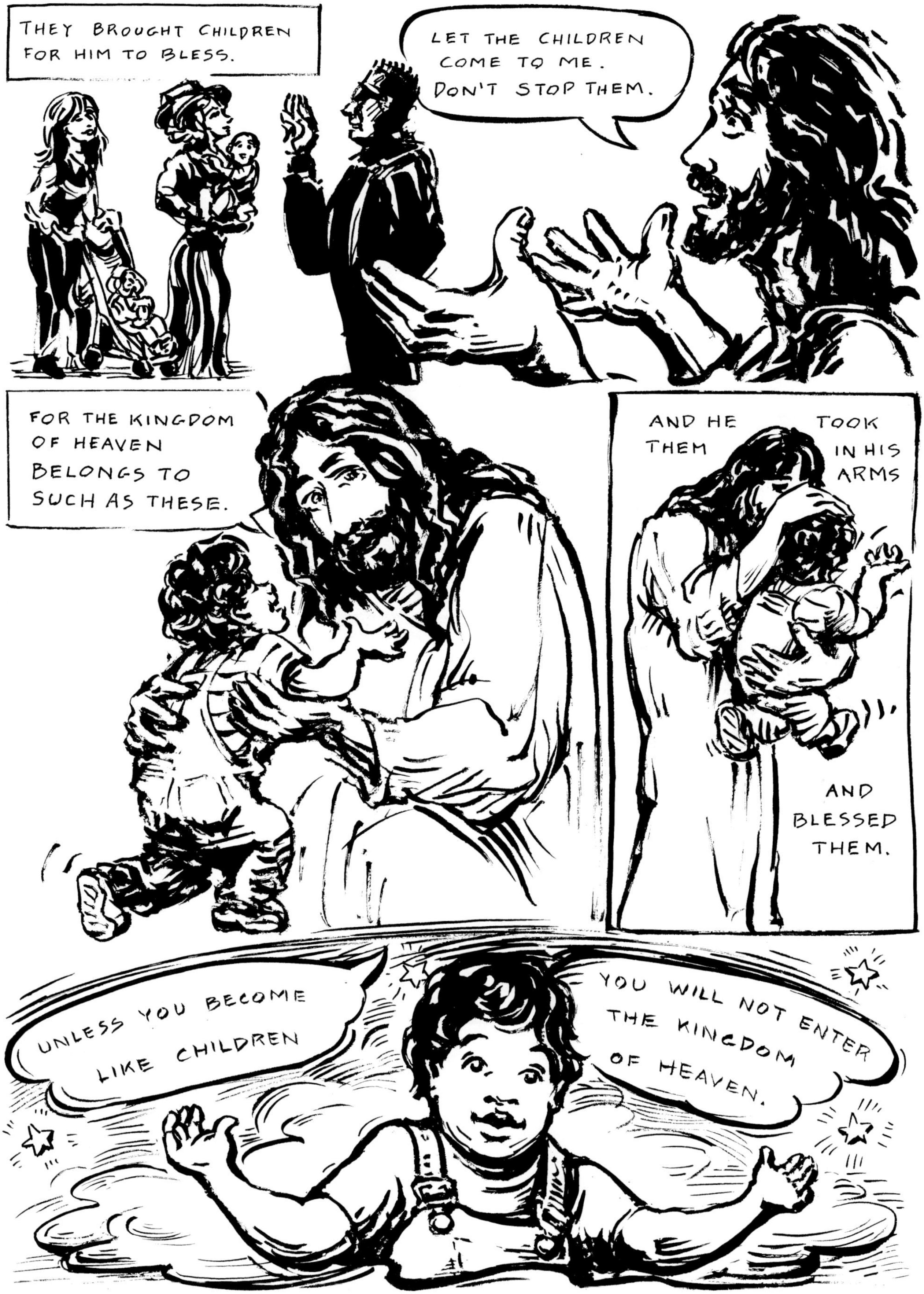
THEY BROUGHT CHILDREN FOR HIM TO BLESS.
LET THE CHILDREN COME TO ME. DON'T STOP THEM.
FOR THE KINGDOM OF HEAVEN BELONGS TO SUCH AS THESE.
AND HE TOOK THEM IN HIS ARMS
AND BLESSED THEM.
UNLESS YOU BECOME LIKE CHILDREN
YOU WILL NOT ENTER THE KINGDOM OF HEAVEN.

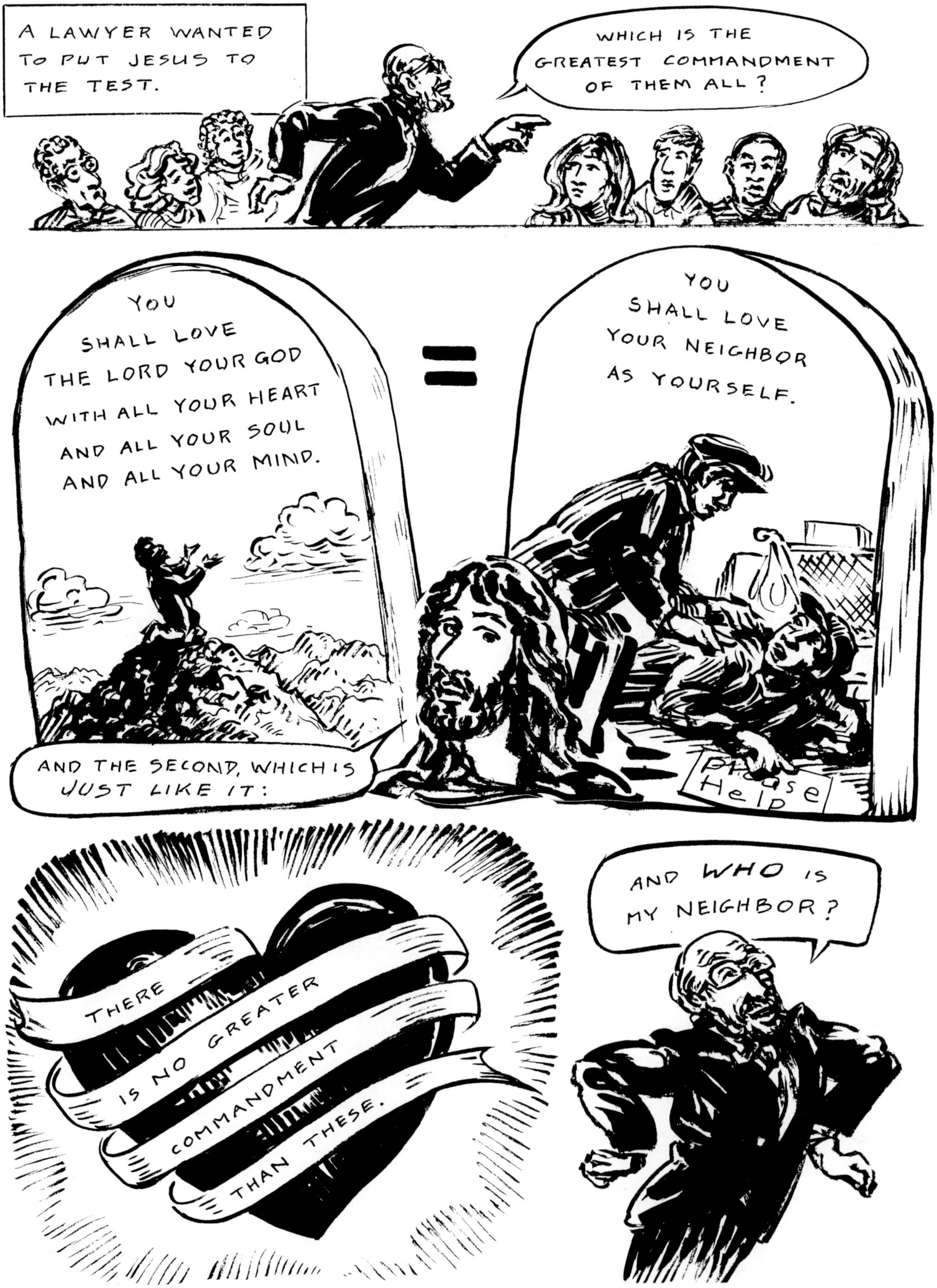
A LAWYER WANTED TO PUT JESUS TO THE TEST.
WHICH IS THE GREATEST COMMANDMENT OF THEM ALL?
YOU SHALL LOVE THE LORD YOUR GOD WITH ALL YOUR HEART AND ALL YOUR SOUL AND ALL YOUR MIND.
=
YOU SHALL LOVE YOUR NEIGHBOR AS YOURSELF.
AND THE SECOND, WHICH IS JUST LIKE IT:
Please Help
THERE IS NO GREATER COMMANDMENT THAN THESE.
AND WHO IS MY NEIGHBOR?

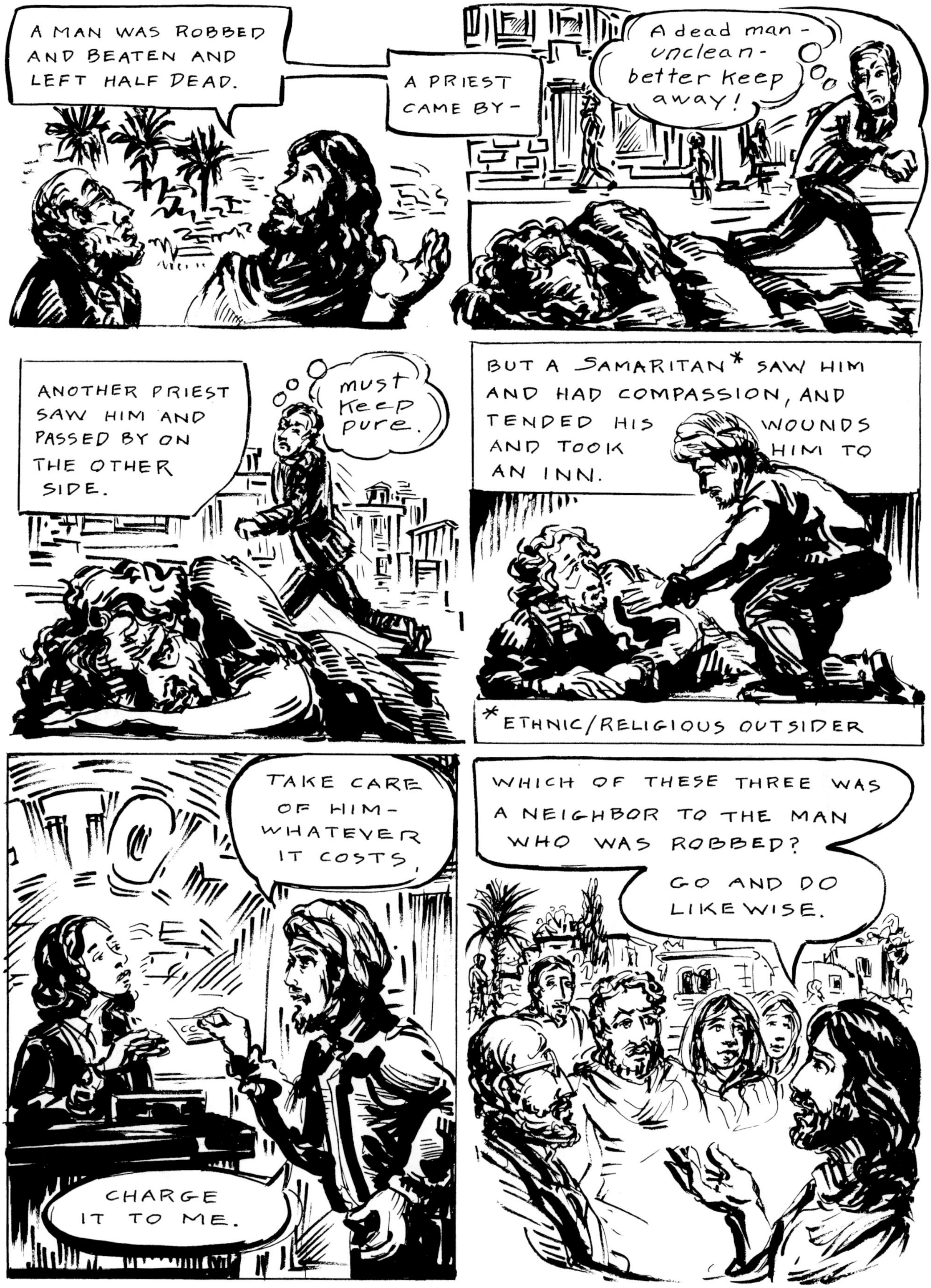
A MAN WAS ROBBED AND BEATEN AND LEFT HALF DEAD.
A PRIEST CAME BY-
A dead man - unclean - better keep away!
ANOTHER PRIEST SAW HIM AND PASSED BY ON THE OTHER SIDE.
must keep pure.
BUT A SAMARITAN* SAW HIM AND HAD COMPASSION, AND TENDED HIS WOUNDS AND TOOK HIM TO AN INN.
*ETHNIC/RELIGIOUS OUTSIDER
TAKE CARE OF HIM- WHATEVER IT COSTS.
CHARGE IT TO ME.
WHICH OF THESE THREE WAS A NEIGHBOR TO THE MAN WHO WAS ROBBED?
GO AND DO LIKEWISE.

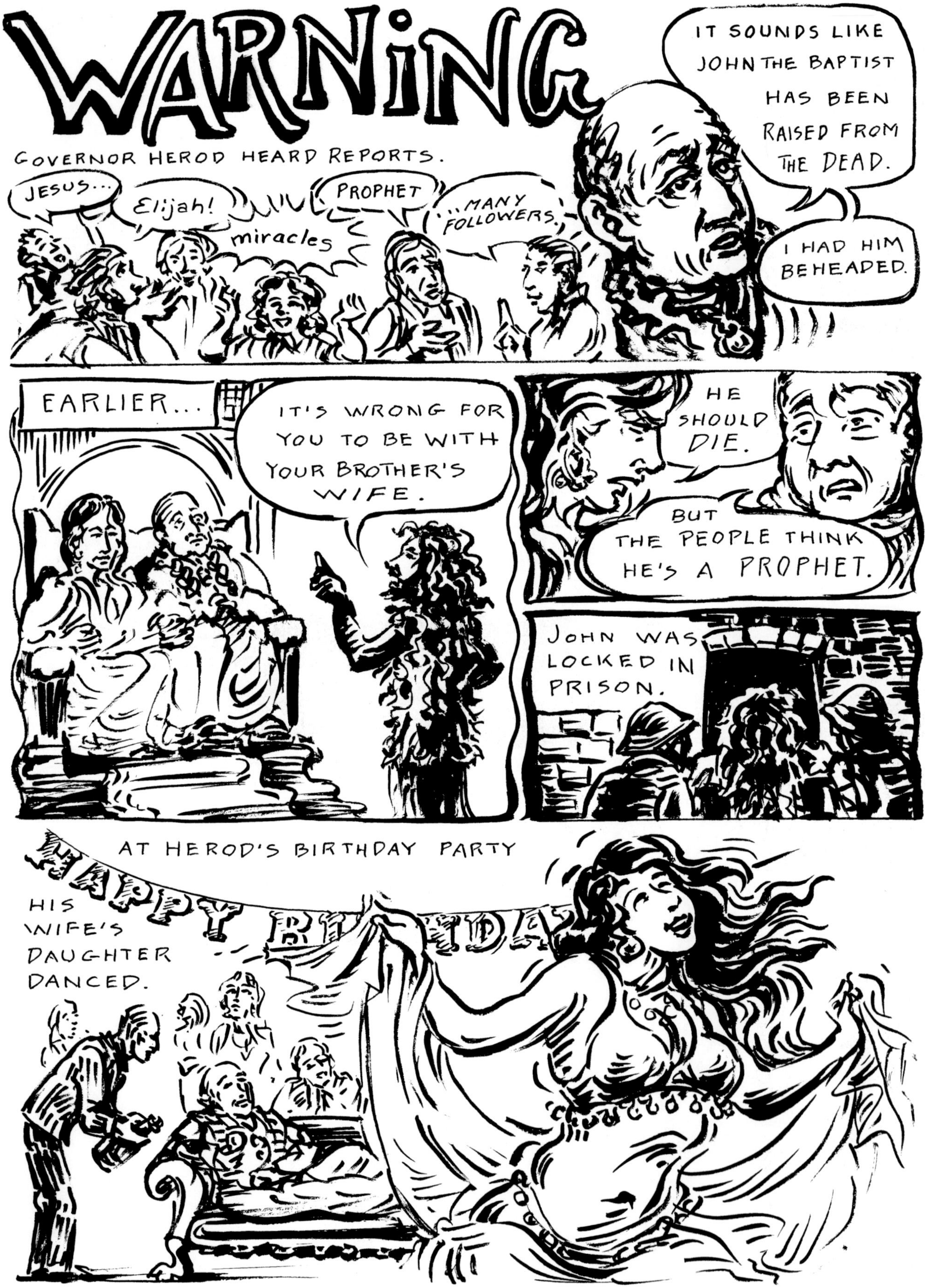
WARNING
GOVERNOR HEROD HEARD REPORTS.
JESUS...
Elijah!
miracles
PROPHET
...MANY FOLLOWERS.
IT SOUNDS LIKE JOHN THE BAPTIST HAS BEEN RAISED FROM THE DEAD.
I HAD HIM BEHEADED.
EARLIER...
IT'S WRONG FOR YOU TO BE WITH YOUR BROTHER'S WIFE.
HE SHOULD DIE.
BUT THE PEOPLE THINK HE'S A PROPHET.
JOHN WAS LOCKED IN PRISON.
AT HEROD'S BIRTHDAY PARTY
HIS WIFE'S DAUGHTER DANCED.

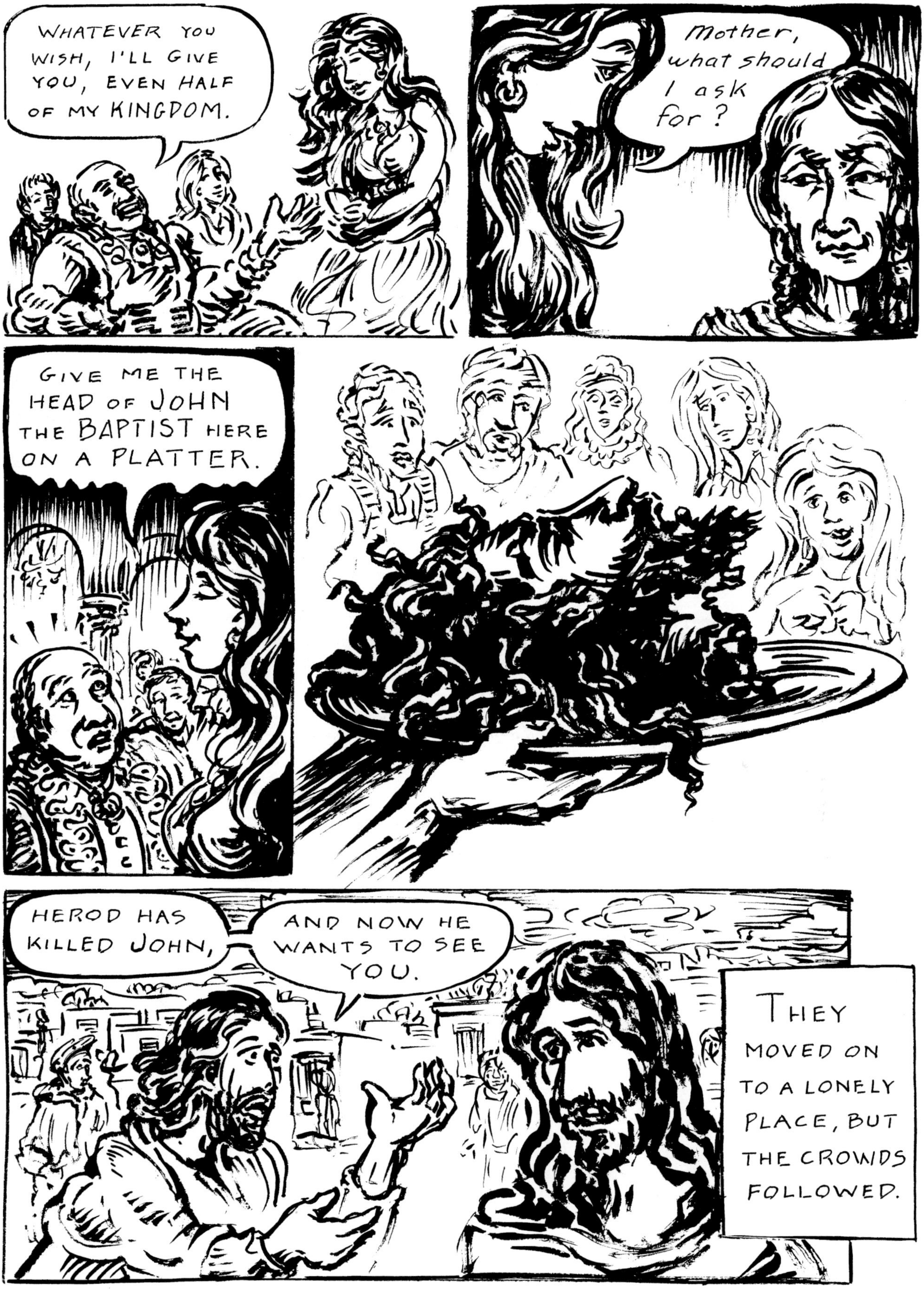
WHATEVER YOU WISH, I'LL GIVE YOU, EVEN HALF OF MY KINGDOM.
Mother, what should I ask for?
GIVE ME THE HEAD OF JOHN THE BAPTIST HERE ON A PLATTER.
HEROD HAS KILLED JOHN,
AND NOW HE WANTS TO SEE YOU.
THEY MOVED ON TO A LONELY PLACE, BUT THE CROWDS FOLLOWED.

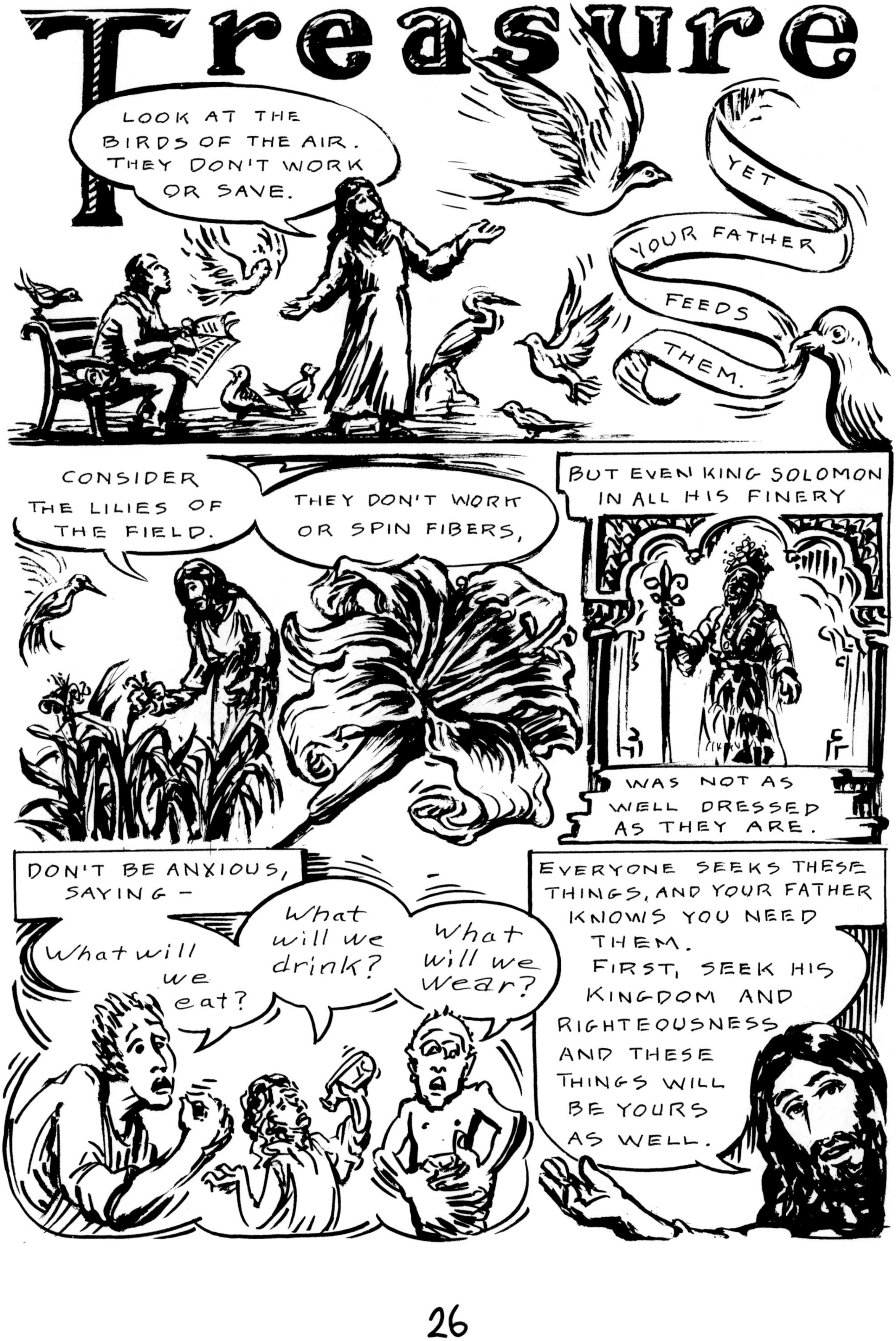

Treasure
LOOK AT THE BIRDS OF THE AIR. THEY DON'T WORK OR SAVE.
YET YOUR FATHER FEEDS THEM.
CONSIDER THE LILIES OF THE FIELD.
THEY DON'T WORK OR SPIN FIBERS,
BUT EVEN KING SOLOMON IN ALL HIS FINERY
WAS NOT AS WELL DRESSED AS THEY ARE.
DON'T BE ANXIOUS, SAYING –
What will we eat?
What will we drink?
What will we wear?
EVERYONE SEEKS THESE THINGS, AND YOUR FATHER KNOWS YOU NEED THEM.
FIRST, SEEK HIS KINGDOM AND RIGHTEOUSNESS AND THESE THINGS WILL BE YOURS AS WELL.

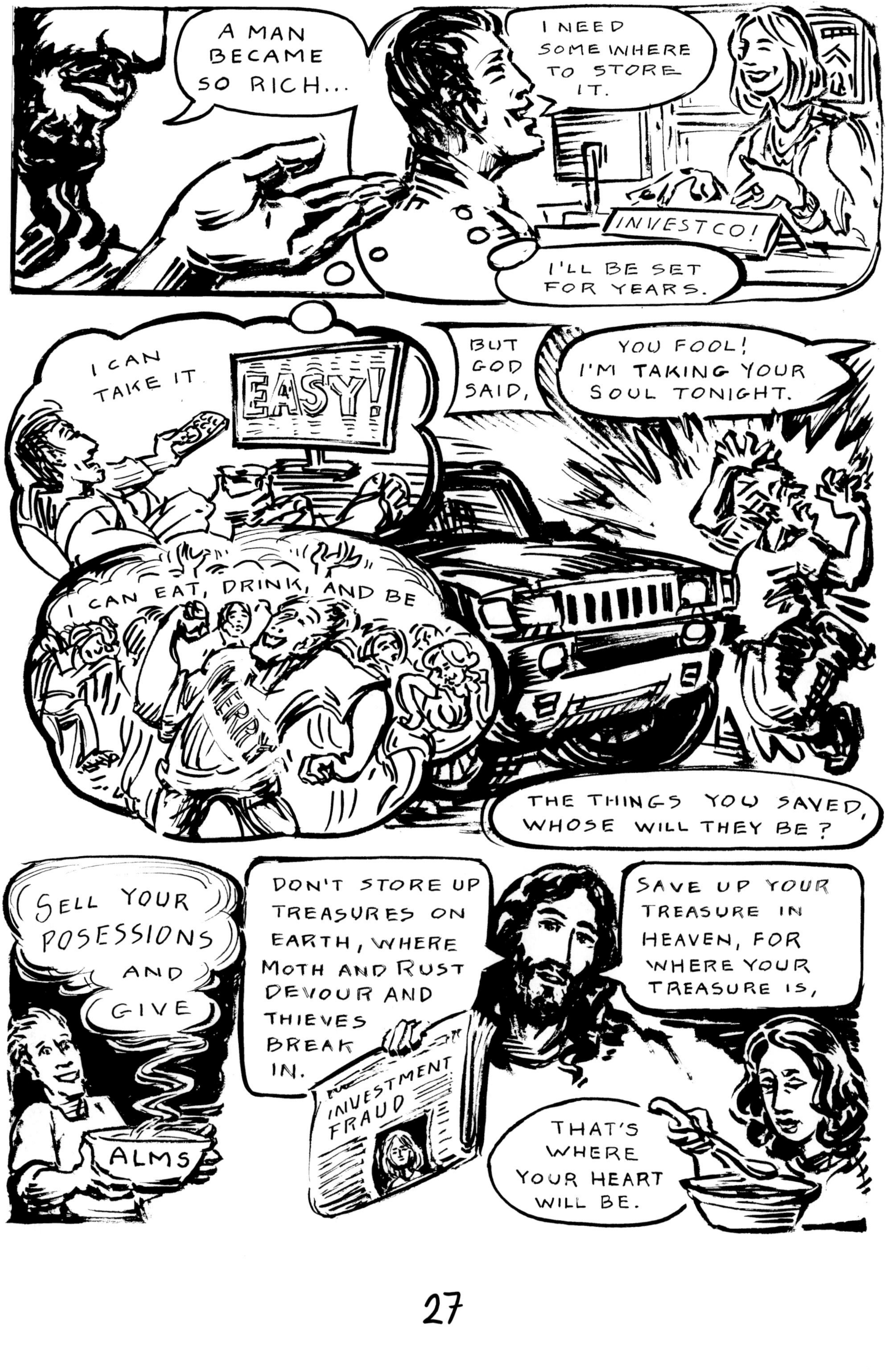
A MAN BECAME SO RICH...
I NEED SOMEWHERE TO STORE IT.
INVESTCO!
I'LL BE SET FOR YEARS.
I CAN TAKE IT
EASY!
BUT GOD SAID,
YOU FOOL! I'M TAKING YOUR SOUL TONIGHT.
I CAN EAT, DRINK, AND BE
MERRY
THE THINGS YOU SAVED, WHOSE WILL THEY BE?
SELL YOUR POSESSIONS AND GIVE
ALMS
DON'T STORE UP TREASURES ON EARTH, WHERE MOTH AND RUST DEVOUR AND THIEVES BREAK IN.
INVESTMENT FRAUD
SAVE UP YOUR TREASURE IN HEAVEN, FOR WHERE YOUR TREASURE IS,
THAT'S WHERE YOUR HEART WILL BE.

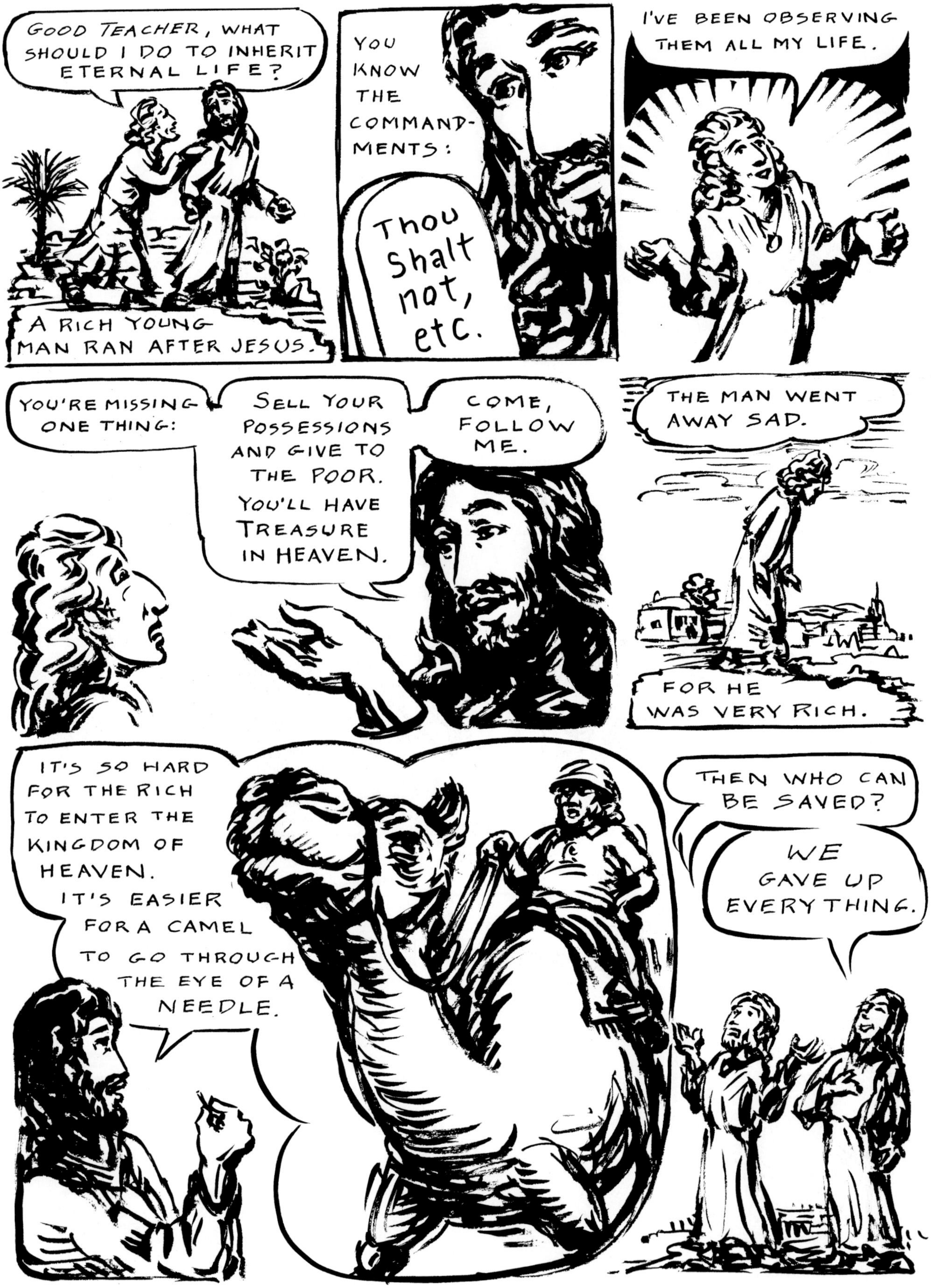

GOOD TEACHER, WHAT SHOULD I DO TO INHERIT ETERNAL LIFE?
A RICH YOUNG MAN RAN AFTER JESUS.
YOU KNOW THE COMMANDMENTS:
Thou Shalt not, etc.
I'VE BEEN OBSERVING THEM ALL MY LIFE.
YOU'RE MISSING ONE THING:
SELL YOUR POSSESSIONS AND GIVE TO THE POOR. YOU'LL HAVE TREASURE IN HEAVEN.
COME, FOLLOW ME.
THE MAN WENT AWAY SAD.
FOR HE WAS VERY RICH.
IT'S SO HARD FOR THE RICH TO ENTER THE KINGDOM OF HEAVEN.
IT'S EASIER FOR A CAMEL TO GO THROUGH THE EYE OF A NEEDLE.
THEN WHO CAN BE SAVED?
WE GAVE UP EVERYTHING.

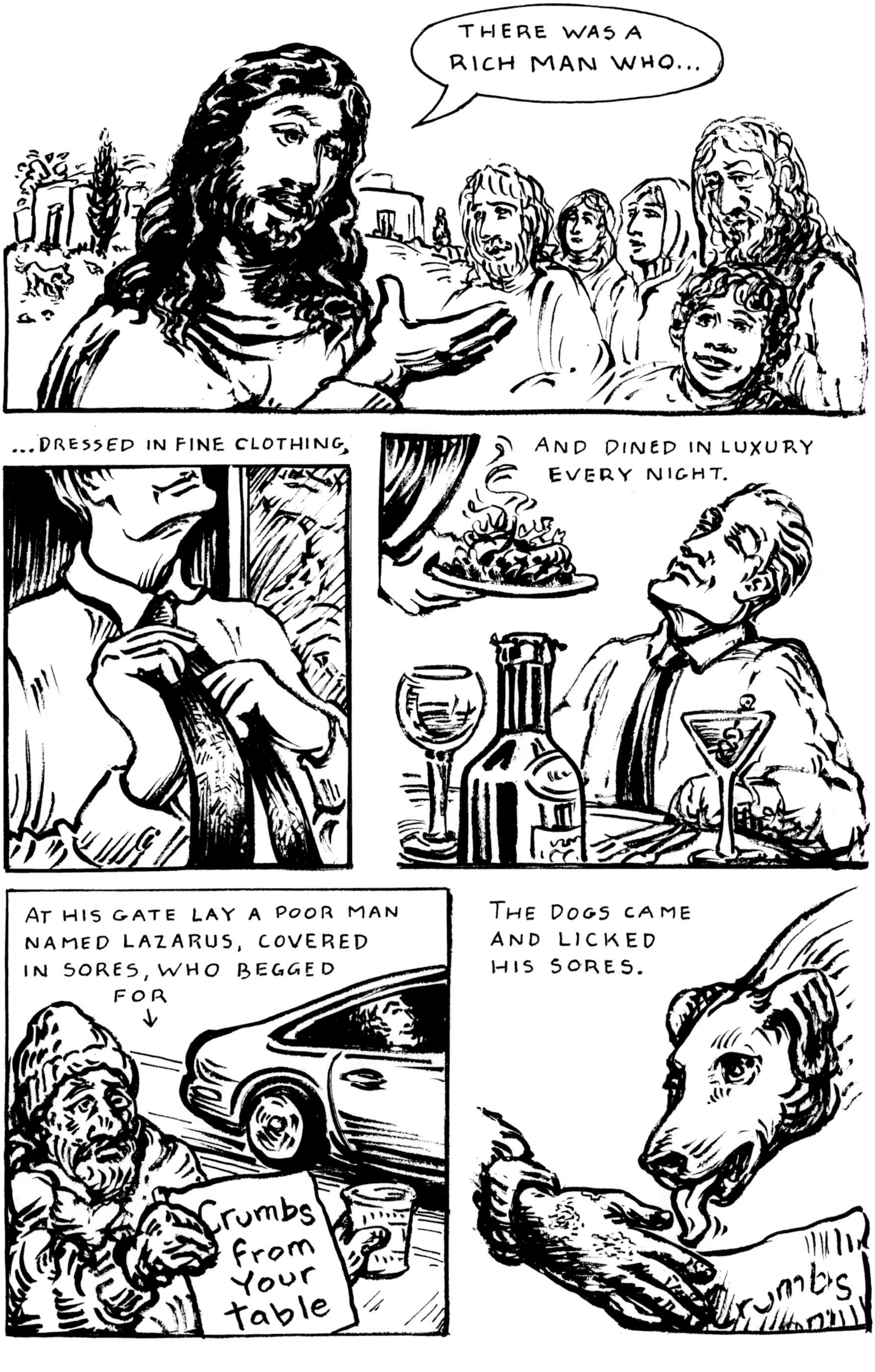
THERE WAS A RICH MAN WHO...
...DRESSED IN FINE CLOTHING,
AND DINED IN LUXURY EVERY NIGHT.
AT HIS GATE LAY A POOR MAN NAMED LAZARUS, COVERED IN SORES, WHO BEGGED FOR
Crumbs from Your table
THE DOGS CAME AND LICKED HIS SORES.
Crumbs

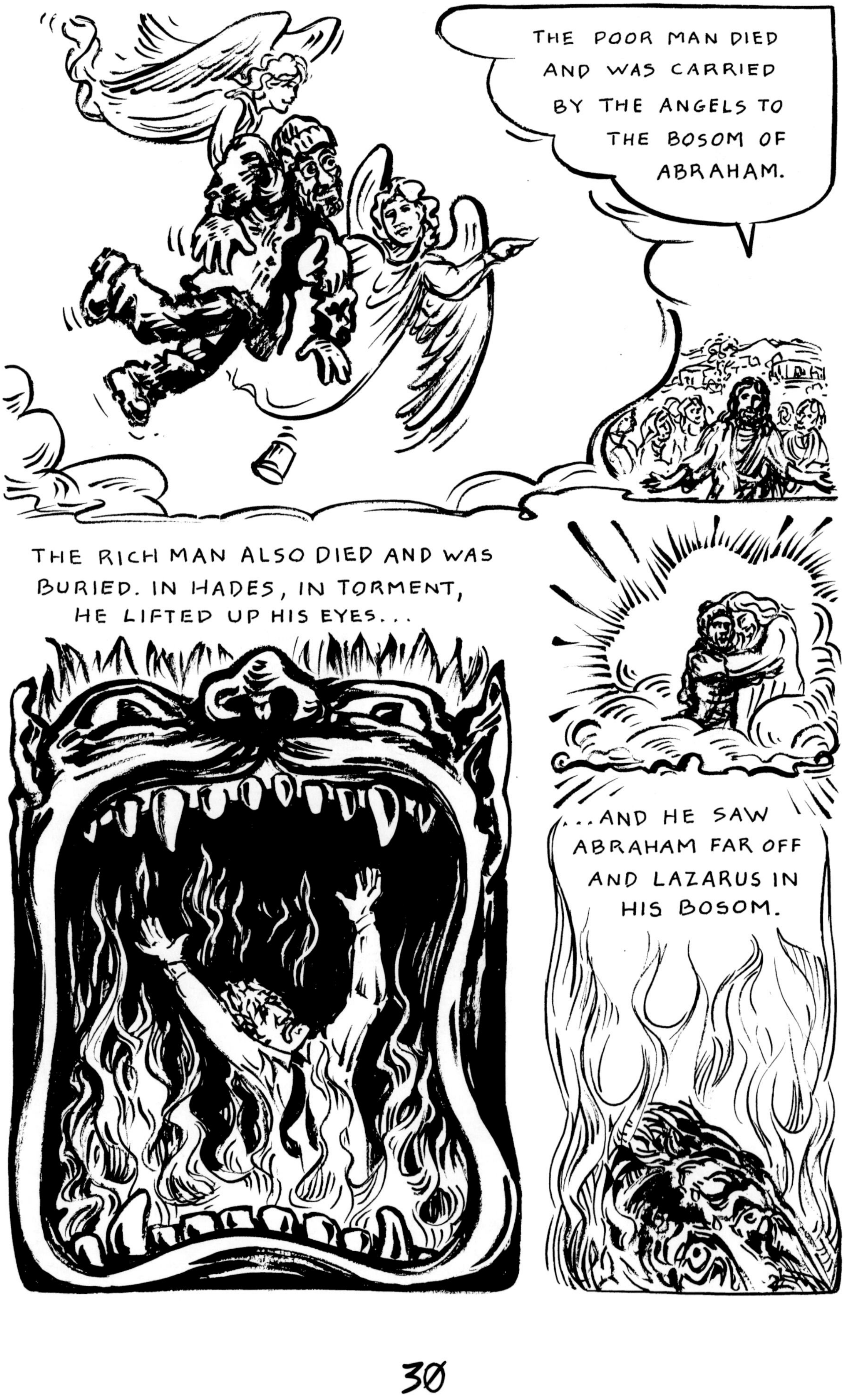
THE POOR MAN DIED AND WAS CARRIED BY THE ANGELS TO THE BOSOM OF ABRAHAM.
THE RICH MAN ALSO DIED AND WAS BURIED. IN HADES, IN TORMENT, HE LIFTED UP HIS EYES...
...AND HE SAW ABRAHAM FAR OFF AND LAZARUS IN HIS BOSOM.

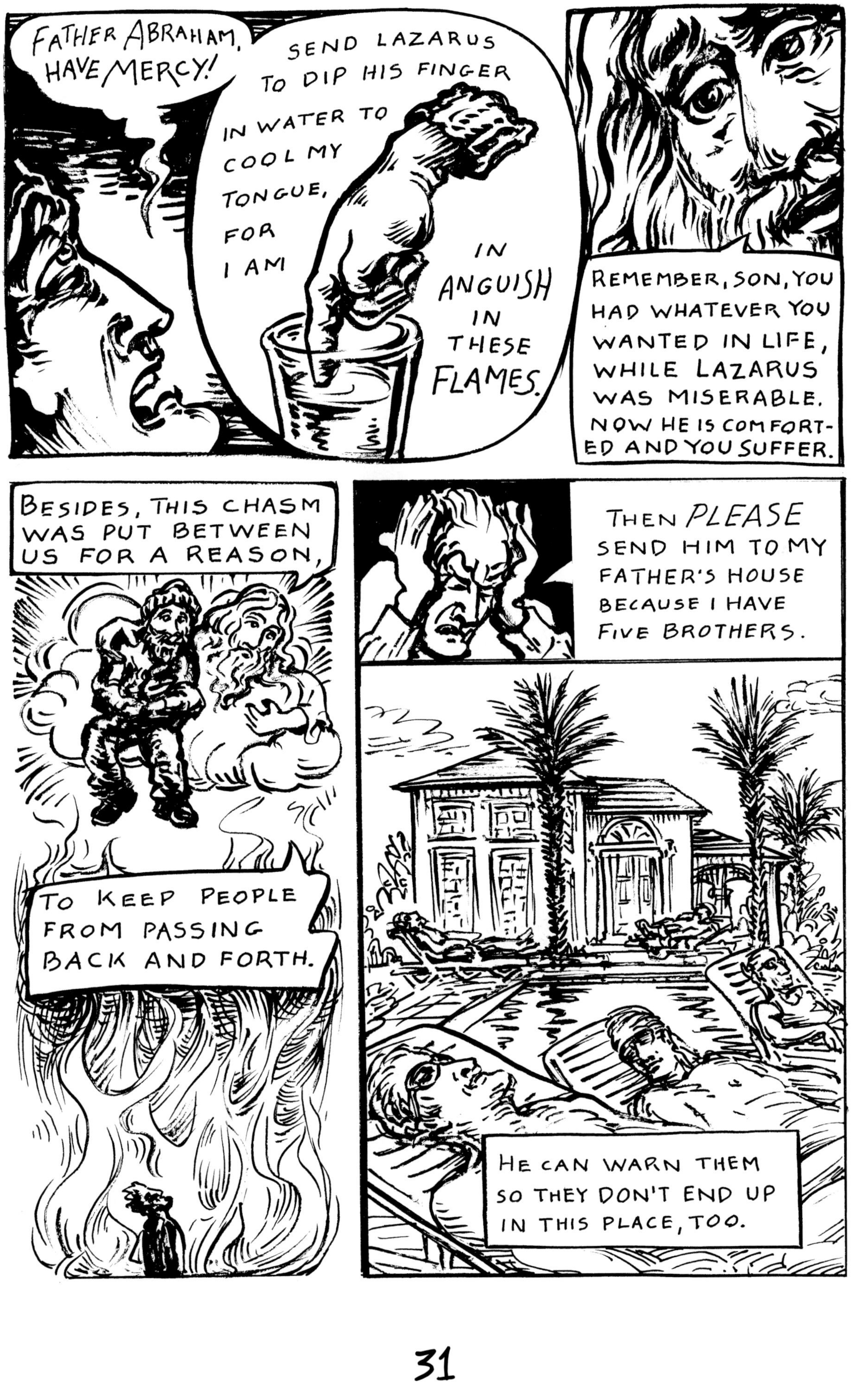
FATHER ABRAHAM, HAVE MERCY!
SEND LAZARUS TO DIP HIS FINGER IN WATER TO COOL MY TONGUE, FOR I AM IN ANGUISH IN THESE FLAMES.
REMEMBER, SON, YOU HAD WHATEVER YOU WANTED IN LIFE, WHILE LAZARUS WAS MISERABLE. NOW HE IS COMFORTED AND YOU SUFFER.
BESIDES, THIS CHASM WAS PUT BETWEEN US FOR A REASON,
TO KEEP PEOPLE FROM PASSING BACK AND FORTH.
THEN PLEASE SEND HIM TO MY FATHER'S HOUSE BECAUSE I HAVE FIVE BROTHERS.
HE CAN WARN THEM SO THEY DON'T END UP IN THIS PLACE, TOO.

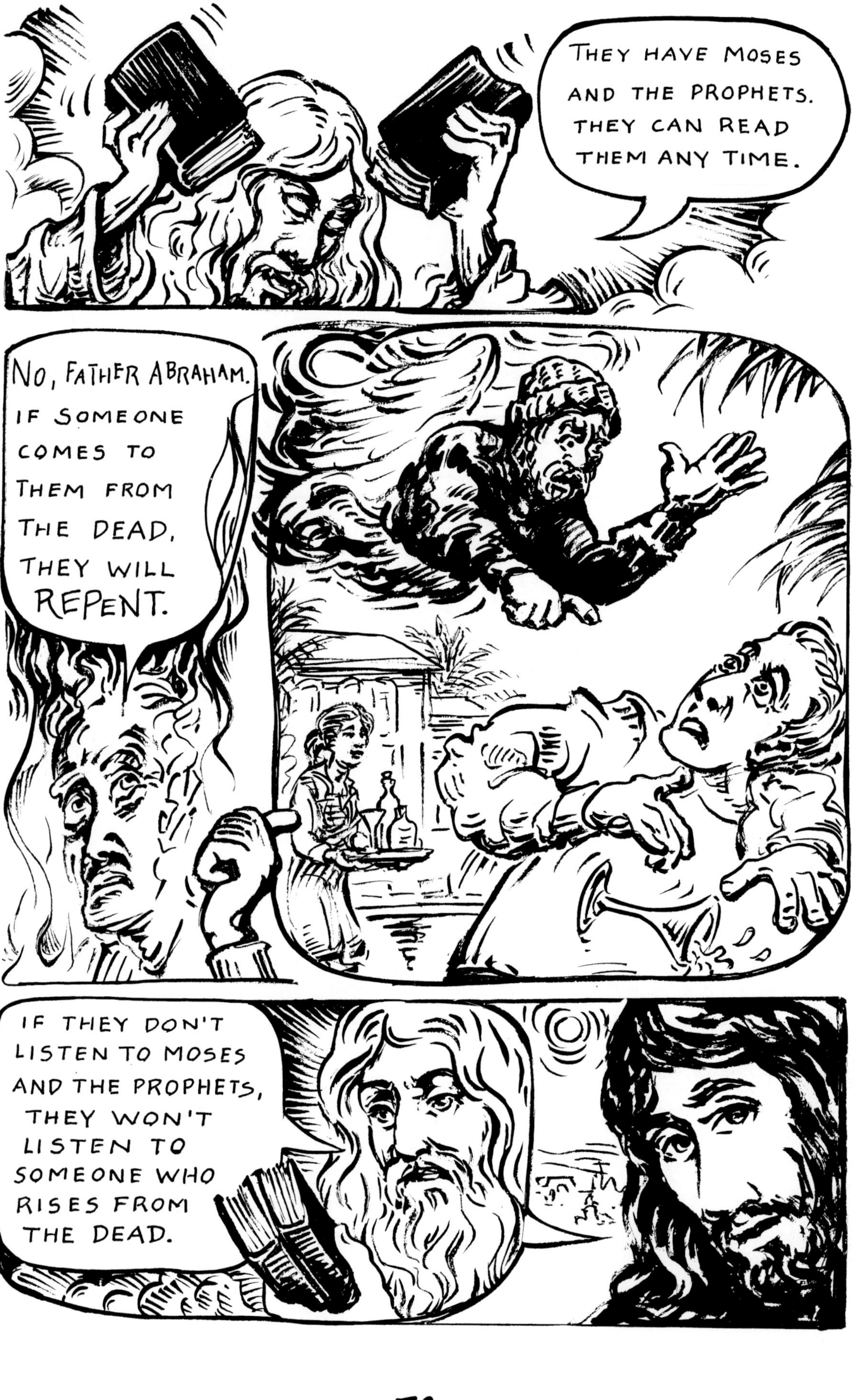
THEY HAVE MOSES AND THE PROPHETS. THEY CAN READ THEM ANY TIME.
NO, FATHER ABRAHAM. IF SOMEONE COMES TO THEM FROM THE DEAD, THEY WILL REPENT.
IF THEY DON'T LISTEN TO MOSES AND THE PROPHETS, THEY WON'T LISTEN TO SOMEONE WHO RISES FROM THE DEAD.

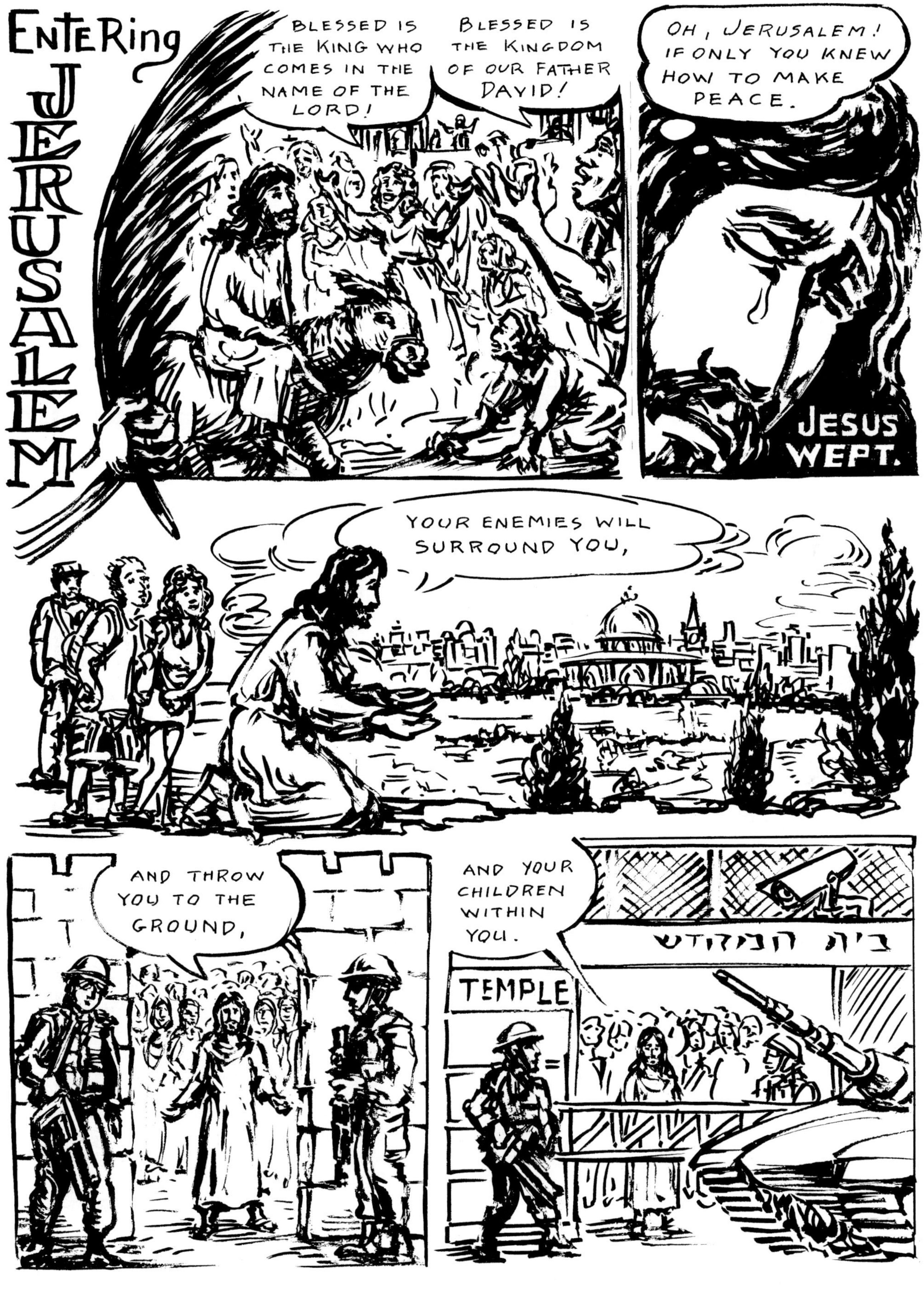

Entering Jerusalem
Blessed is the King who comes in the name of the Lord!
Blessed is the Kingdom of our father David!
Oh, Jerusalem! If only you knew how to make peace.
JESUS WEPT.
Your enemies will surround you,
And throw you to the ground,
And your children within you.
בית המקדש
TEMPLE

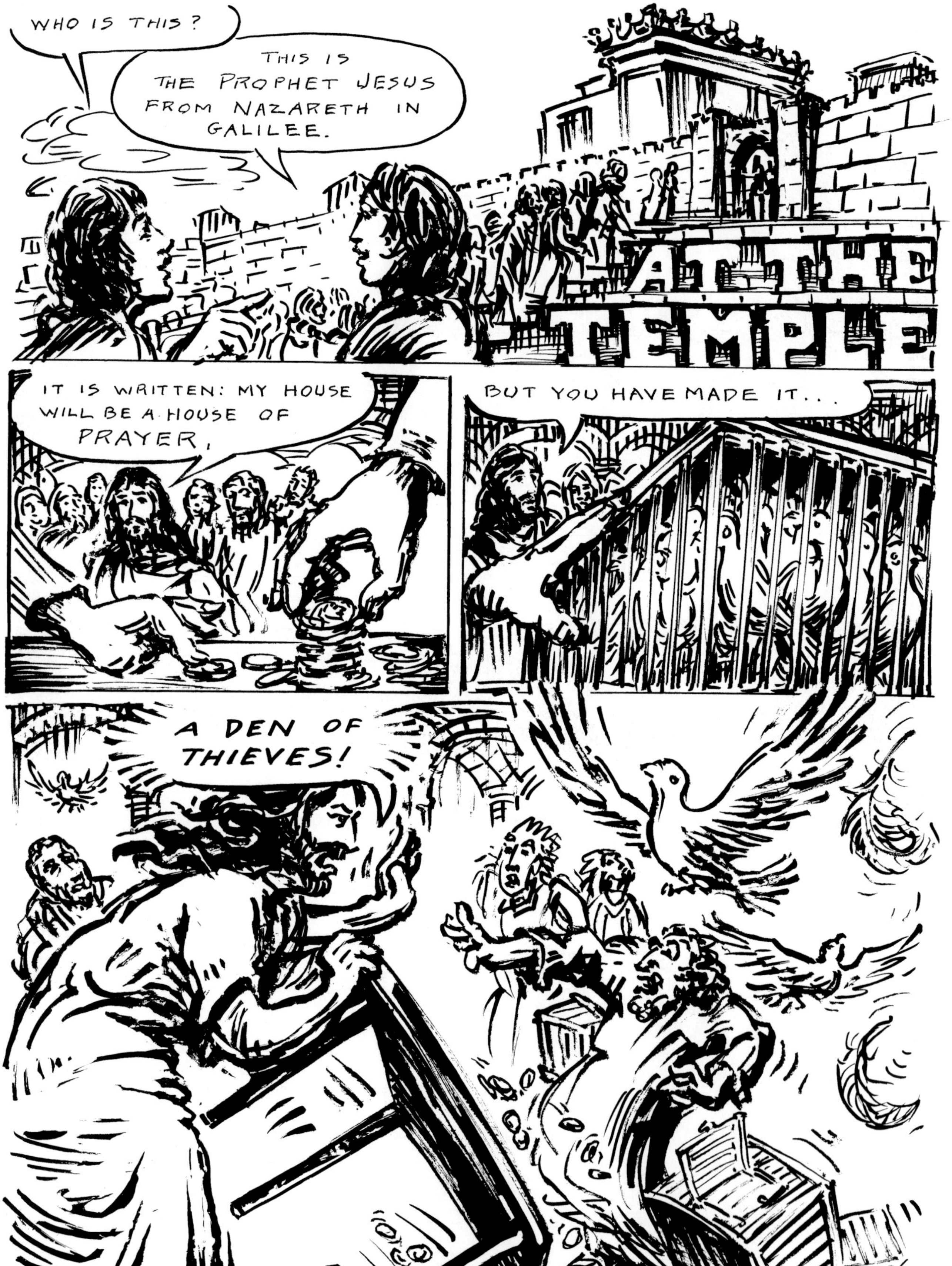
WHO IS THIS?
THIS IS THE PROPHET JESUS FROM NAZARETH IN GALILEE.
AT THE TEMPLE
IT IS WRITTEN: MY HOUSE WILL BE A HOUSE OF PRAYER,
BUT YOU HAVE MADE IT...
A DEN OF THIEVES!

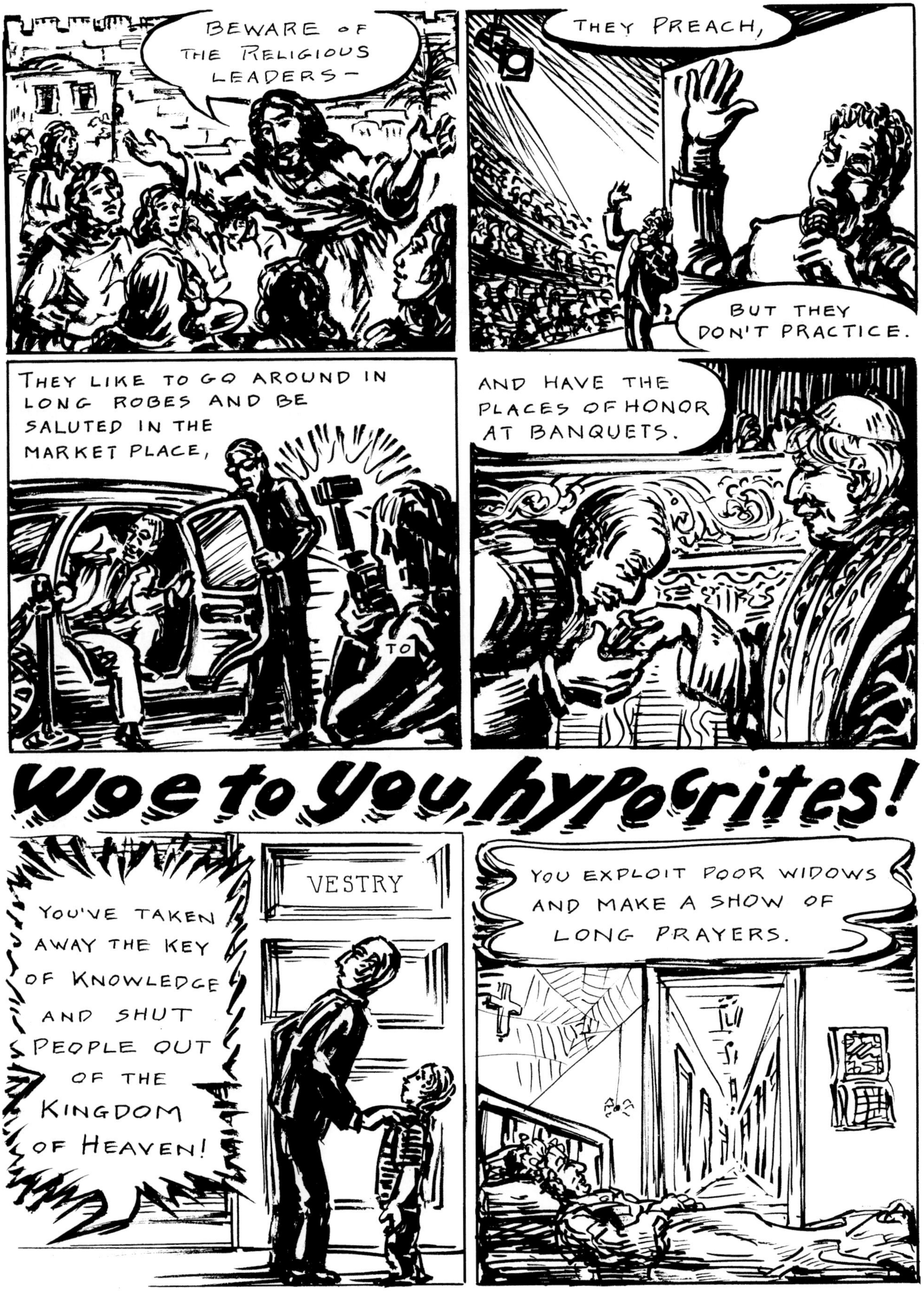
BEWARE OF THE RELIGIOUS LEADERS—
THEY PREACH,
BUT THEY DON'T PRACTICE.
THEY LIKE TO GO AROUND IN LONG ROBES AND BE SALUTED IN THE MARKET PLACE,
TO
AND HAVE THE PLACES OF HONOR AT BANQUETS.
Woe to you, hypocrites!
VESTRY
YOU'VE TAKEN AWAY THE KEY OF KNOWLEDGE AND SHUT PEOPLE OUT OF THE KINGDOM OF HEAVEN!
YOU EXPLOIT POOR WIDOWS AND MAKE A SHOW OF LONG PRAYERS.

JESUS WATCHED THE CROWDS PUTTING MONEY IN THE
TREASURY
SOME RICH PEOPLE PUT IN LARGE SUMS
A POOR WIDOW CAME.
TWO COPPER COINS
THIS POOR WIDOW HAS PUT IN MORE THAN ALL OF THEM.
FOR THEY CONTRIBUTED OUT OF THEIR ABUNDANCE,
BUT SHE, OUT OF HER POVERTY, GAVE EVERYTHING SHE HAD.

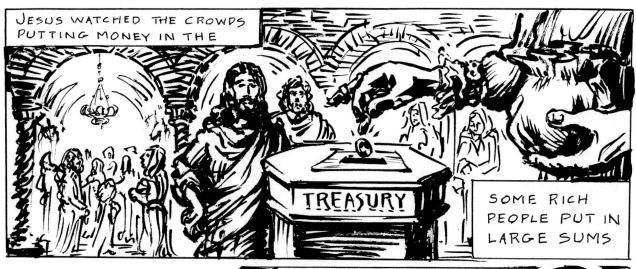

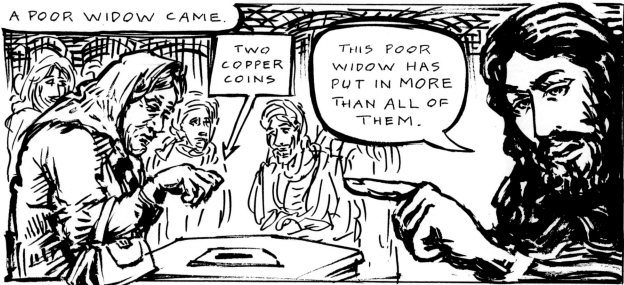

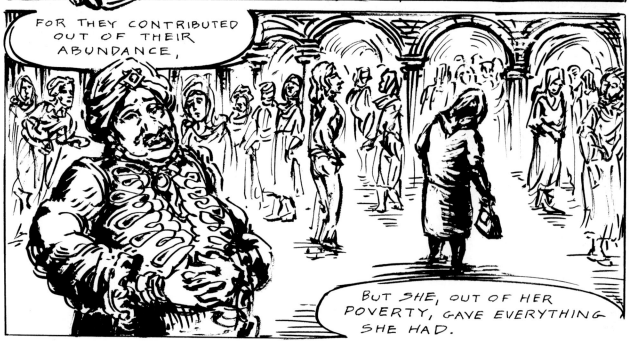

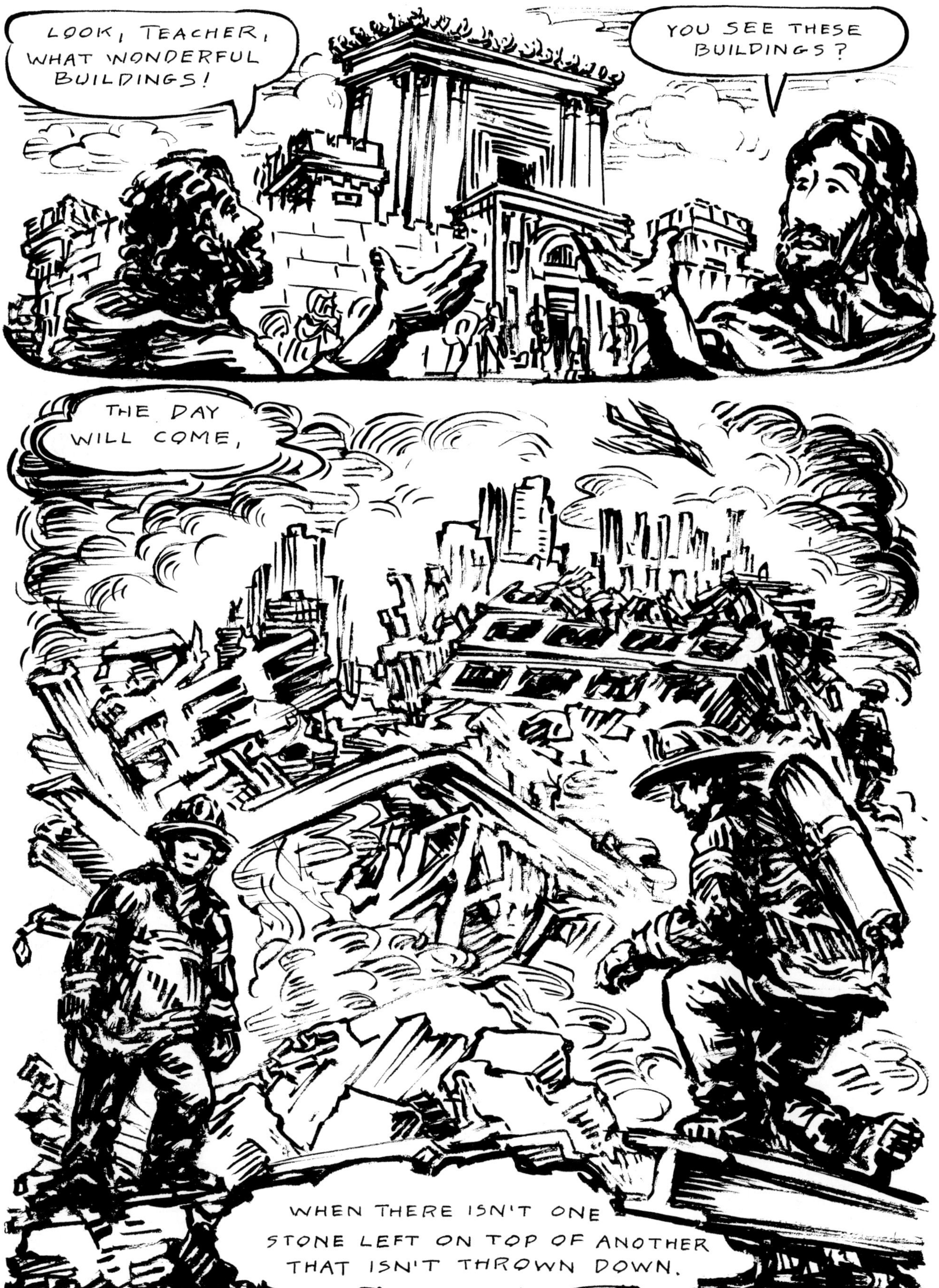
LOOK, TEACHER, WHAT WONDERFUL BUILDINGS!
YOU SEE THESE BUILDINGS?
THE DAY WILL COME,
WHEN THERE ISN'T ONE STONE LEFT ON TOP OF ANOTHER THAT ISN'T THROWN DOWN.

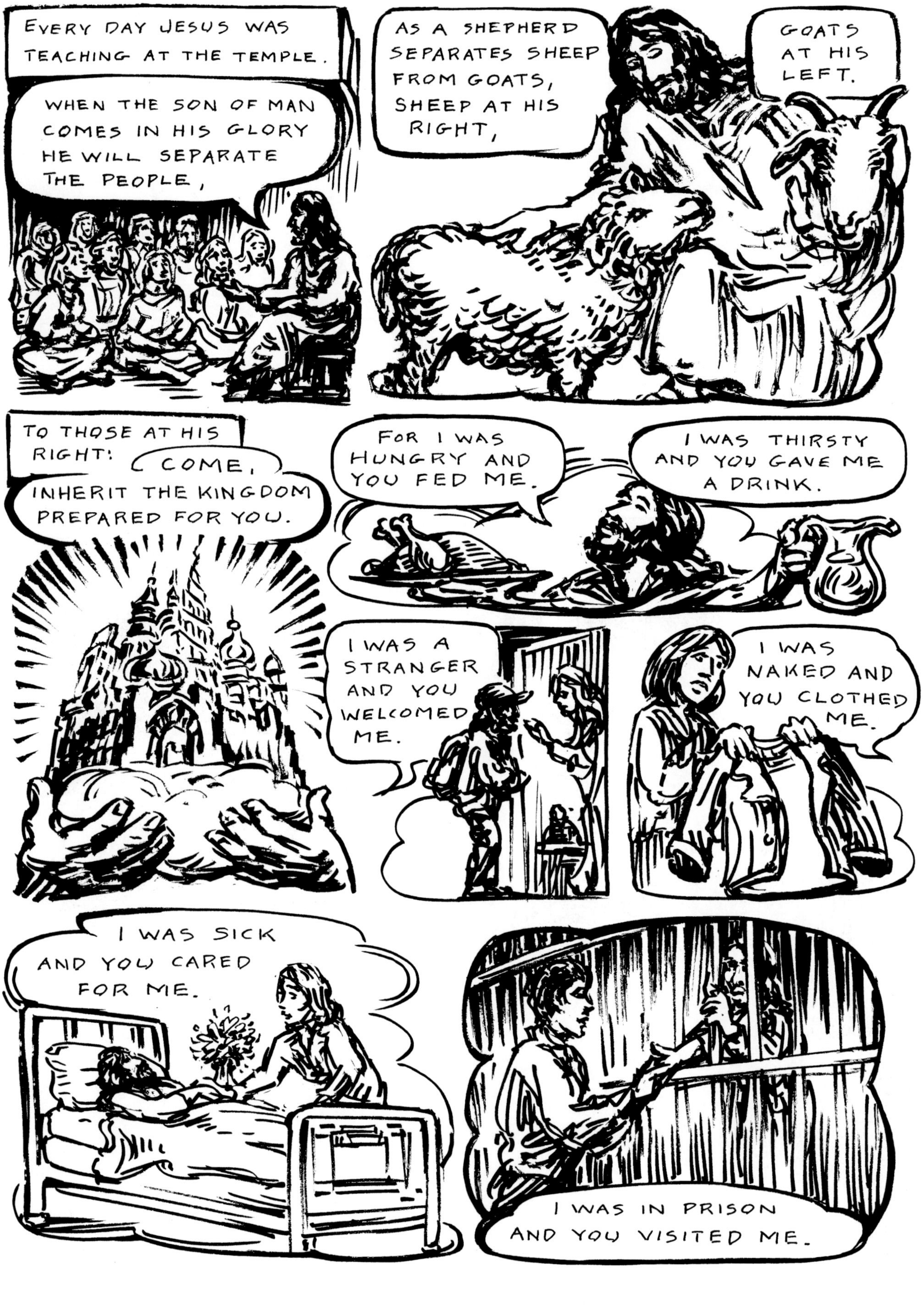
EVERY DAY JESUS WAS TEACHING AT THE TEMPLE.
WHEN THE SON OF MAN COMES IN HIS GLORY HE WILL SEPARATE THE PEOPLE,
AS A SHEPHERD SEPARATES SHEEP FROM GOATS, SHEEP AT HIS RIGHT,
GOATS AT HIS LEFT.
TO THOSE AT HIS RIGHT:
COME, INHERIT THE KINGDOM PREPARED FOR YOU.
FOR I WAS HUNGRY AND YOU FED ME.
I WAS THIRSTY AND YOU GAVE ME A DRINK.
I WAS A STRANGER AND YOU WELCOMED ME.
I WAS NAKED AND YOU CLOTHED ME.
I WAS SICK AND YOU CARED FOR ME.
I WAS IN PRISON AND YOU VISITED ME.

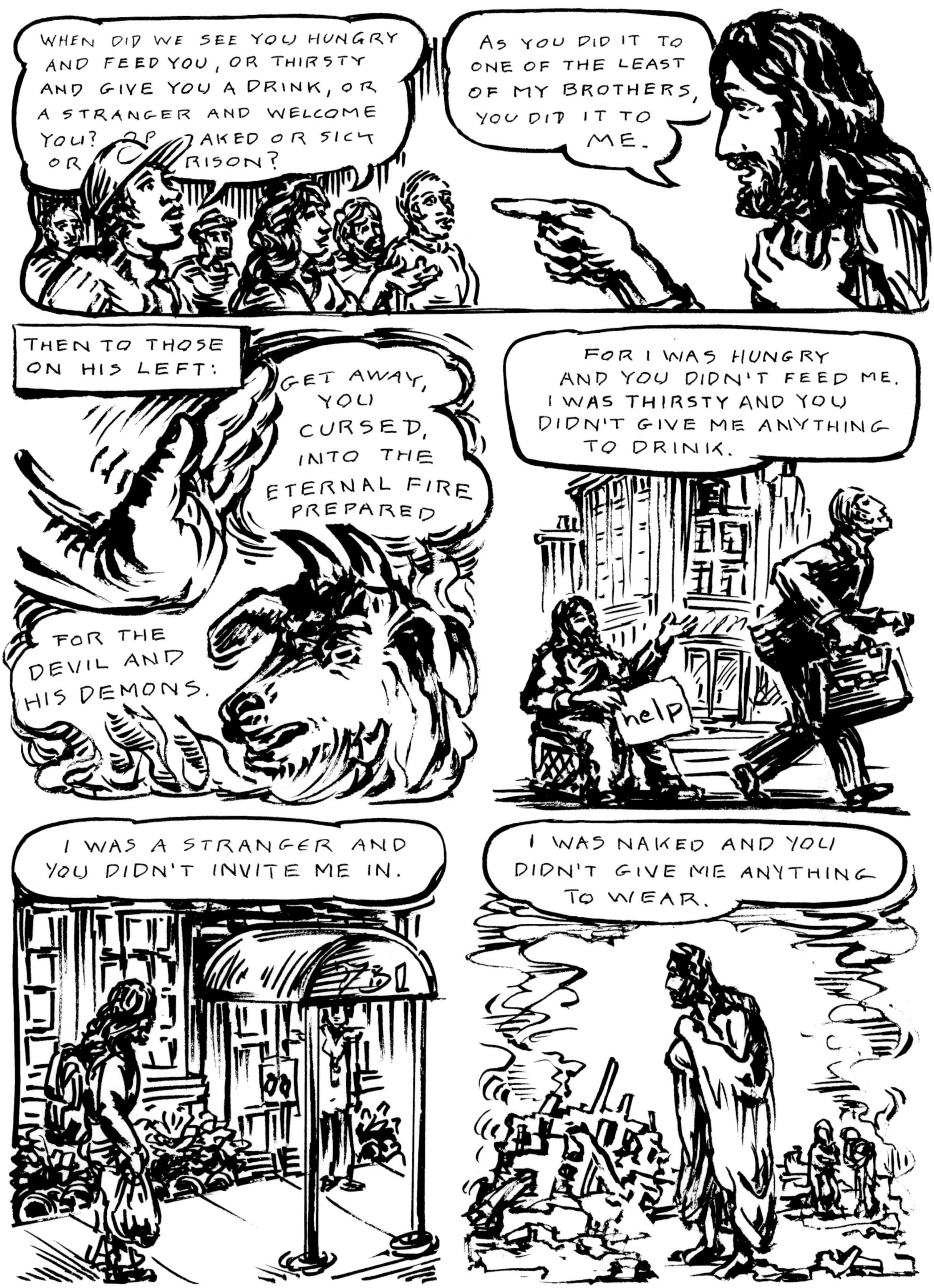
WHEN DID WE SEE YOU HUNGRY AND FEED YOU, OR THIRSTY AND GIVE YOU A DRINK, OR A STRANGER AND WELCOME YOU? OR AKED OR SICK OR RISON?
AS YOU DID IT TO ONE OF THE LEAST OF MY BROTHERS, YOU DID IT TO ME.
THEN TO THOSE ON HIS LEFT:
GET AWAY, YOU CURSED, INTO THE ETERNAL FIRE PREPARED
FOR THE DEVIL AND HIS DEMONS.
FOR I WAS HUNGRY AND YOU DIDN'T FEED ME. I WAS THIRSTY AND YOU DIDN'T GIVE ME ANYTHING TO DRINK.
help
I WAS A STRANGER AND YOU DIDN'T INVITE ME IN.
I WAS NAKED AND YOU DIDN'T GIVE ME ANYTHING TO WEAR.

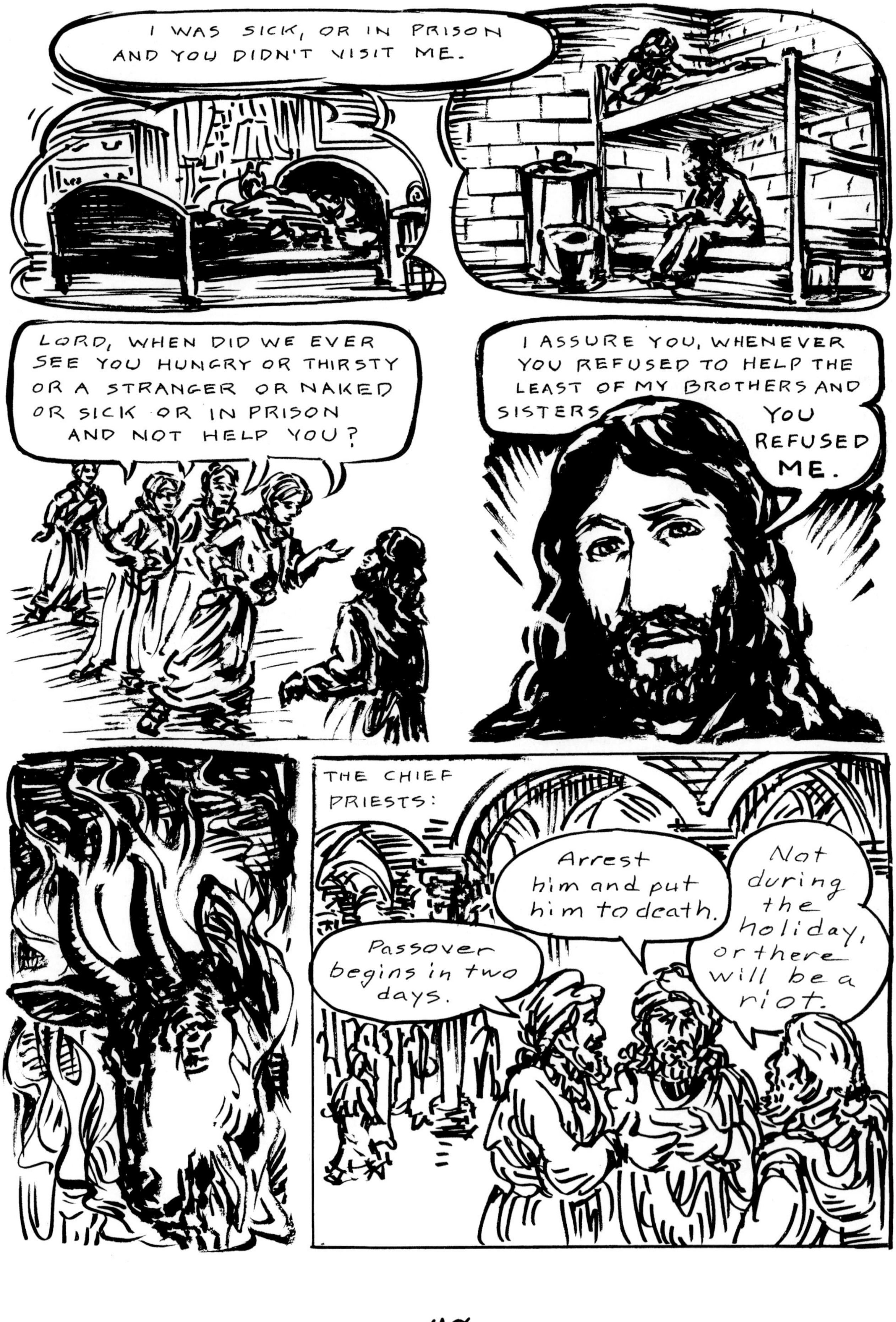
I WAS SICK, OR IN PRISON AND YOU DIDN'T VISIT ME.
LORD, WHEN DID WE EVER SEE YOU HUNGRY OR THIRSTY OR A STRANGER OR NAKED OR SICK OR IN PRISON AND NOT HELP YOU?
I ASSURE YOU, WHENEVER YOU REFUSED TO HELP THE LEAST OF MY BROTHERS AND SISTERS YOU REFUSED ME.
THE CHIEF PRIESTS:
Arrest him and put him to death.
Not during the holiday, or there will be a riot.
Passover begins in two days.

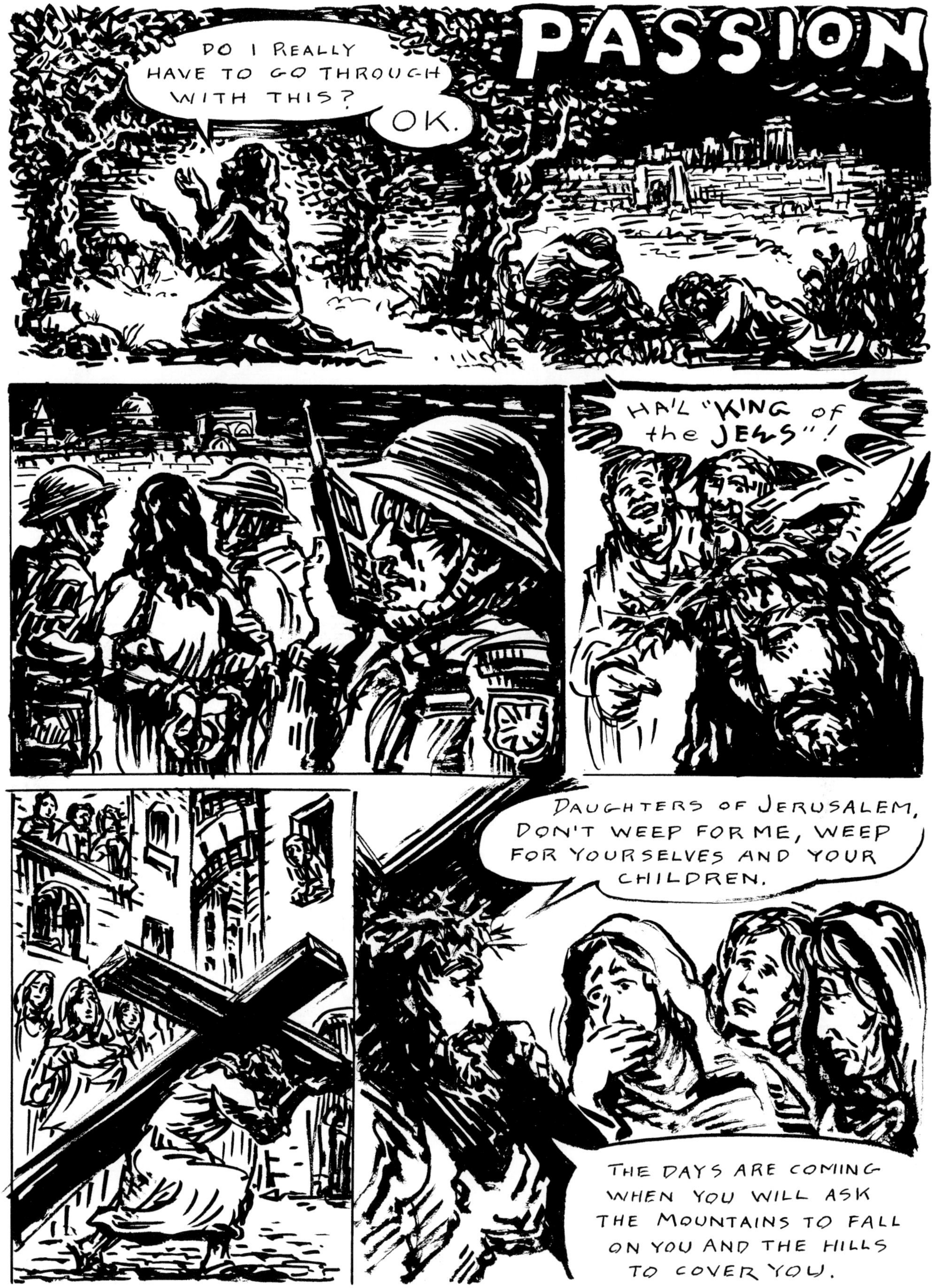
PASSION
DO I REALLY HAVE TO GO THROUGH WITH THIS?
OK.
HAIL "KING of the JEWS"!
DAUGHTERS OF JERUSALEM, DON'T WEEP FOR ME, WEEP FOR YOURSELVES AND YOUR CHILDREN.
THE DAYS ARE COMING WHEN YOU WILL ASK THE MOUNTAINS TO FALL ON YOU AND THE HILLS TO COVER YOU.

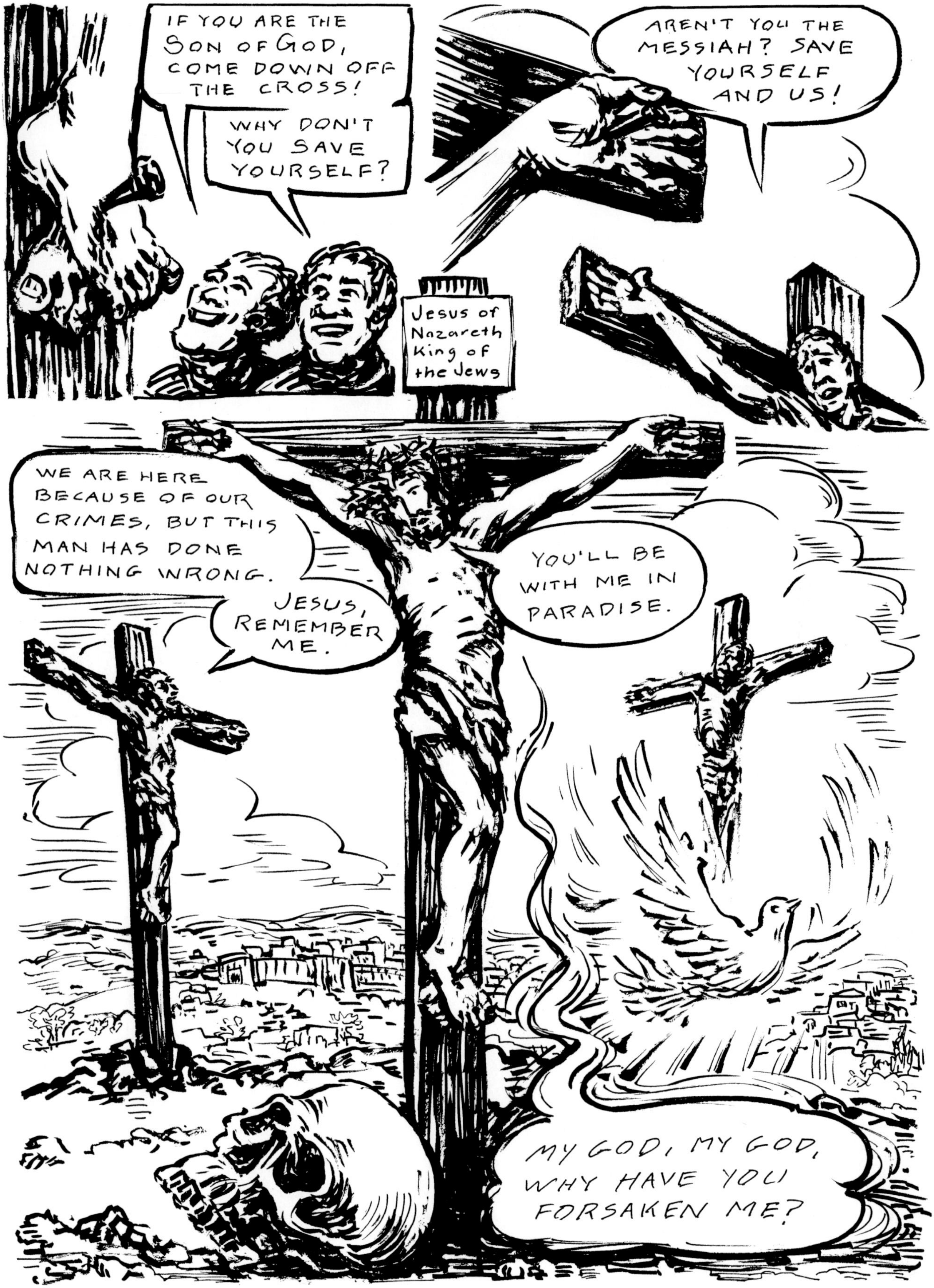
IF YOU ARE THE SON OF GOD, COME DOWN OFF THE CROSS!
WHY DON'T YOU SAVE YOURSELF?
AREN'T YOU THE MESSIAH? SAVE YOURSELF AND US!
Jesus of Nazareth King of the Jews
WE ARE HERE BECAUSE OF OUR CRIMES, BUT THIS MAN HAS DONE NOTHING WRONG.
JESUS, REMEMBER ME.
YOU'LL BE WITH ME IN PARADISE.
MY GOD, MY GOD, WHY HAVE YOU FORSAKEN ME?

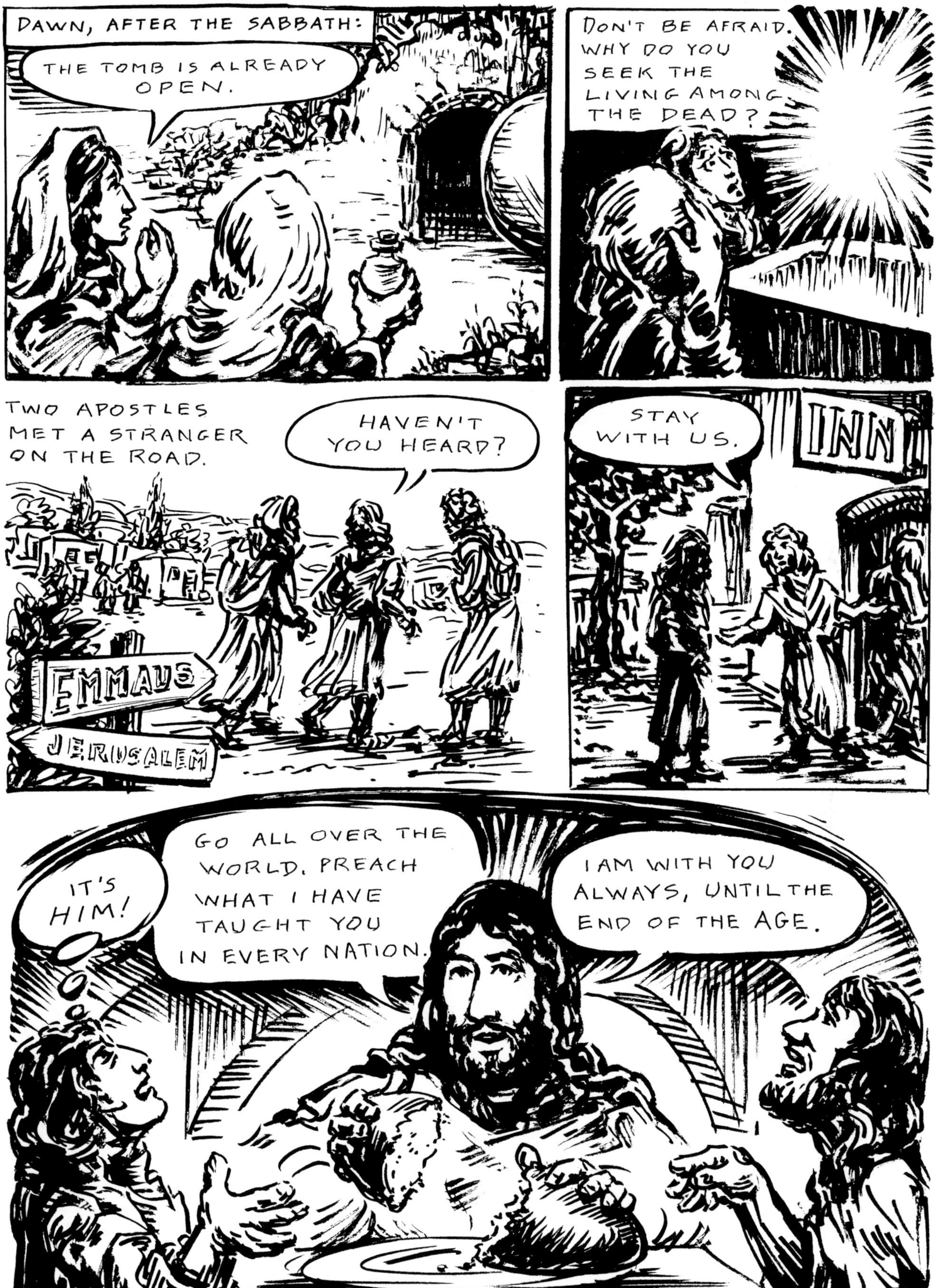
DAWN, AFTER THE SABBATH:
THE TOMB IS ALREADY OPEN.
DON'T BE AFRAID. WHY DO YOU SEEK THE LIVING AMONG THE DEAD?
TWO APOSTLES MET A STRANGER ON THE ROAD.
HAVEN'T YOU HEARD?
EMMAUS
JERUSALEM
STAY WITH US.
INN
IT'S HIM!
GO ALL OVER THE WORLD. PREACH WHAT I HAVE TAUGHT YOU IN EVERY NATION.
I AM WITH YOU ALWAYS, UNTIL THE END OF THE AGE.

# Radical History

By Gary Dumm
with Laura Dumm and others

# THE LOLLARDS

## THE SCRIPTURES SPEAK A NEW LANGUAGE

THE BLACK PLAGUE KILLED 30%–60% OF EUROPE'S POPULATION BETWEEN 1348 AND 1350.

WAT TYLER LED THE PEASANTS' REVOLT OF 1381 AND WAS BETRAYED AND MURDERED.

...THIS 14TH CENTURY OF OUR LORD WAS A TIME OF GREAT CHANGE AND TRIBULATION...

TRAVELING PREACHER JOHN BALL SPREAD A MESSAGE OF EQUALITY DURING THE ENGLISH PEASANT REVOLT.

JOHN WYCLIFFE TRANSLATED THE BIBLE INTO ENGLISH FOR THE COMMON PEOPLE IN THE 1380S.

STORY BY PAUL BUHLE & GARY DUMM
ART BY GARY DUMM · COLOR BY LAURA DUMM

THE PEOPLE PROTESTED INJUSTICE...

THE CHURCH HAS ACQUIRED GREAT WEALTH. IT IMPOSES CHURCH TAXES UPON VILLAGERS WHO ALREADY PAY TAXES TO THE KING.

DISPUTES AROSE IN THE BRITISH PARLIAMENT...

THE POPE HAS NO RIGHT TO TAX US WHEN WE ARE ALREADY PRESSED FOR MONEY!

I WAS TRAINED IN THEOLOGY BUT WAS DRAWN INTO POLITICS IN 1365 OVER A DISPUTE ABOUT TAXES BETWEEN POPE URBAN AND KING JOHN. AFTER THAT, I STARTED THINKING IN NEW WAYS ABOUT THE CHURCH'S ROLE IN SOCIETY. I FELT THE CHURCH WAS MAKING MONEY OFF THE BACKS OF PEASANTS.

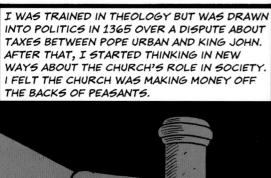

BY 1377 I HAD WRITTEN TRACTS ABOUT THE CORRUPT CHURCH SYSTEM—FULL OF COMMISSIONS, TAXES, AND THE SQUANDERING OF MONEY BY PRIESTS. ON FEBRUARY 19 I WAS CALLED TO ANSWER QUESTIONS IN COURT ABOUT MY BELIEFS. NOTHING WAS RESOLVED.

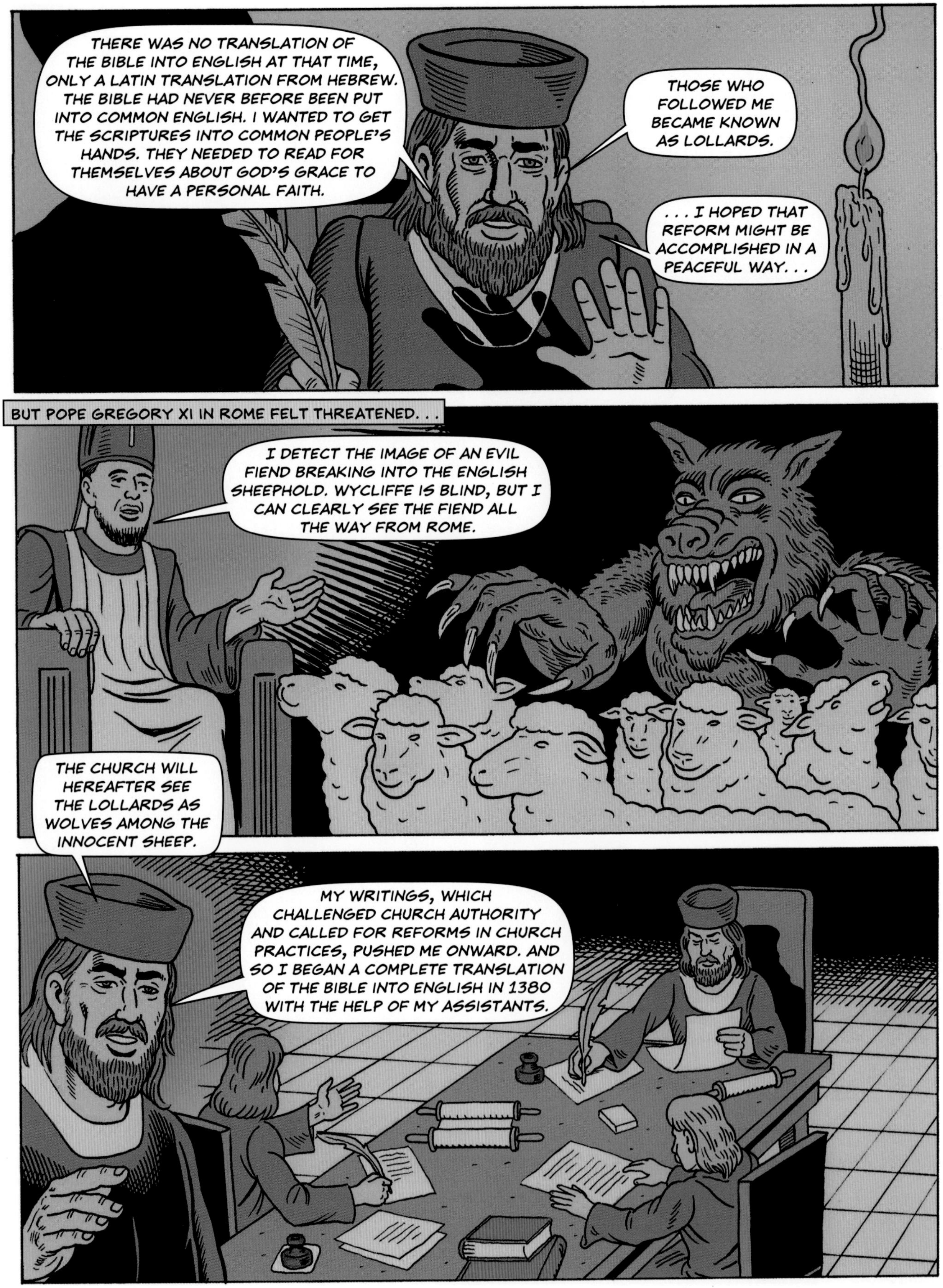
THERE WAS NO TRANSLATION OF THE BIBLE INTO ENGLISH AT THAT TIME, ONLY A LATIN TRANSLATION FROM HEBREW. THE BIBLE HAD NEVER BEFORE BEEN PUT INTO COMMON ENGLISH. I WANTED TO GET THE SCRIPTURES INTO COMMON PEOPLE'S HANDS. THEY NEEDED TO READ FOR THEMSELVES ABOUT GOD'S GRACE TO HAVE A PERSONAL FAITH.
THOSE WHO FOLLOWED ME BECAME KNOWN AS LOLLARDS.
. . . I HOPED THAT REFORM MIGHT BE ACCOMPLISHED IN A PEACEFUL WAY. . .
BUT POPE GREGORY XI IN ROME FELT THREATENED. . .
I DETECT THE IMAGE OF AN EVIL FIEND BREAKING INTO THE ENGLISH SHEEPHOLD. WYCLIFFE IS BLIND, BUT I CAN CLEARLY SEE THE FIEND ALL THE WAY FROM ROME.
THE CHURCH WILL HEREAFTER SEE THE LOLLARDS AS WOLVES AMONG THE INNOCENT SHEEP.
MY WRITINGS, WHICH CHALLENGED CHURCH AUTHORITY AND CALLED FOR REFORMS IN CHURCH PRACTICES, PUSHED ME ONWARD. AND SO I BEGAN A COMPLETE TRANSLATION OF THE BIBLE INTO ENGLISH IN 1380 WITH THE HELP OF MY ASSISTANTS.

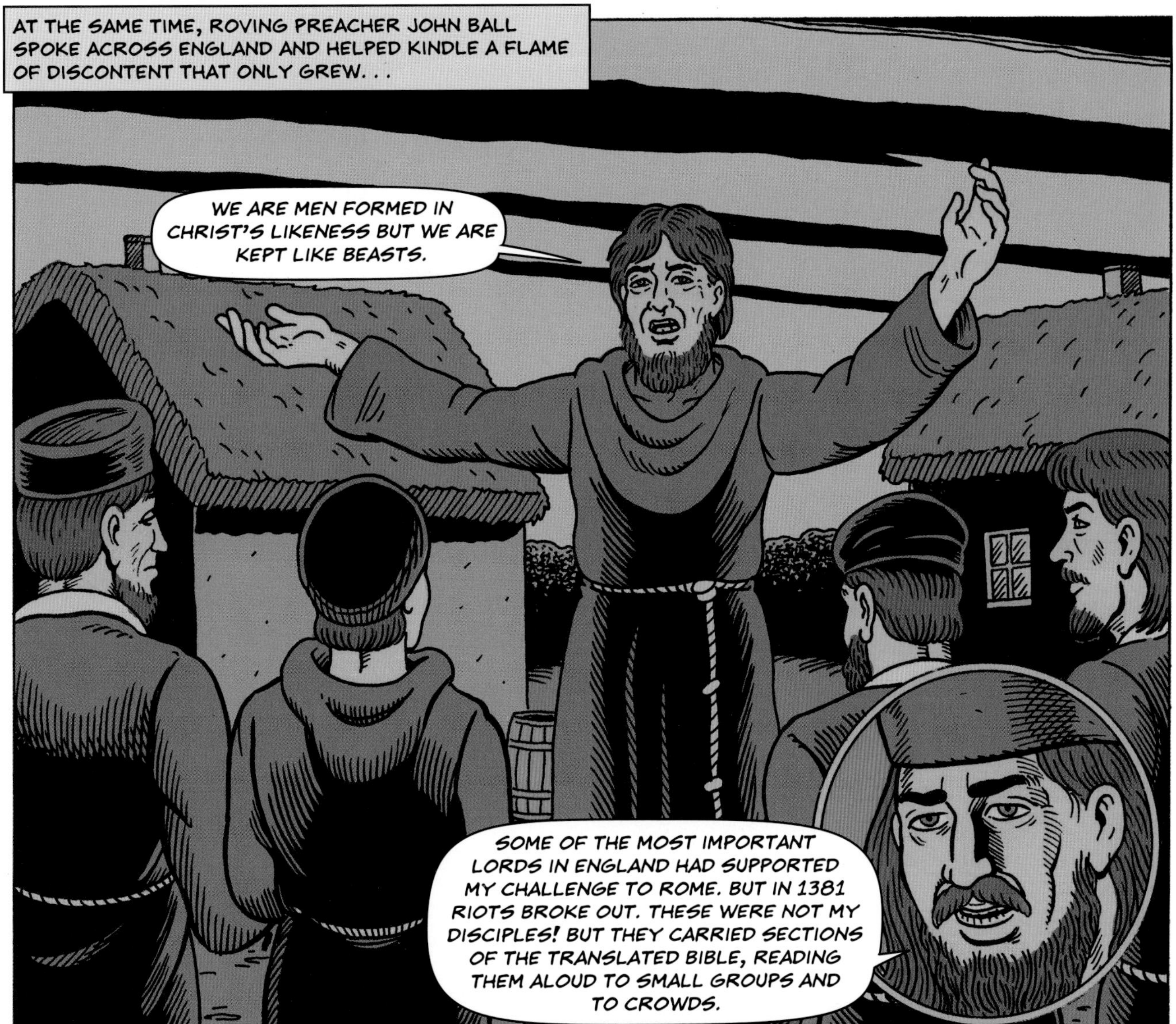
AT THE SAME TIME, ROVING PREACHER JOHN BALL SPOKE ACROSS ENGLAND AND HELPED KINDLE A FLAME OF DISCONTENT THAT ONLY GREW. . .
WE ARE MEN FORMED IN CHRIST'S LIKENESS BUT WE ARE KEPT LIKE BEASTS.
SOME OF THE MOST IMPORTANT LORDS IN ENGLAND HAD SUPPORTED MY CHALLENGE TO ROME. BUT IN 1381 RIOTS BROKE OUT. THESE WERE NOT MY DISCIPLES! BUT THEY CARRIED SECTIONS OF THE TRANSLATED BIBLE, READING THEM ALOUD TO SMALL GROUPS AND TO CROWDS.

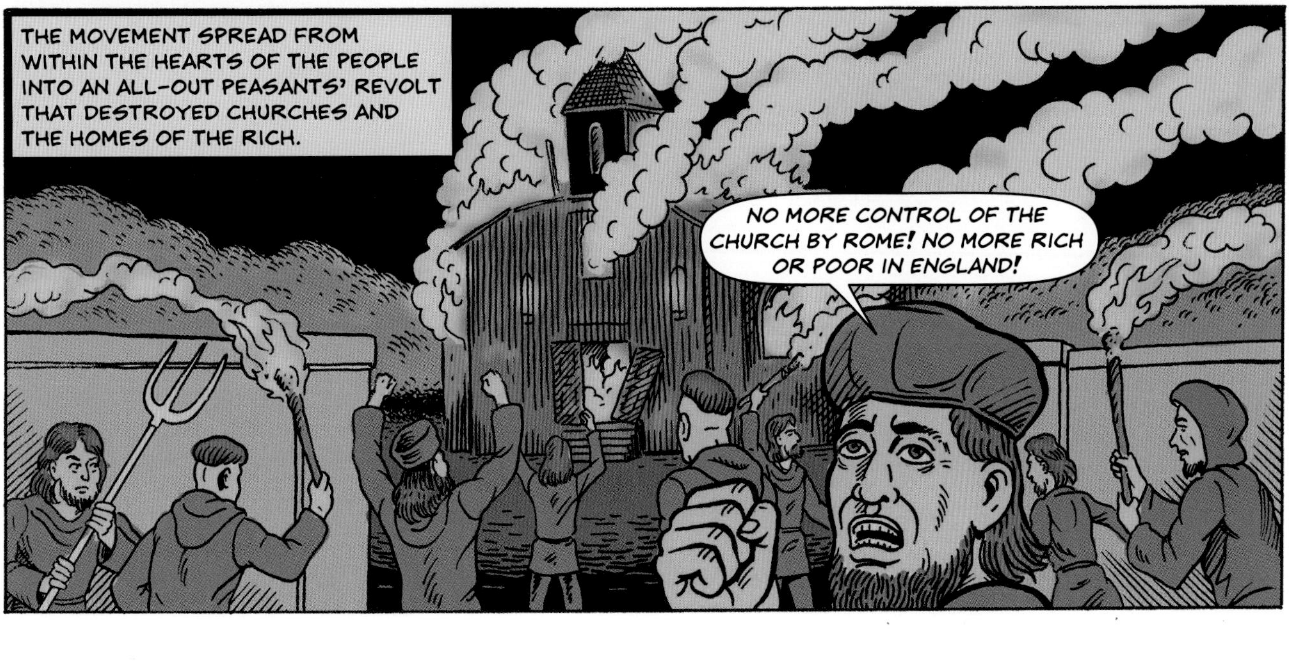
THE MOVEMENT SPREAD FROM WITHIN THE HEARTS OF THE PEOPLE INTO AN ALL-OUT PEASANTS' REVOLT THAT DESTROYED CHURCHES AND THE HOMES OF THE RICH.
NO MORE CONTROL OF THE CHURCH BY ROME! NO MORE RICH OR POOR IN ENGLAND!

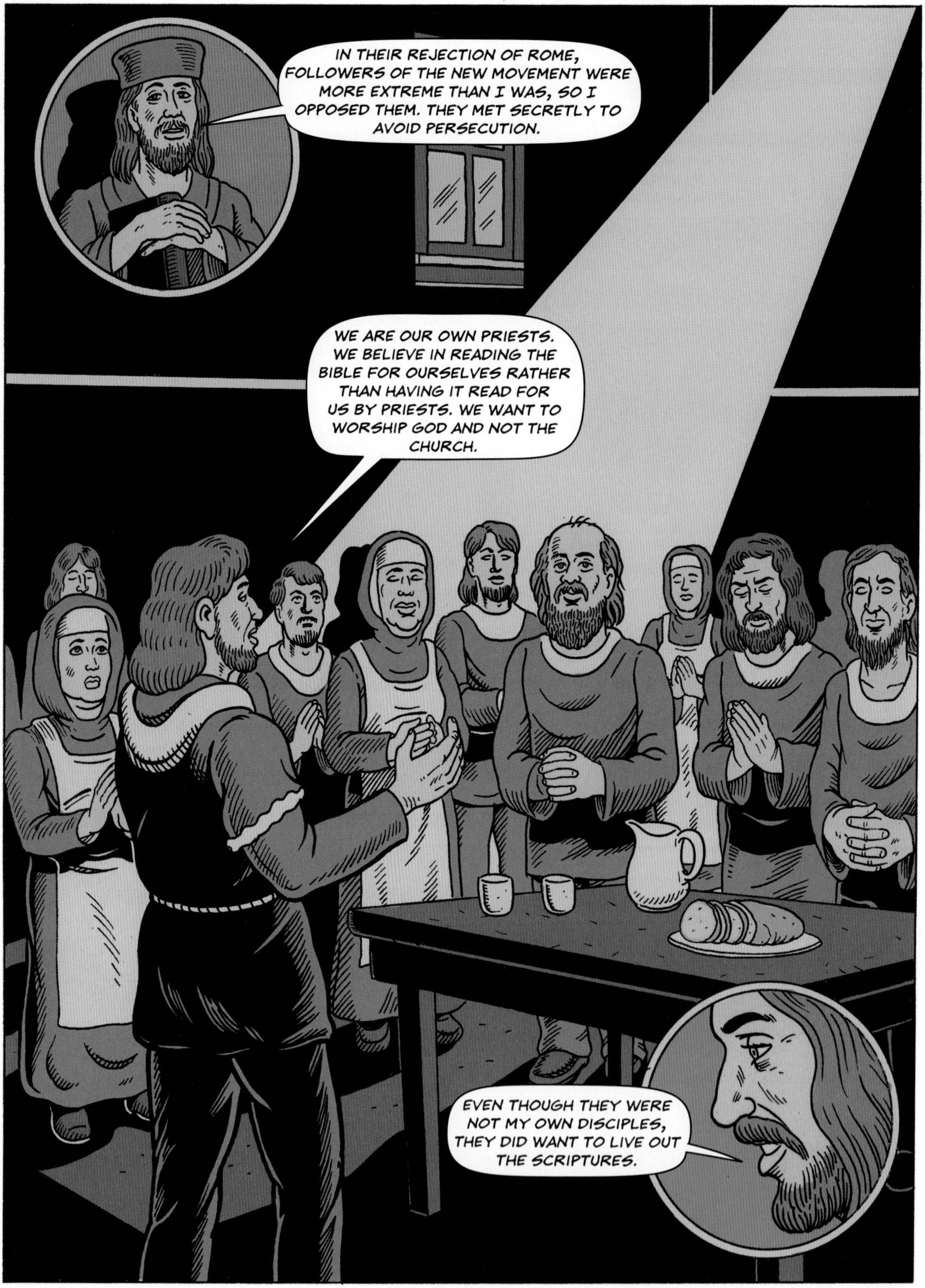
IN THEIR REJECTION OF ROME, FOLLOWERS OF THE NEW MOVEMENT WERE MORE EXTREME THAN I WAS, SO I OPPOSED THEM. THEY MET SECRETLY TO AVOID PERSECUTION.
WE ARE OUR OWN PRIESTS. WE BELIEVE IN READING THE BIBLE FOR OURSELVES RATHER THAN HAVING IT READ FOR US BY PRIESTS. WE WANT TO WORSHIP GOD AND NOT THE CHURCH.
EVEN THOUGH THEY WERE NOT MY OWN DISCIPLES, THEY DID WANT TO LIVE OUT THE SCRIPTURES.

JOHN WYCLIFFE DIED IN 1384, BOTH EXCOMMUNICATED FROM THE CHURCH AND CUT OFF FROM THE POLITICAL RADICALS OF THE AGE. HE WAS, HOWEVER, AN IMPORTANT INTERNATIONAL FIGURE. FOR CENTURIES HERETICS WERE KNOWN AS "WYCLIFFITES" AND "LOLLARDS," AMONG OTHER NAMES. THE RADICAL IDEAS HE PLANTED IN ENGLAND SPREAD ACROSS EUROPE.

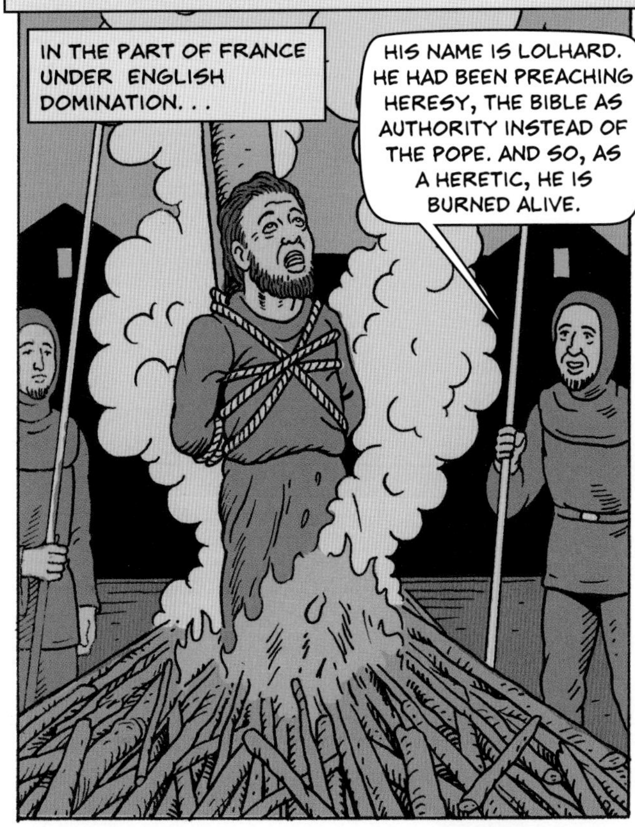
IN THE PART OF FRANCE UNDER ENGLISH DOMINATION. . .
HIS NAME IS LOLHARD. HE HAD BEEN PREACHING HERESY, THE BIBLE AS AUTHORITY INSTEAD OF THE POPE. AND SO, AS A HERETIC, HE IS BURNED ALIVE.

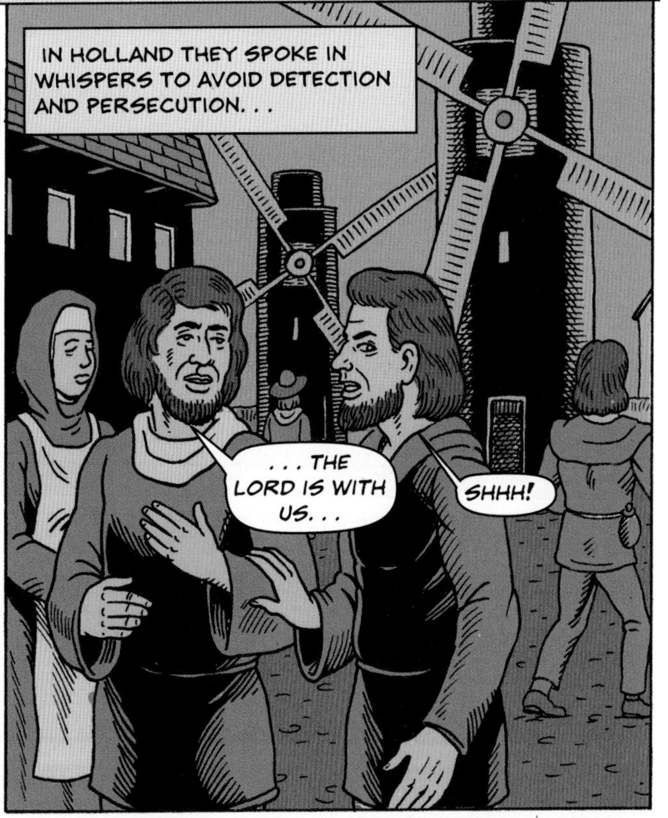
IN HOLLAND THEY SPOKE IN WHISPERS TO AVOID DETECTION AND PERSECUTION. . .
. . . THE LORD IS WITH US. . .
SHHH!

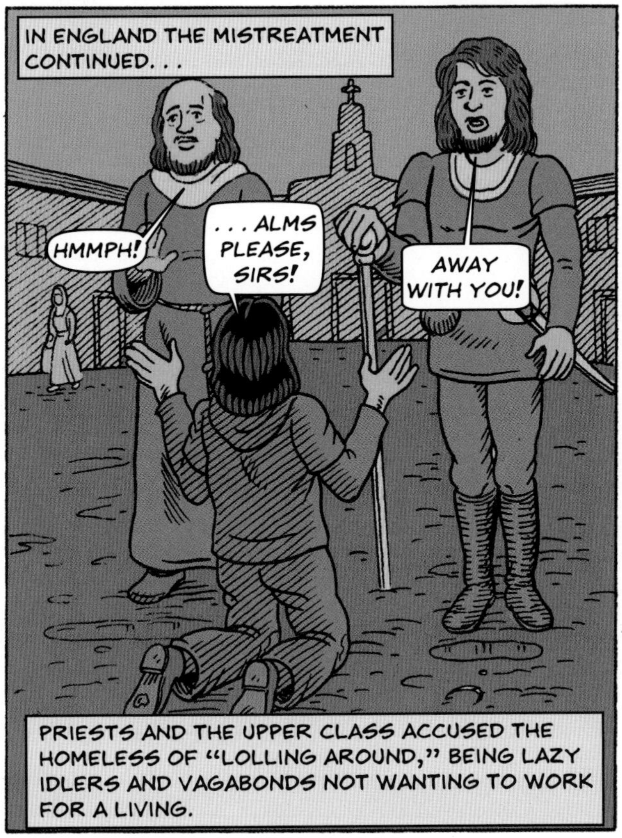
IN ENGLAND THE MISTREATMENT CONTINUED. . .
HMMPH!
. . . ALMS PLEASE, SIRS!
AWAY WITH YOU!
PRIESTS AND THE UPPER CLASS ACCUSED THE HOMELESS OF "LOLLING AROUND," BEING LAZY IDLERS AND VAGABONDS NOT WANTING TO WORK FOR A LIVING.

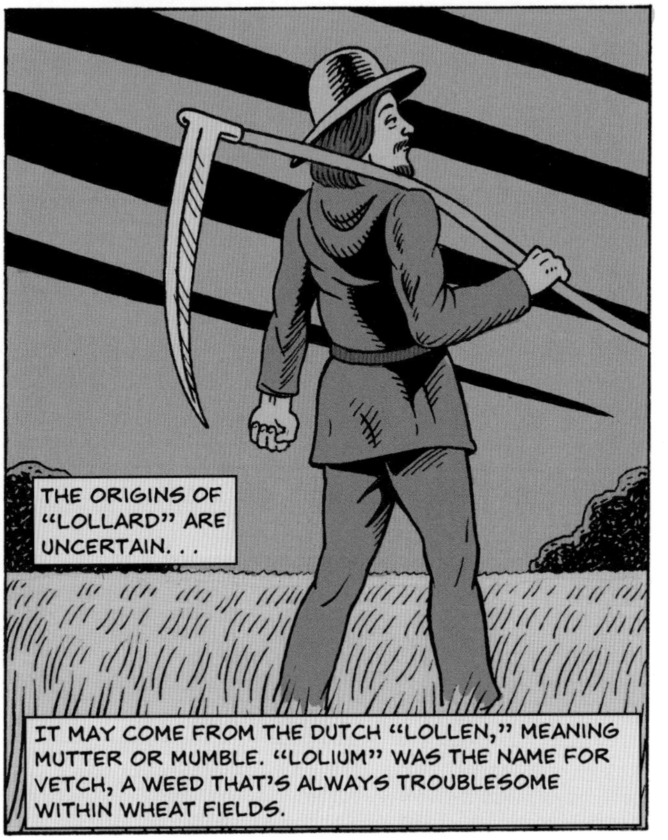
THE ORIGINS OF "LOLLARD" ARE UNCERTAIN. . .
IT MAY COME FROM THE DUTCH "LOLLEN," MEANING MUTTER OR MUMBLE. "LOLIUM" WAS THE NAME FOR VETCH, A WEED THAT'S ALWAYS TROUBLESOME WITHIN WHEAT FIELDS.

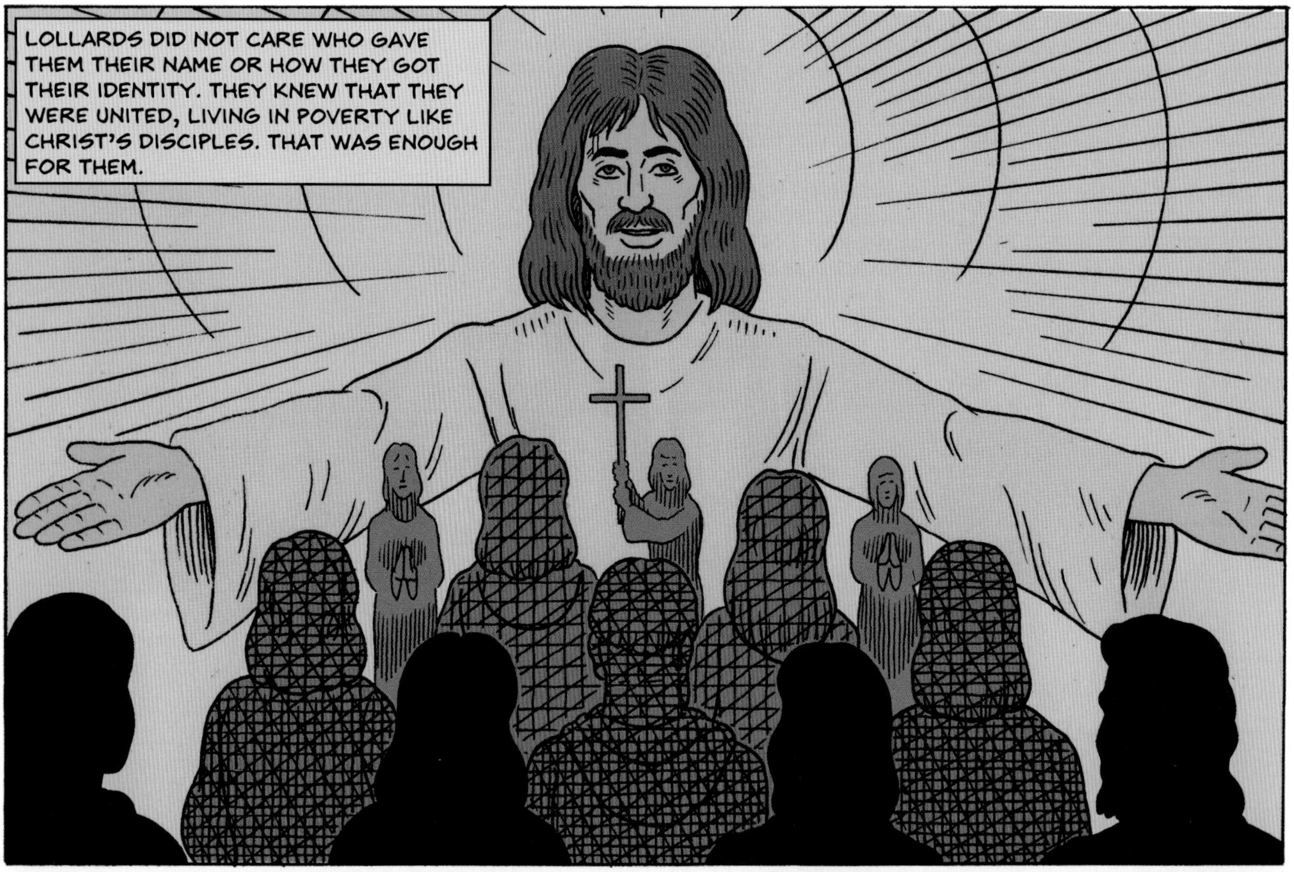
LOLLARDS DID NOT CARE WHO GAVE THEM THEIR NAME OR HOW THEY GOT THEIR IDENTITY. THEY KNEW THAT THEY WERE UNITED, LIVING IN POVERTY LIKE CHRIST'S DISCIPLES. THAT WAS ENOUGH FOR THEM.

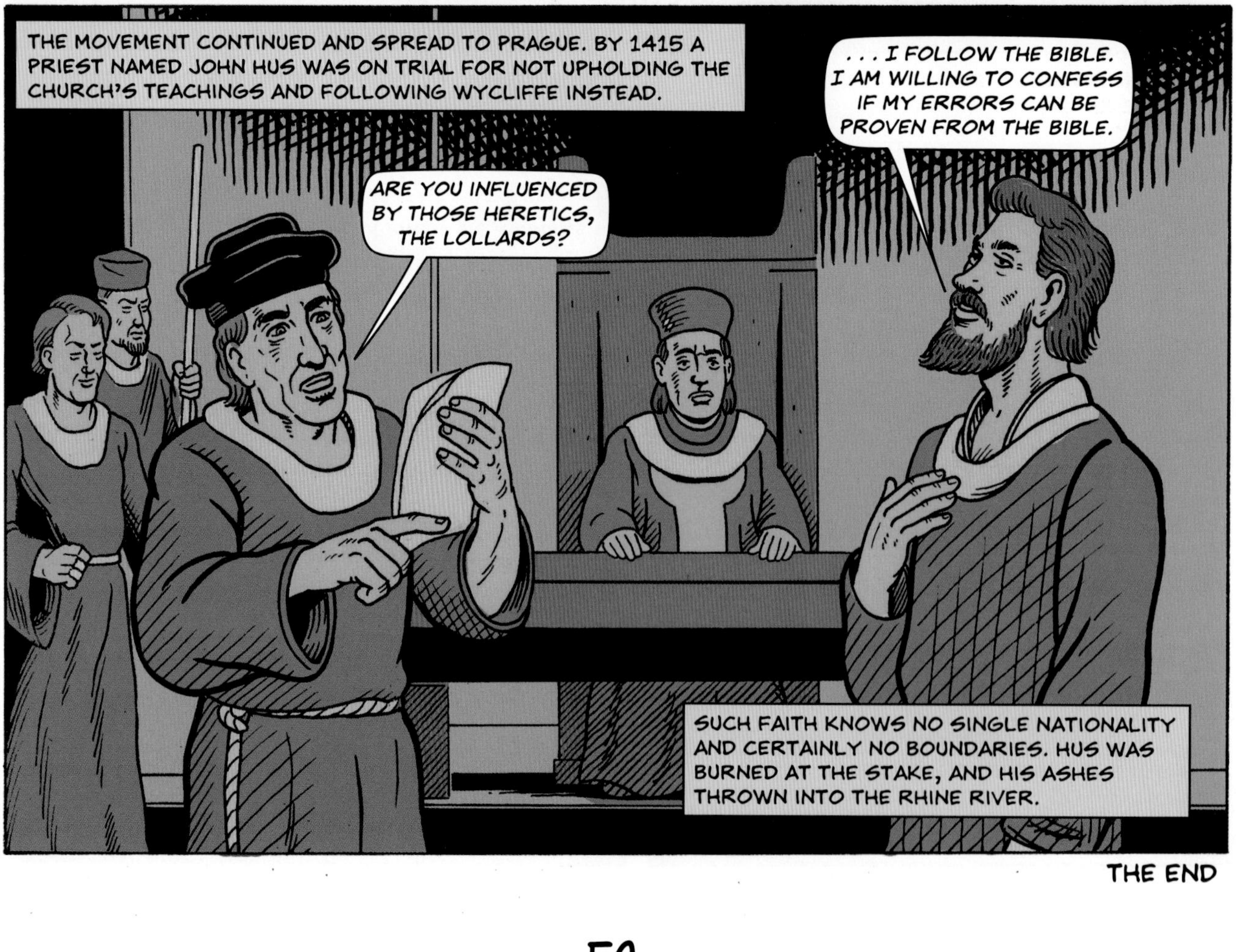
THE MOVEMENT CONTINUED AND SPREAD TO PRAGUE. BY 1415 A PRIEST NAMED JOHN HUS WAS ON TRIAL FOR NOT UPHOLDING THE CHURCH'S TEACHINGS AND FOLLOWING WYCLIFFE INSTEAD.
ARE YOU INFLUENCED BY THOSE HERETICS, THE LOLLARDS?
. . . I FOLLOW THE BIBLE. I AM WILLING TO CONFESS IF MY ERRORS CAN BE PROVEN FROM THE BIBLE.
SUCH FAITH KNOWS NO SINGLE NATIONALITY AND CERTAINLY NO BOUNDARIES. HUS WAS BURNED AT THE STAKE, AND HIS ASHES THROWN INTO THE RHINE RIVER.

THE END

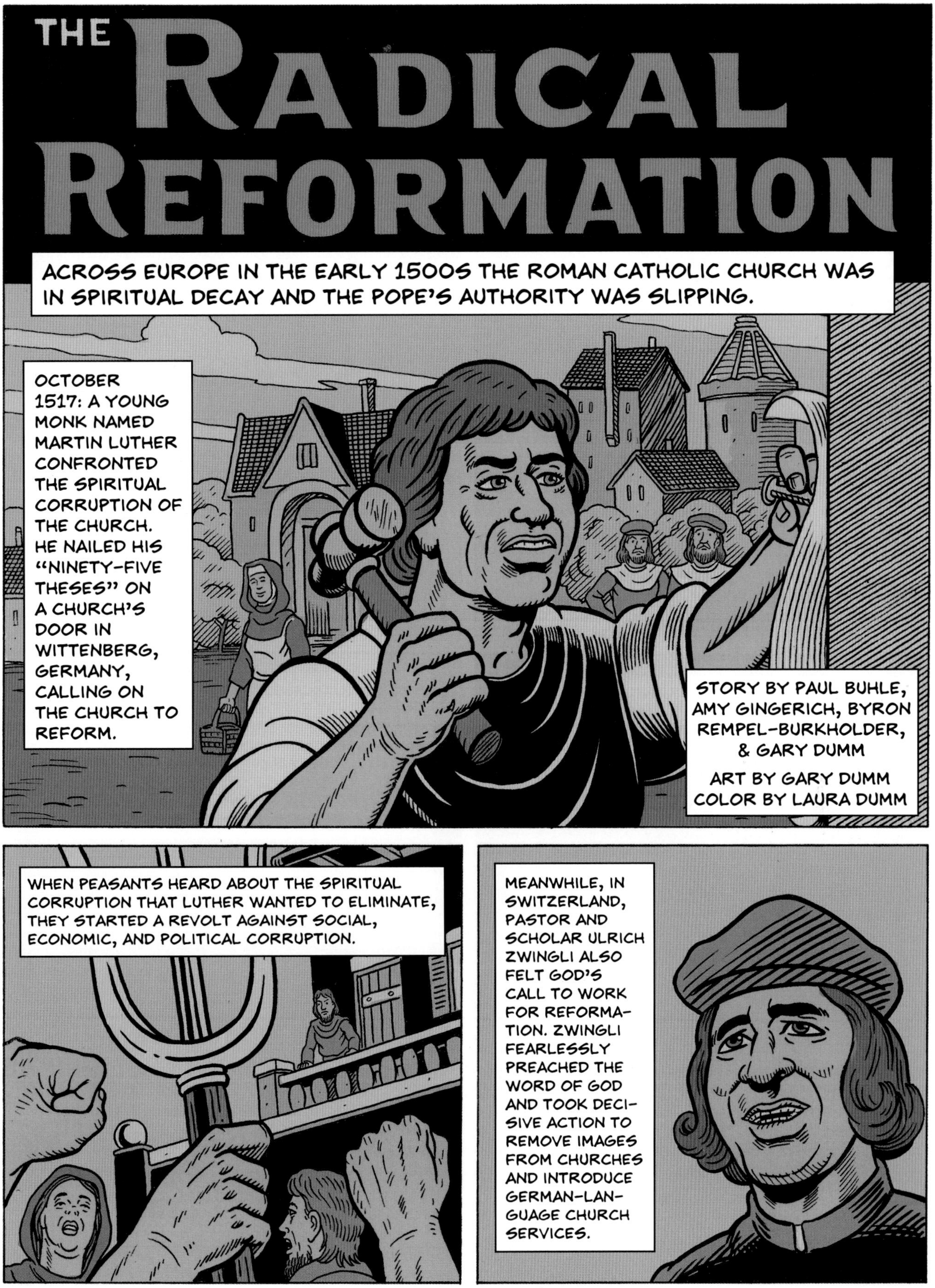
THE RADICAL REFORMATION
ACROSS EUROPE IN THE EARLY 1500S THE ROMAN CATHOLIC CHURCH WAS IN SPIRITUAL DECAY AND THE POPE'S AUTHORITY WAS SLIPPING.
OCTOBER 1517: A YOUNG MONK NAMED MARTIN LUTHER CONFRONTED THE SPIRITUAL CORRUPTION OF THE CHURCH. HE NAILED HIS "NINETY-FIVE THESES" ON A CHURCH'S DOOR IN WITTENBERG, GERMANY, CALLING ON THE CHURCH TO REFORM.
STORY BY PAUL BUHLE, AMY GINGERICH, BYRON REMPEL-BURKHOLDER, & GARY DUMM
ART BY GARY DUMM
COLOR BY LAURA DUMM
WHEN PEASANTS HEARD ABOUT THE SPIRITUAL CORRUPTION THAT LUTHER WANTED TO ELIMINATE, THEY STARTED A REVOLT AGAINST SOCIAL, ECONOMIC, AND POLITICAL CORRUPTION.
MEANWHILE, IN SWITZERLAND, PASTOR AND SCHOLAR ULRICH ZWINGLI ALSO FELT GOD'S CALL TO WORK FOR REFORMATION. ZWINGLI FEARLESSLY PREACHED THE WORD OF GOD AND TOOK DECISIVE ACTION TO REMOVE IMAGES FROM CHURCHES AND INTRODUCE GERMAN-LANGUAGE CHURCH SERVICES.

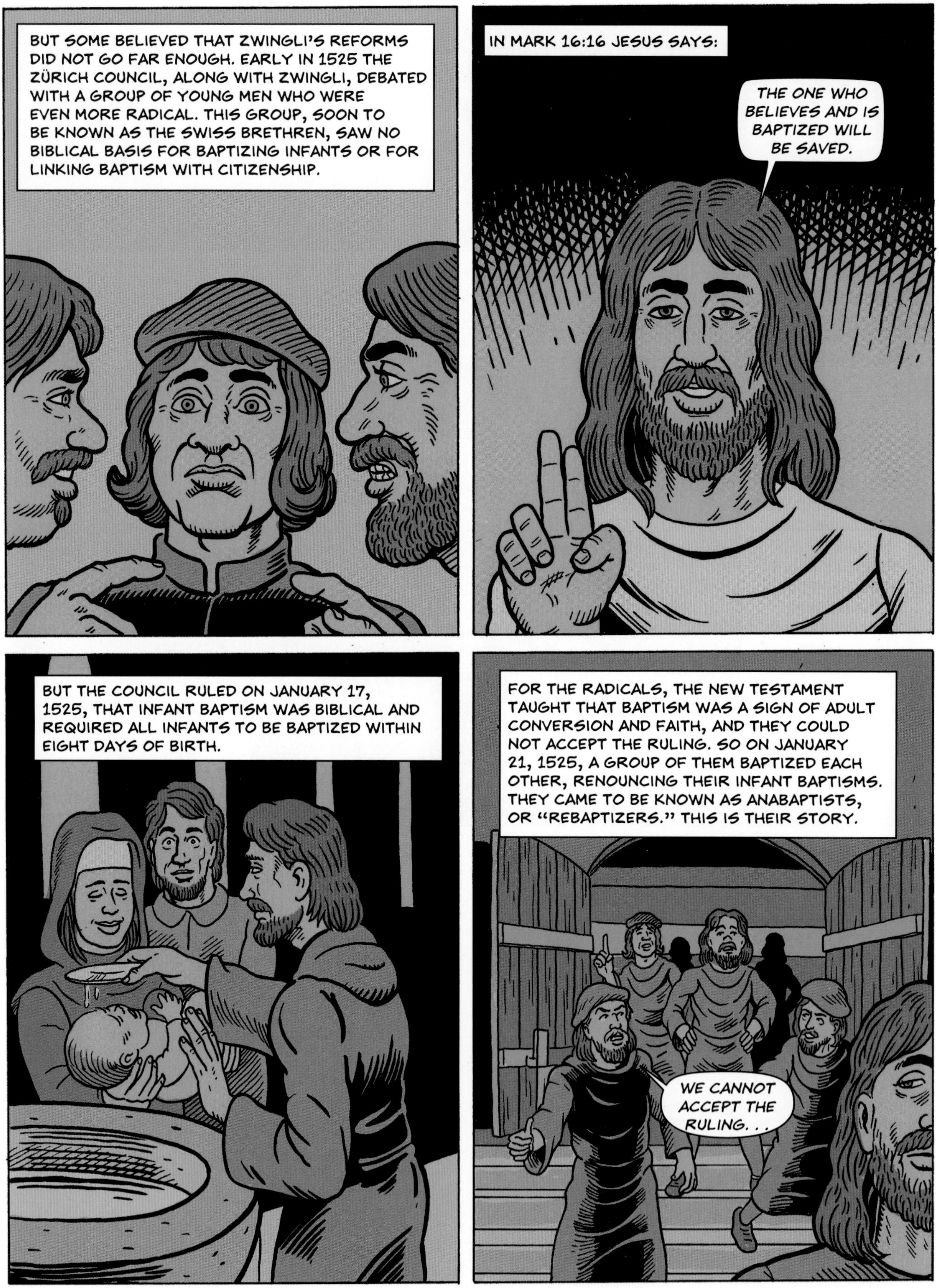
BUT SOME BELIEVED THAT ZWINGLI'S REFORMS DID NOT GO FAR ENOUGH. EARLY IN 1525 THE ZÜRICH COUNCIL, ALONG WITH ZWINGLI, DEBATED WITH A GROUP OF YOUNG MEN WHO WERE EVEN MORE RADICAL. THIS GROUP, SOON TO BE KNOWN AS THE SWISS BRETHREN, SAW NO BIBLICAL BASIS FOR BAPTIZING INFANTS OR FOR LINKING BAPTISM WITH CITIZENSHIP.
IN MARK 16:16 JESUS SAYS:
THE ONE WHO BELIEVES AND IS BAPTIZED WILL BE SAVED.
BUT THE COUNCIL RULED ON JANUARY 17, 1525, THAT INFANT BAPTISM WAS BIBLICAL AND REQUIRED ALL INFANTS TO BE BAPTIZED WITHIN EIGHT DAYS OF BIRTH.
FOR THE RADICALS, THE NEW TESTAMENT TAUGHT THAT BAPTISM WAS A SIGN OF ADULT CONVERSION AND FAITH, AND THEY COULD NOT ACCEPT THE RULING. SO ON JANUARY 21, 1525, A GROUP OF THEM BAPTIZED EACH OTHER, RENOUNCING THEIR INFANT BAPTISMS. THEY CAME TO BE KNOWN AS ANABAPTISTS, OR "REBAPTIZERS." THIS IS THEIR STORY.
WE CANNOT ACCEPT THE RULING. . .

I, GEORGE BLAUROCK, HAD FIRST COME TO ZÜRICH TO CONSULT WITH ZWINGLI ABOUT THE TRUTH OF THE GOSPEL. BUT I DIDN'T AGREE WITH EVERYTHING THAT ZWINGLI WAS TEACHING. I SOON JOINED THE RADICALS.

CONRAD GREBEL AND FELIX MANZ CHALLENGED ME FROM THE WORD OF GOD TO PRACTICE A TRUE FAITH, LOVE ALL PEOPLE, AND REMAIN STEADFAST IN TRIBULATION.

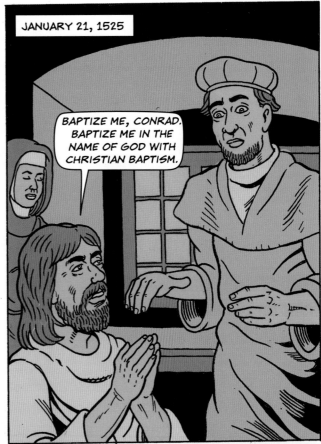

JANUARY 21, 1525

BAPTIZE ME, CONRAD. BAPTIZE ME IN THE NAME OF GOD WITH CHRISTIAN BAPTISM.

I BAPTIZE YOU IN THE NAME OF THE FATHER, THE SON, AND THE HOLY SPIRIT.

55

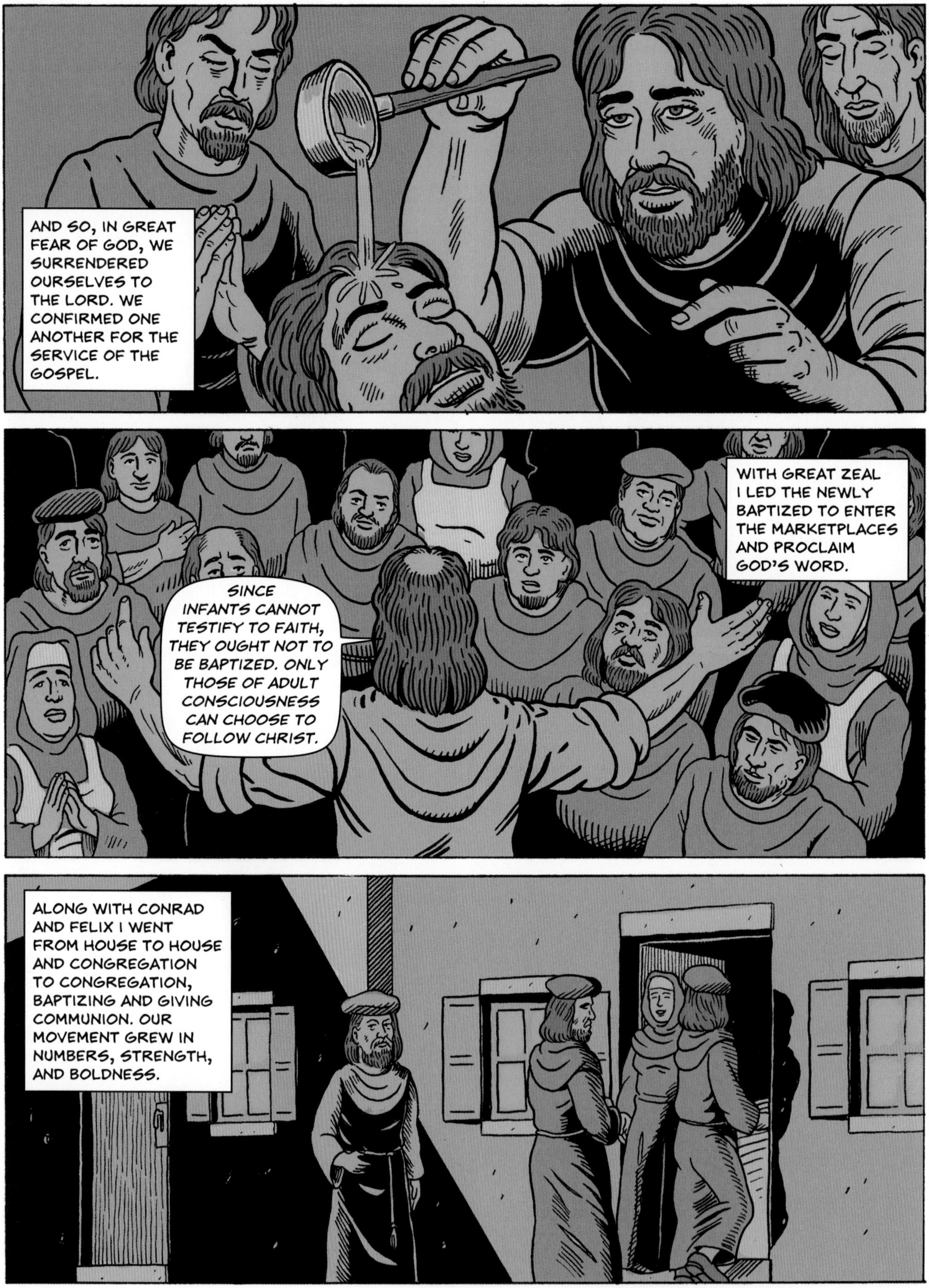
AND SO, IN GREAT FEAR OF GOD, WE SURRENDERED OURSELVES TO THE LORD. WE CONFIRMED ONE ANOTHER FOR THE SERVICE OF THE GOSPEL.
WITH GREAT ZEAL I LED THE NEWLY BAPTIZED TO ENTER THE MARKETPLACES AND PROCLAIM GOD'S WORD.
SINCE INFANTS CANNOT TESTIFY TO FAITH, THEY OUGHT NOT TO BE BAPTIZED. ONLY THOSE OF ADULT CONSCIOUSNESS CAN CHOOSE TO FOLLOW CHRIST.
ALONG WITH CONRAD AND FELIX I WENT FROM HOUSE TO HOUSE AND CONGREGATION TO CONGREGATION, BAPTIZING AND GIVING COMMUNION. OUR MOVEMENT GREW IN NUMBERS, STRENGTH, AND BOLDNESS.

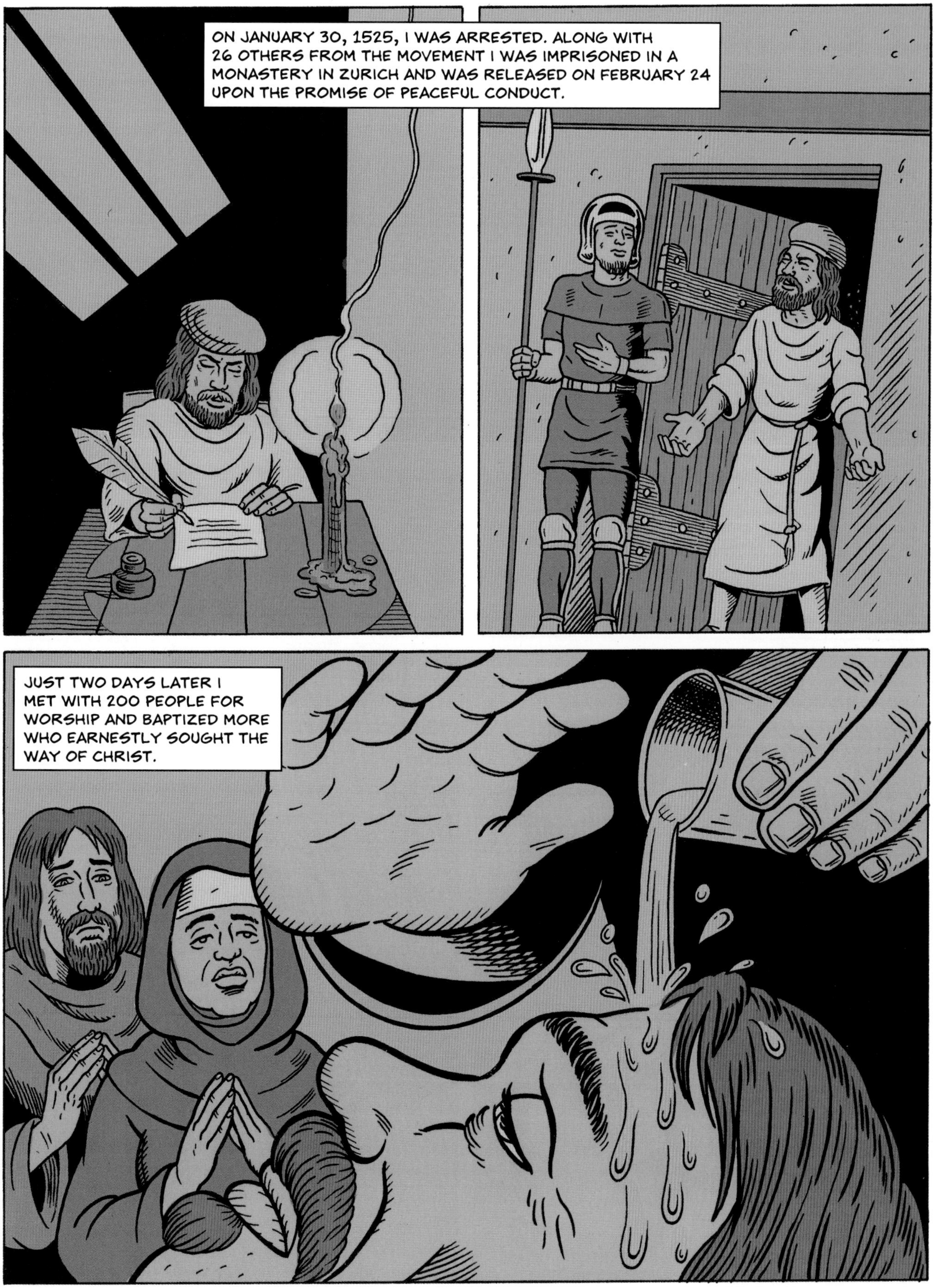
ON JANUARY 30, 1525, I WAS ARRESTED. ALONG WITH 26 OTHERS FROM THE MOVEMENT I WAS IMPRISONED IN A MONASTERY IN ZURICH AND WAS RELEASED ON FEBRUARY 24 UPON THE PROMISE OF PEACEFUL CONDUCT.
JUST TWO DAYS LATER I MET WITH 200 PEOPLE FOR WORSHIP AND BAPTIZED MORE WHO EARNESTLY SOUGHT THE WAY OF CHRIST.

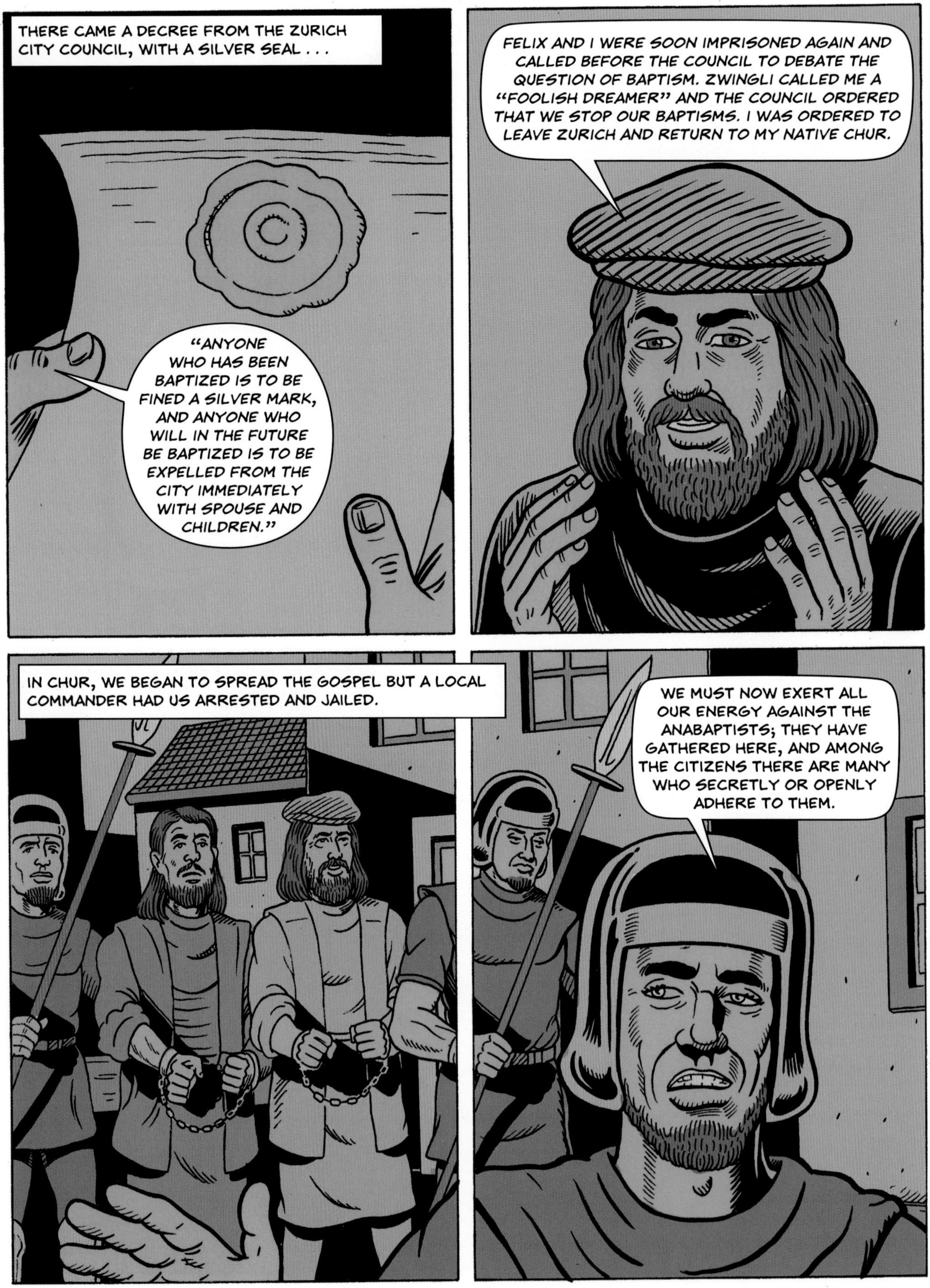
THERE CAME A DECREE FROM THE ZURICH CITY COUNCIL, WITH A SILVER SEAL . . .
"ANYONE WHO HAS BEEN BAPTIZED IS TO BE FINED A SILVER MARK, AND ANYONE WHO WILL IN THE FUTURE BE BAPTIZED IS TO BE EXPELLED FROM THE CITY IMMEDIATELY WITH SPOUSE AND CHILDREN."
FELIX AND I WERE SOON IMPRISONED AGAIN AND CALLED BEFORE THE COUNCIL TO DEBATE THE QUESTION OF BAPTISM. ZWINGLI CALLED ME A "FOOLISH DREAMER" AND THE COUNCIL ORDERED THAT WE STOP OUR BAPTISMS. I WAS ORDERED TO LEAVE ZURICH AND RETURN TO MY NATIVE CHUR.
IN CHUR, WE BEGAN TO SPREAD THE GOSPEL BUT A LOCAL COMMANDER HAD US ARRESTED AND JAILED.
WE MUST NOW EXERT ALL OUR ENERGY AGAINST THE ANABAPTISTS; THEY HAVE GATHERED HERE, AND AMONG THE CITIZENS THERE ARE MANY WHO SECRETLY OR OPENLY ADHERE TO THEM.

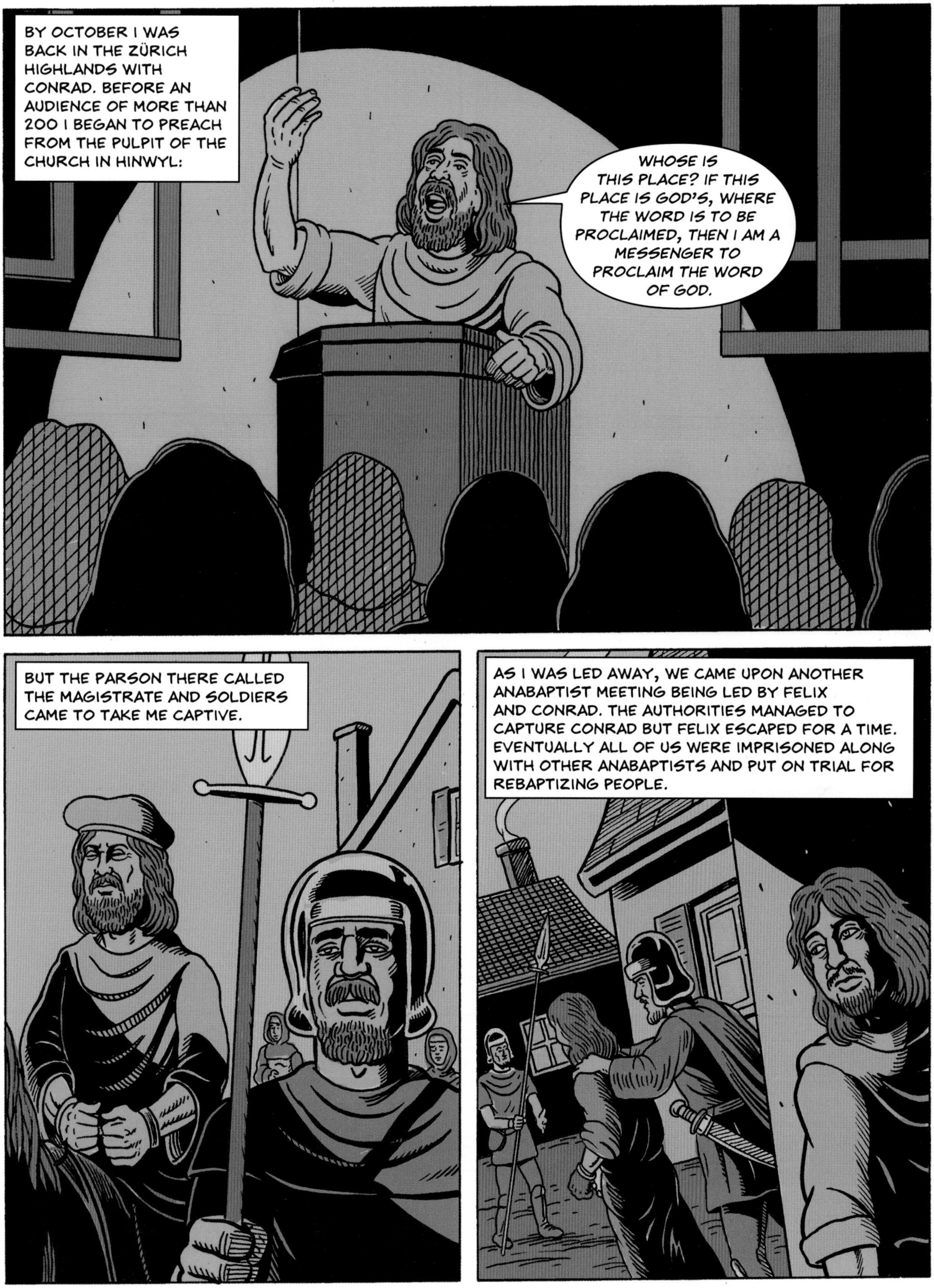
BY OCTOBER I WAS BACK IN THE ZÜRICH HIGHLANDS WITH CONRAD. BEFORE AN AUDIENCE OF MORE THAN 200 I BEGAN TO PREACH FROM THE PULPIT OF THE CHURCH IN HINWYL:
WHOSE IS THIS PLACE? IF THIS PLACE IS GOD'S, WHERE THE WORD IS TO BE PROCLAIMED, THEN I AM A MESSENGER TO PROCLAIM THE WORD OF GOD.
BUT THE PARSON THERE CALLED THE MAGISTRATE AND SOLDIERS CAME TO TAKE ME CAPTIVE.
AS I WAS LED AWAY, WE CAME UPON ANOTHER ANABAPTIST MEETING BEING LED BY FELIX AND CONRAD. THE AUTHORITIES MANAGED TO CAPTURE CONRAD BUT FELIX ESCAPED FOR A TIME. EVENTUALLY ALL OF US WERE IMPRISONED ALONG WITH OTHER ANABAPTISTS AND PUT ON TRIAL FOR REBAPTIZING PEOPLE.

AFTER OUR CAPTURE ONE OF THEIR MEMBERS ADDRESSED THE REST OF THE COUNCIL...

WE MUST PUT AN END TO THIS CORNER PREACHING AND RABBLE-ROUSING.

ON MARCH 7, 1526, WE WERE SENTENCED TO LIFE IN PRISON. THE COUNCIL RULED THAT REBAPTIZING WAS FORBIDDEN, AND DEATH BY DROWNING WAS SET AS THE PUNISHMENT FOR ALL THOSE WHO PERFORMED IT.

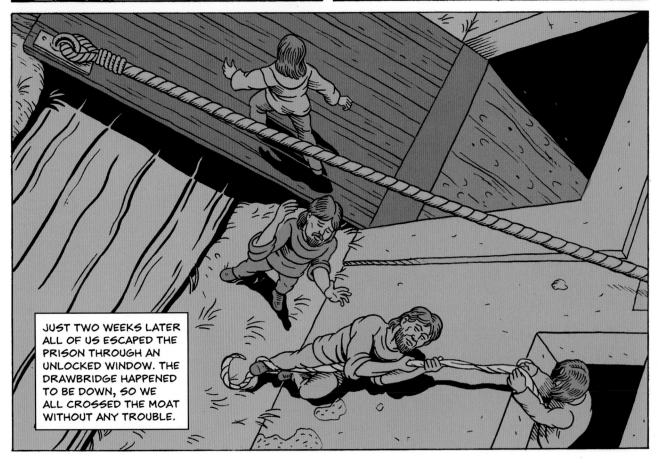

JUST TWO WEEKS LATER ALL OF US ESCAPED THE PRISON THROUGH AN UNLOCKED WINDOW. THE DRAWBRIDGE HAPPENED TO BE DOWN, SO WE ALL CROSSED THE MOAT WITHOUT ANY TROUBLE.

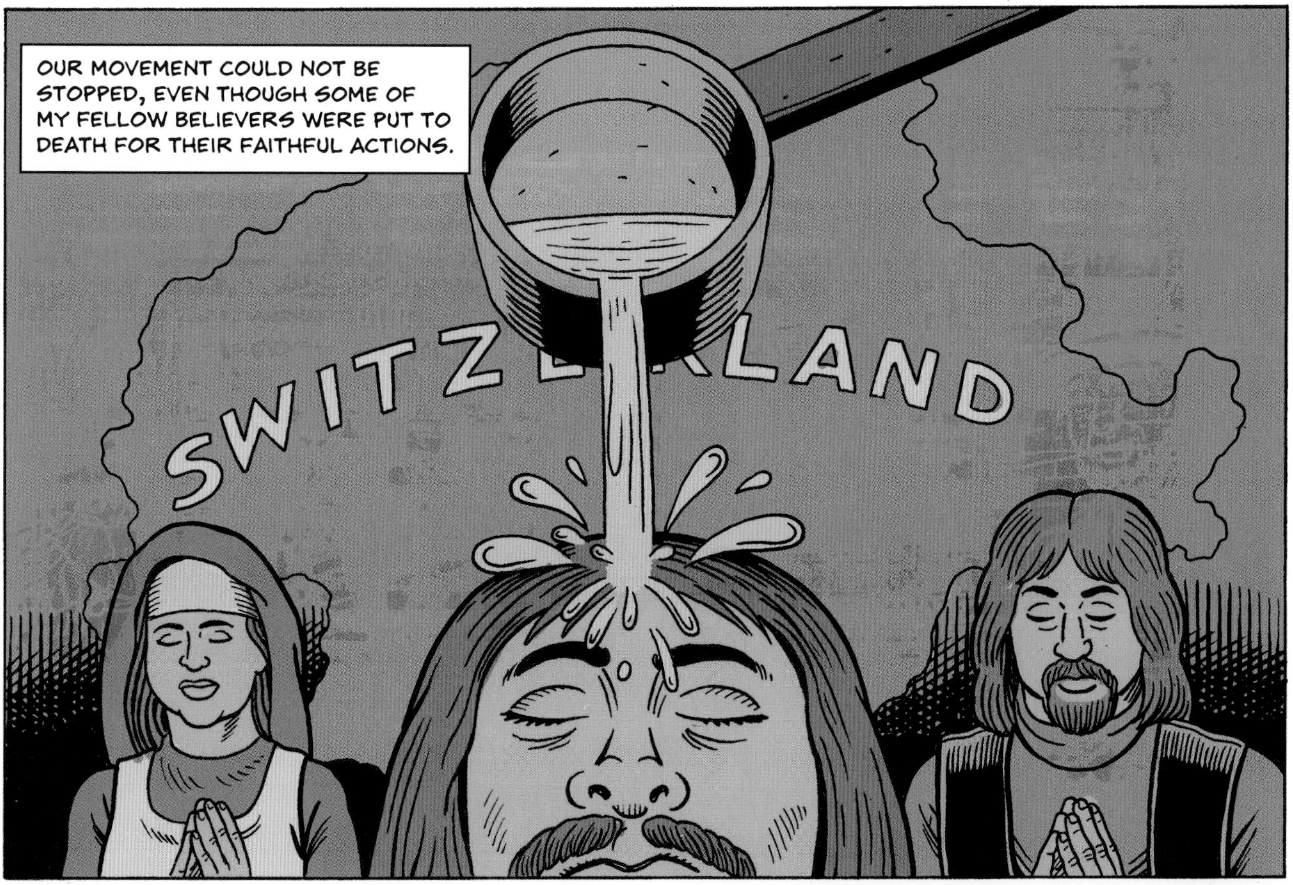
OUR MOVEMENT COULD NOT BE STOPPED, EVEN THOUGH SOME OF MY FELLOW BELIEVERS WERE PUT TO DEATH FOR THEIR FAITHFUL ACTIONS.
SWITZERLAND

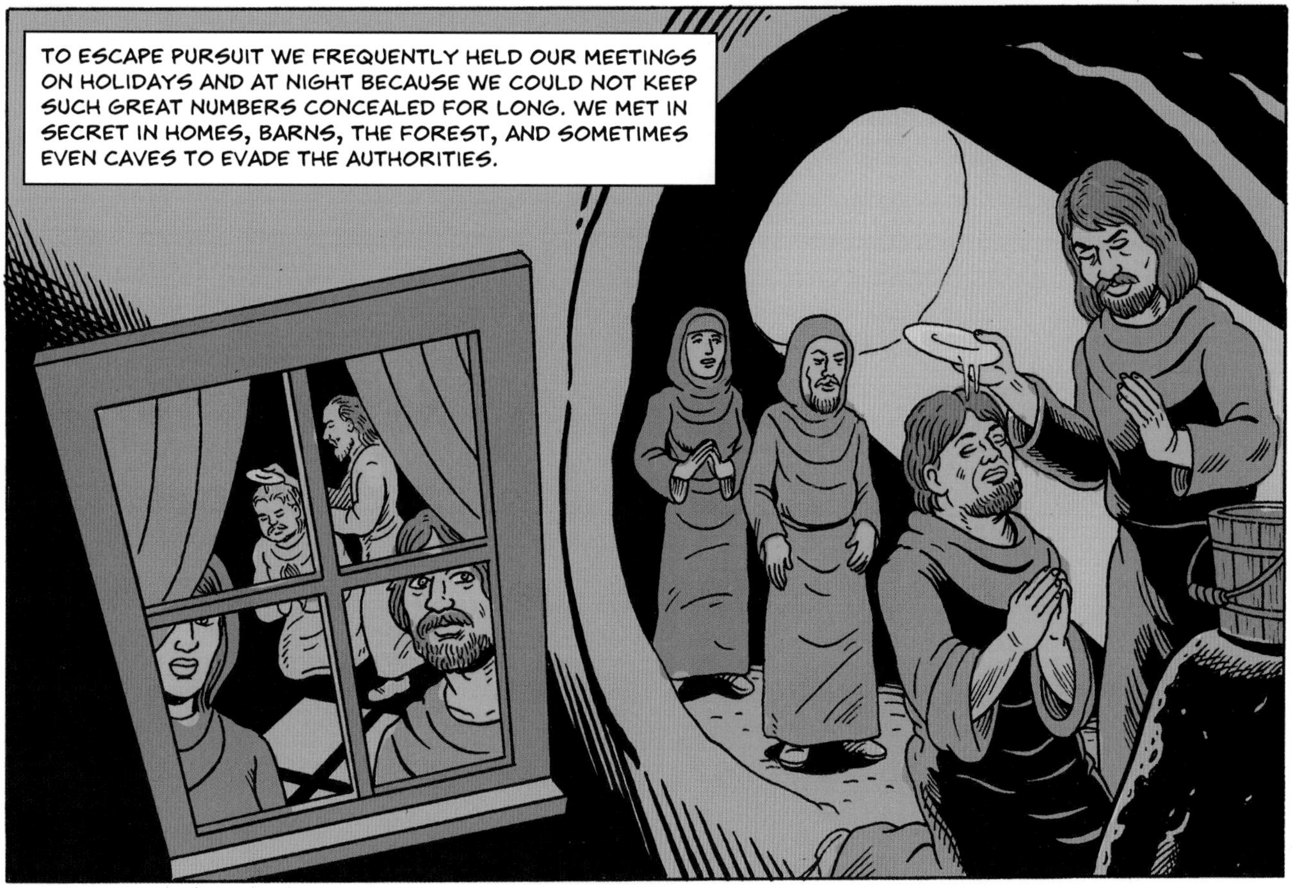
TO ESCAPE PURSUIT WE FREQUENTLY HELD OUR MEETINGS ON HOLIDAYS AND AT NIGHT BECAUSE WE COULD NOT KEEP SUCH GREAT NUMBERS CONCEALED FOR LONG. WE MET IN SECRET IN HOMES, BARNS, THE FOREST, AND SOMETIMES EVEN CAVES TO EVADE THE AUTHORITIES.

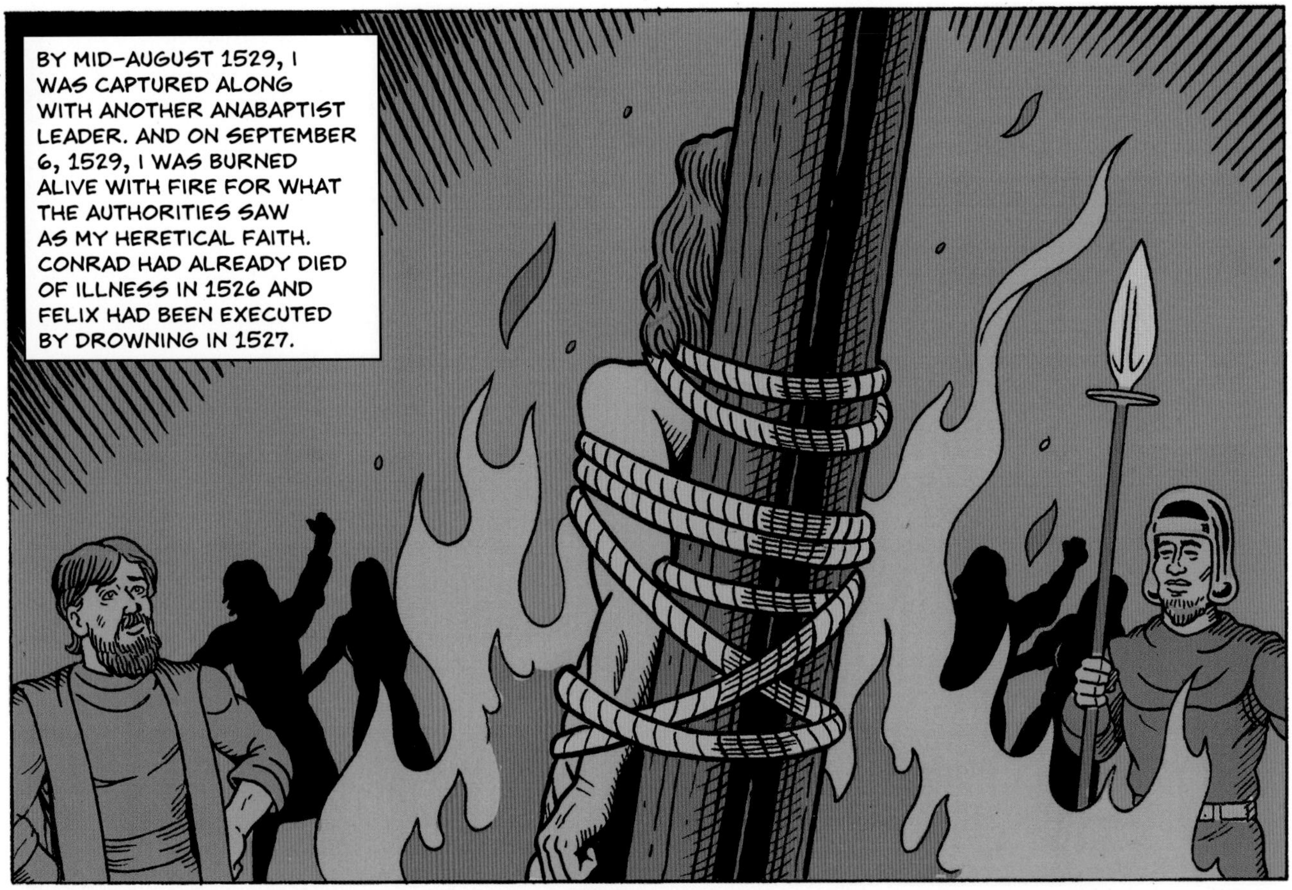
BY MID-AUGUST 1529, I WAS CAPTURED ALONG WITH ANOTHER ANABAPTIST LEADER. AND ON SEPTEMBER 6, 1529, I WAS BURNED ALIVE WITH FIRE FOR WHAT THE AUTHORITIES SAW AS MY HERETICAL FAITH. CONRAD HAD ALREADY DIED OF ILLNESS IN 1526 AND FELIX HAD BEEN EXECUTED BY DROWNING IN 1527.

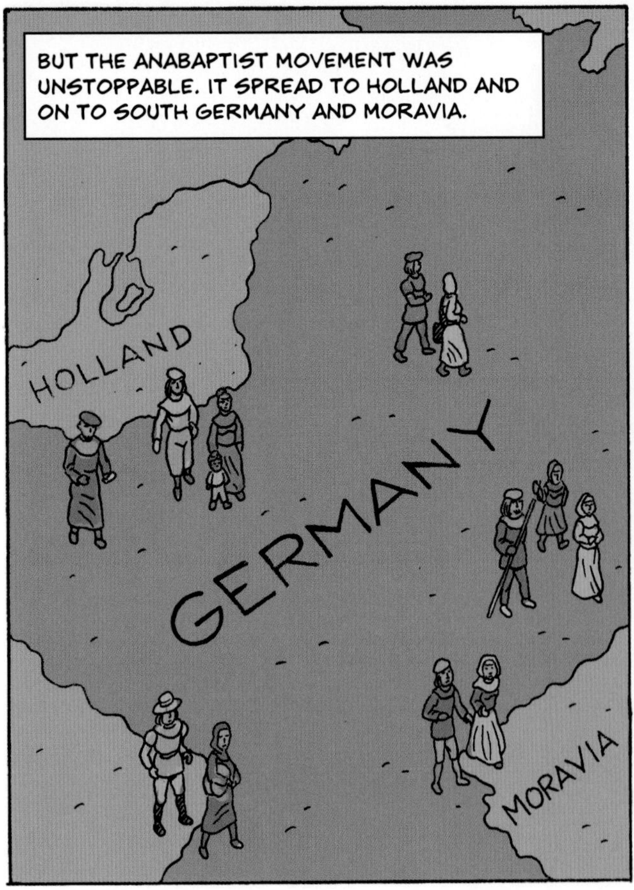
BUT THE ANABAPTIST MOVEMENT WAS UNSTOPPABLE. IT SPREAD TO HOLLAND AND ON TO SOUTH GERMANY AND MORAVIA.
HOLLAND
GERMANY
MORAVIA

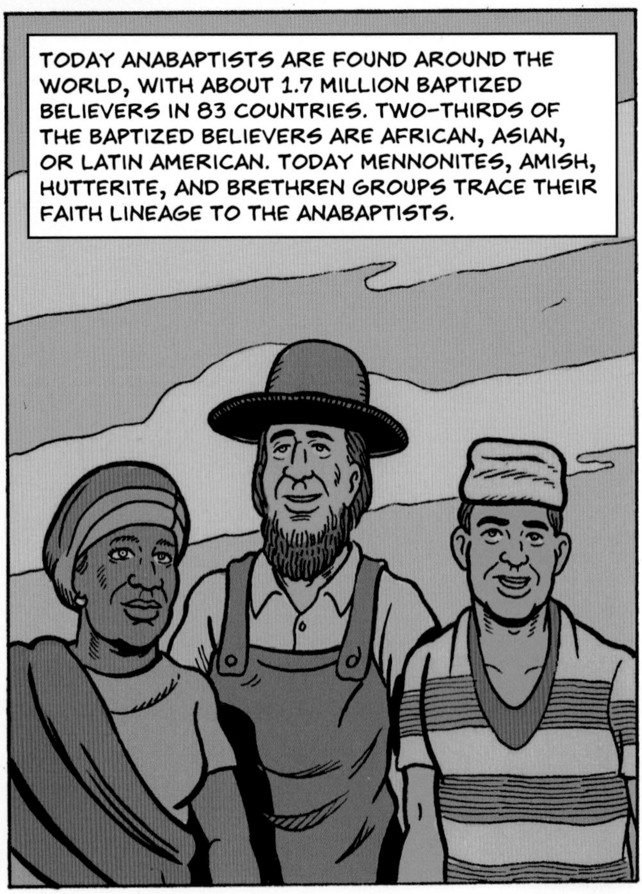
TODAY ANABAPTISTS ARE FOUND AROUND THE WORLD, WITH ABOUT 1.7 MILLION BAPTIZED BELIEVERS IN 83 COUNTRIES. TWO-THIRDS OF THE BAPTIZED BELIEVERS ARE AFRICAN, ASIAN, OR LATIN AMERICAN. TODAY MENNONITES, AMISH, HUTTERITE, AND BRETHREN GROUPS TRACE THEIR FAITH LINEAGE TO THE ANABAPTISTS.

THE END

# ESCAPE FROM GALLEY SLAVERY

## A STORY OF THE HUTTERITE BRETHREN

STORY BY PAUL BUHLE · ART BY GARY DUMM · COLOR BY LAURA DUMM

ANABAPTISTS WERE OFTEN DUBBED "THE RADICALS," AN EPITHET THEY CAME TO EMBRACE. THEIR EXECUTIONS IN PUBLIC WERE MEANT TO SERVE AS A LESSON TO INSTILL FEAR IN OTHERS. PERVERSELY, THE KILLINGS ALSO SERVED AS BRUTAL PUBLIC ENTERTAINMENT, MUCH LIKE THE LIFE–AND–DEATH SPECTACLES OF THE ROMAN COLISEUMS. IN AN ERA OF FEW ENTERTAINMENTS, CROWDS GATHERED WILLINGLY TO WATCH THE BODIES OF THE CONDEMNED BEING MUTILATED WHILE THEIR SOULS WERE SUPPOSEDLY SENT OFF TO HADES.

SOME MARTYRS WERE BURNED AT THE STAKE, OTHERS WERE DROWNED, DECAPITATED, HAD THEIR TONGUES RIPPED OUT, OR THEIR MOUTHS FILLED WITH GUNPOWDER. TO GO TO A VIOLENT DEATH WITH COLD DETERMINATION OR EVEN GOOD CHEER WAS TO PROVE TO ALL PRESENT THAT THE BELIEVER PLACED ULTIMATE TRUST IN GOD'S JUDGMENT.

NO, I WILL DRINK THE NEW WINE IN THE KINGDOM OF THE FATHER. . .

FRENCH AND BELGIAN ROYAL COURTS SOMETIMES OFFERED "BANQUETS" FOR THE INTENDED VICTIM A DAY BEFORE THE EXECUTION. IN THE CITY HALL, THE ACCUSED WOULD BE COMPELLED TO TAKE THE SEAT OF HONOR BETWEEN THE MAYOR AND A LOCAL RELIGIOUS LEADER WHILE BEING MOCKED AND OFFERED EXPENSIVE FOOD AND WINE.

ONE FAMOUS MARTYR OF 1557, GERRIT HAZENPOET OF NIJMEGEN, THE NETHERLANDS, REFUSED TO ACCEPT THE WINE. AT THE STAKE WHERE HE WAS TO BE BURNED, HAZENPOET BOLDLY SANG OUT A HYMN OF FAREWELL TO ENCOURAGE HIS FELLOW CHRISTIANS AS THEY BORE WITNESS TO HIS EXECUTION.

BUT NOT ALL MARTYRS WERE SACRIFICED AT STATE EXPENSE FOR PUBLIC ENTERTAINMENT. THIS STORY IS ABOUT A GROUP OF HUTTERITES, AN ANABAPTIST GROUP IN AUSTRIA, FORCED TO ROW MASSIVE GALLEY SHIPS INTO BATTLES. AS SLAVES OF THE CROWN, THEY PERFORMED BACKBREAKING WORK UNTIL THEY WERE "WORKED TO DEATH." MANY DIED OF HUNGER AND EXHAUSTION, WHILE OTHERS WERE KILLED IN BATTLE WHEN CANNON FIRE TORE THROUGH THEIR SHIPS.

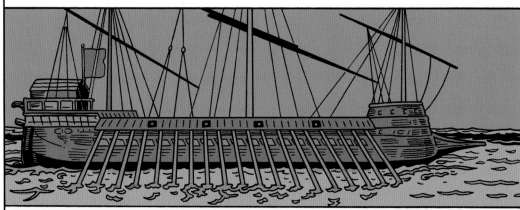

SOME ANABAPTISTS HAD STUDIED THE BIBLE AND RELATED LITERATURE CLOSELY. THEY TOOK LITERALLY WHAT JESUS SAID IN THE NEW TESTAMENT . . .

"LOVE YOUR ENEMIES, DO GOOD TO THOSE WHO HATE YOU, BLESS THOSE WHO CURSE YOU, PRAY FOR THOSE WHO MISTREAT YOU."

MEN OF STEINABRUNN! IMPERIAL ADMIRAL ANDREA DORIC HAS GIVEN THE COMMAND THAT WE MUST HAVE 80 OF YOU FOR OUR OARSMEN. WHOEVER WILL RENOUNCE HIS FAITH DOES NOT NEED TO GO.

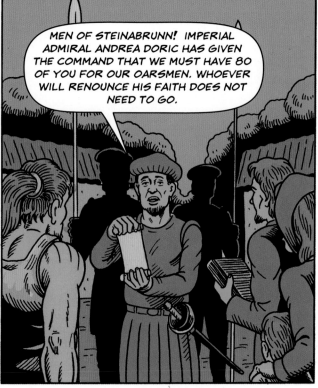

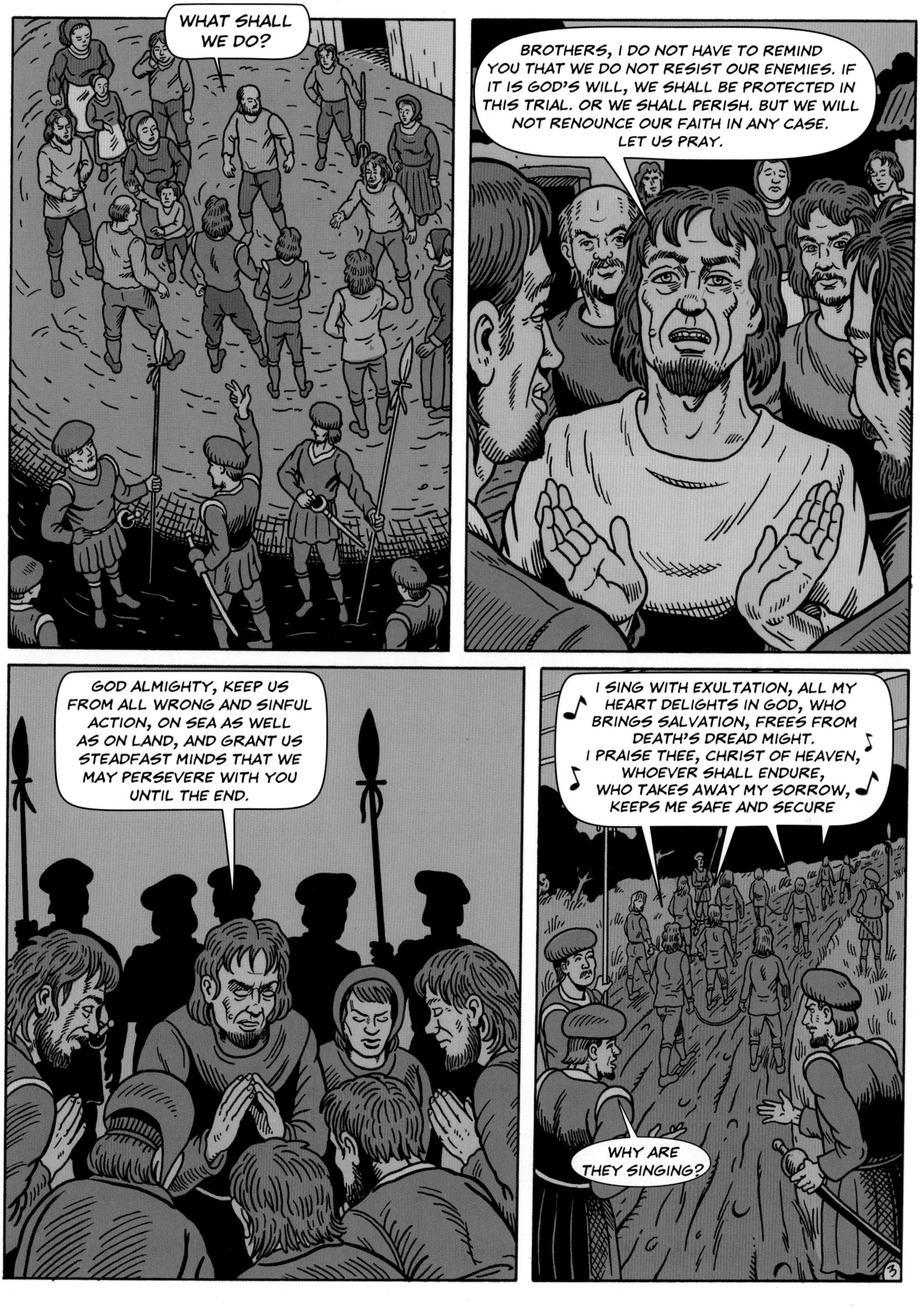
WHAT SHALL WE DO?
BROTHERS, I DO NOT HAVE TO REMIND YOU THAT WE DO NOT RESIST OUR ENEMIES. IF IT IS GOD'S WILL, WE SHALL BE PROTECTED IN THIS TRIAL. OR WE SHALL PERISH. BUT WE WILL NOT RENOUNCE OUR FAITH IN ANY CASE. LET US PRAY.
GOD ALMIGHTY, KEEP US FROM ALL WRONG AND SINFUL ACTION, ON SEA AS WELL AS ON LAND, AND GRANT US STEADFAST MINDS THAT WE MAY PERSEVERE WITH YOU UNTIL THE END.
I SING WITH EXULTATION, ALL MY HEART DELIGHTS IN GOD, WHO BRINGS SALVATION, FREES FROM DEATH'S DREAD MIGHT. I PRAISE THEE, CHRIST OF HEAVEN, WHOEVER SHALL ENDURE, WHO TAKES AWAY MY SORROW, KEEPS ME SAFE AND SECURE
WHY ARE THEY SINGING?
3

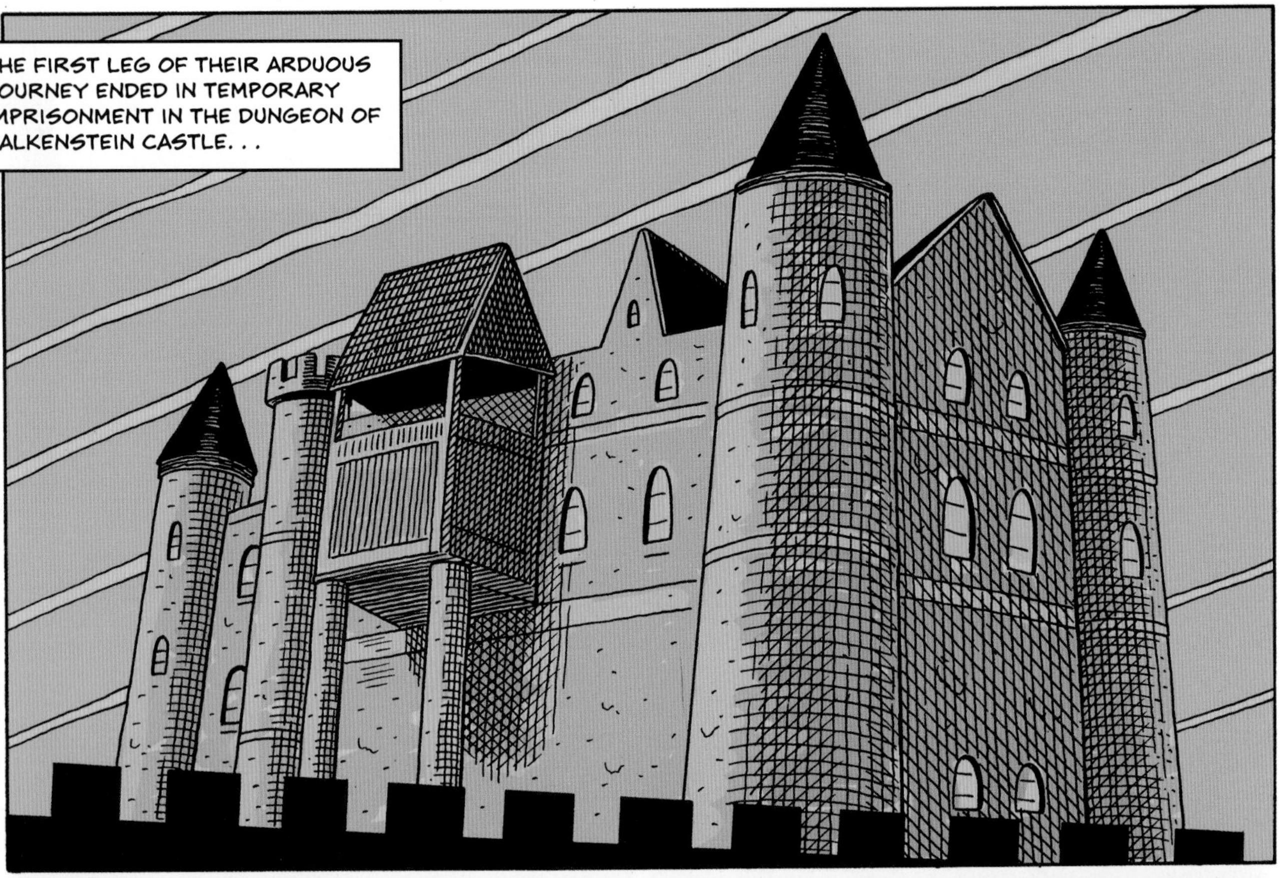
THE FIRST LEG OF THEIR ARDUOUS JOURNEY ENDED IN TEMPORARY IMPRISONMENT IN THE DUNGEON OF FALKENSTEIN CASTLE. . .

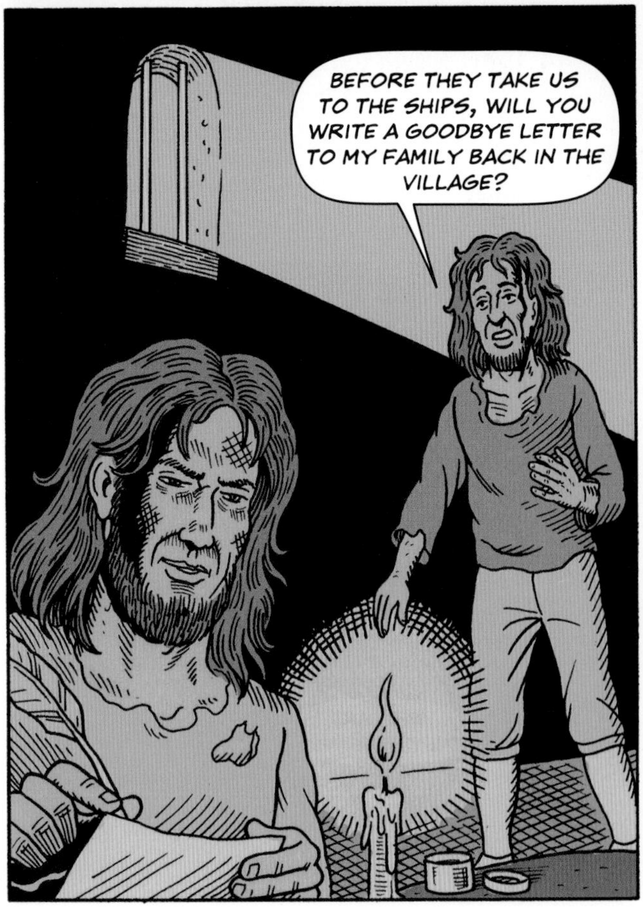
BEFORE THEY TAKE US TO THE SHIPS, WILL YOU WRITE A GOODBYE LETTER TO MY FAMILY BACK IN THE VILLAGE?

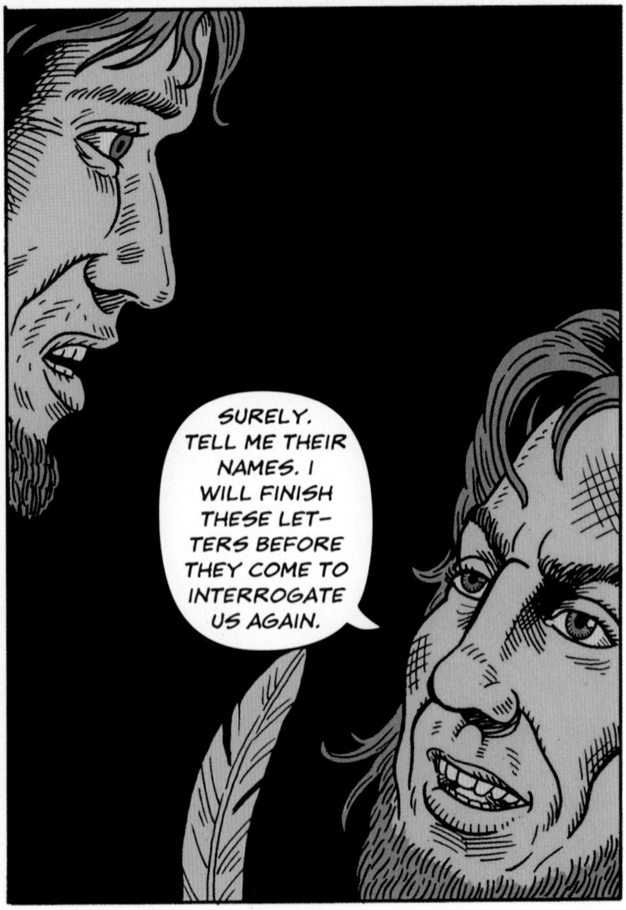
SURELY. TELL ME THEIR NAMES. I WILL FINISH THESE LET-TERS BEFORE THEY COME TO INTERROGATE US AGAIN.

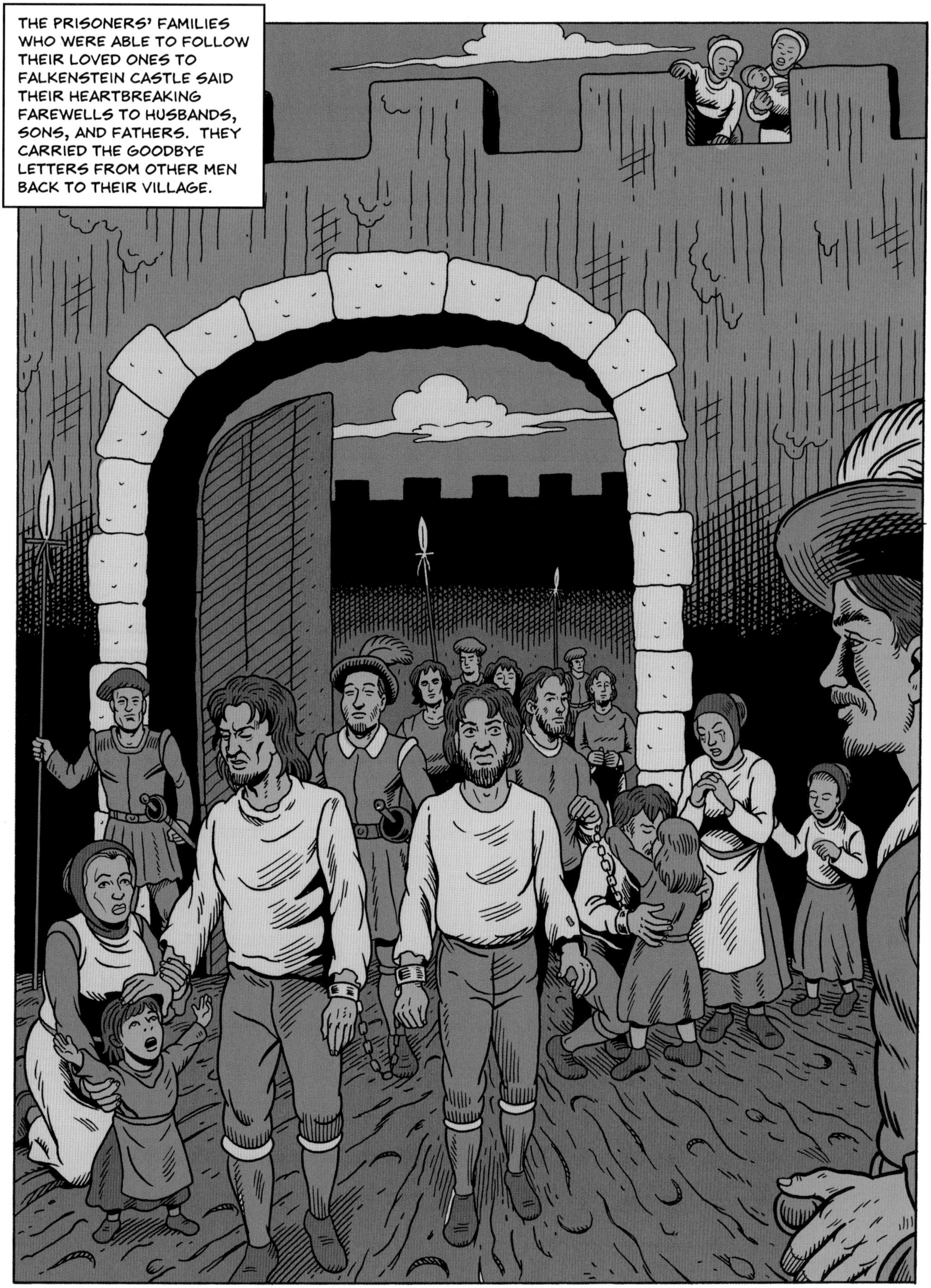
THE PRISONERS' FAMILIES WHO WERE ABLE TO FOLLOW THEIR LOVED ONES TO FALKENSTEIN CASTLE SAID THEIR HEARTBREAKING FAREWELLS TO HUSBANDS, SONS, AND FATHERS. THEY CARRIED THE GOODBYE LETTERS FROM OTHER MEN BACK TO THEIR VILLAGE.

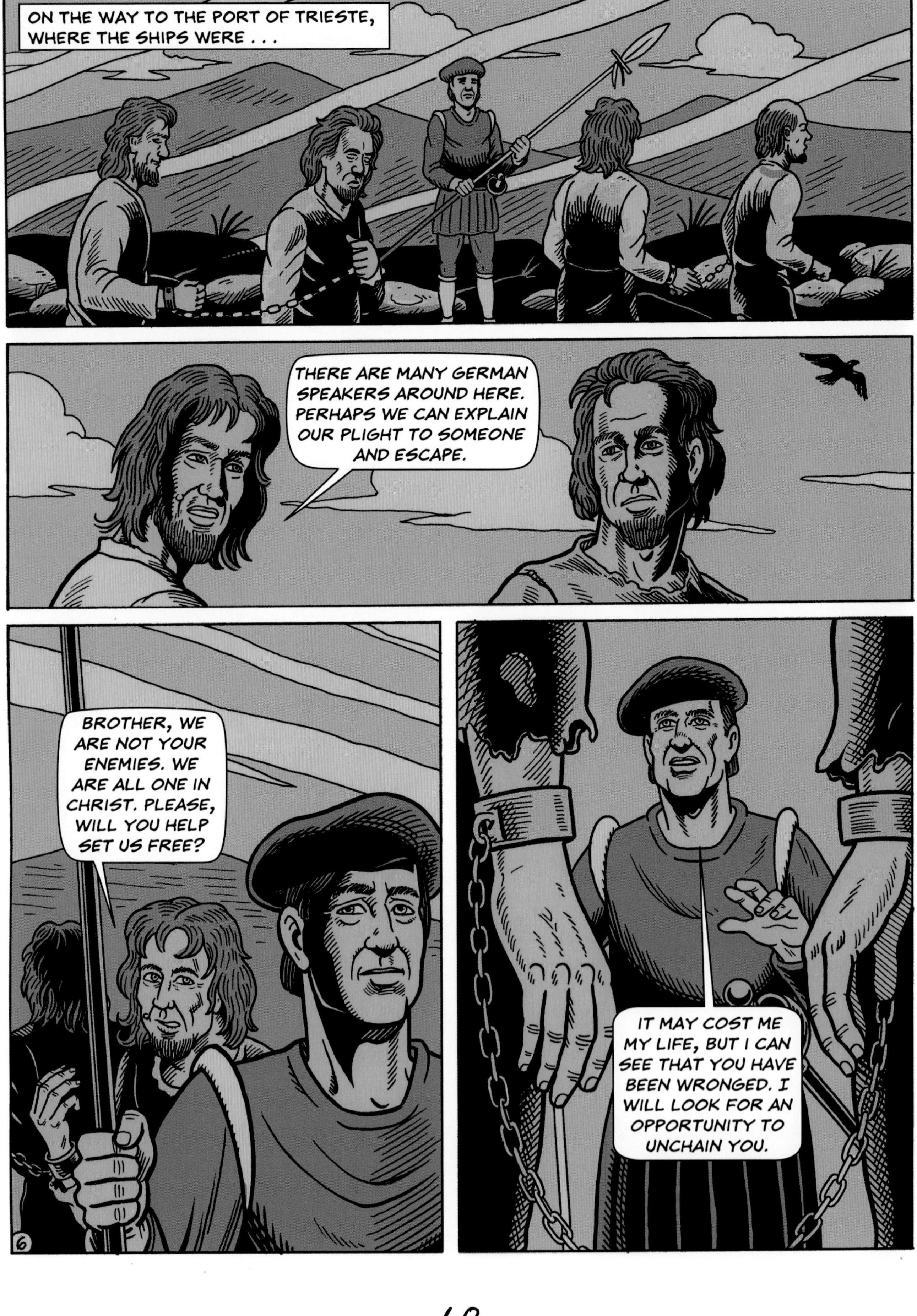

ON THE WAY TO THE PORT OF TRIESTE, WHERE THE SHIPS WERE . . .
THERE ARE MANY GERMAN SPEAKERS AROUND HERE. PERHAPS WE CAN EXPLAIN OUR PLIGHT TO SOMEONE AND ESCAPE.
BROTHER, WE ARE NOT YOUR ENEMIES. WE ARE ALL ONE IN CHRIST. PLEASE, WILL YOU HELP SET US FREE?
IT MAY COST ME MY LIFE, BUT I CAN SEE THAT YOU HAVE BEEN WRONGED. I WILL LOOK FOR AN OPPORTUNITY TO UNCHAIN YOU.

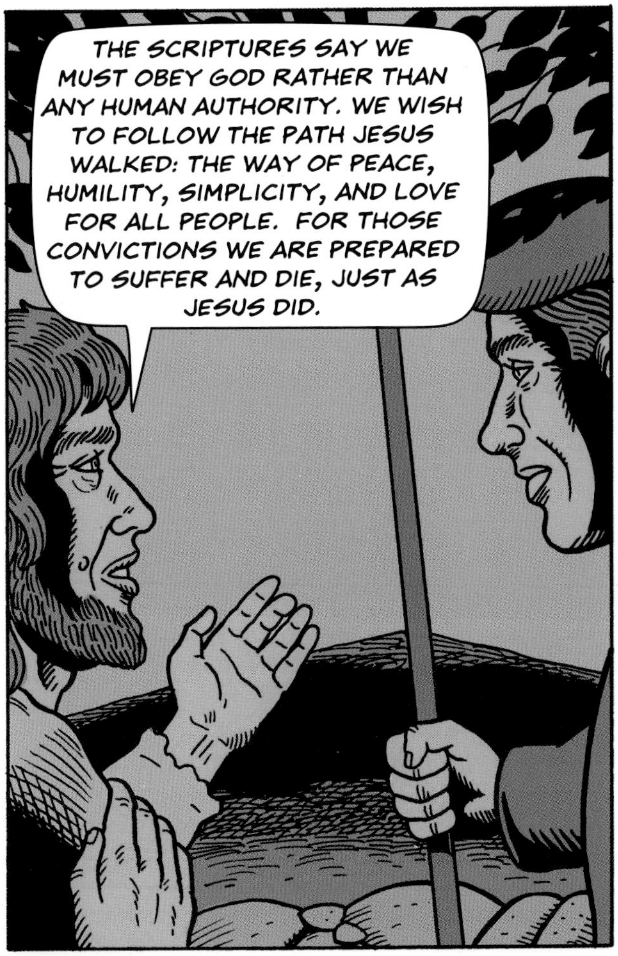
THE SCRIPTURES SAY WE MUST OBEY GOD RATHER THAN ANY HUMAN AUTHORITY. WE WISH TO FOLLOW THE PATH JESUS WALKED: THE WAY OF PEACE, HUMILITY, SIMPLICITY, AND LOVE FOR ALL PEOPLE. FOR THOSE CONVICTIONS WE ARE PREPARED TO SUFFER AND DIE, JUST AS JESUS DID.

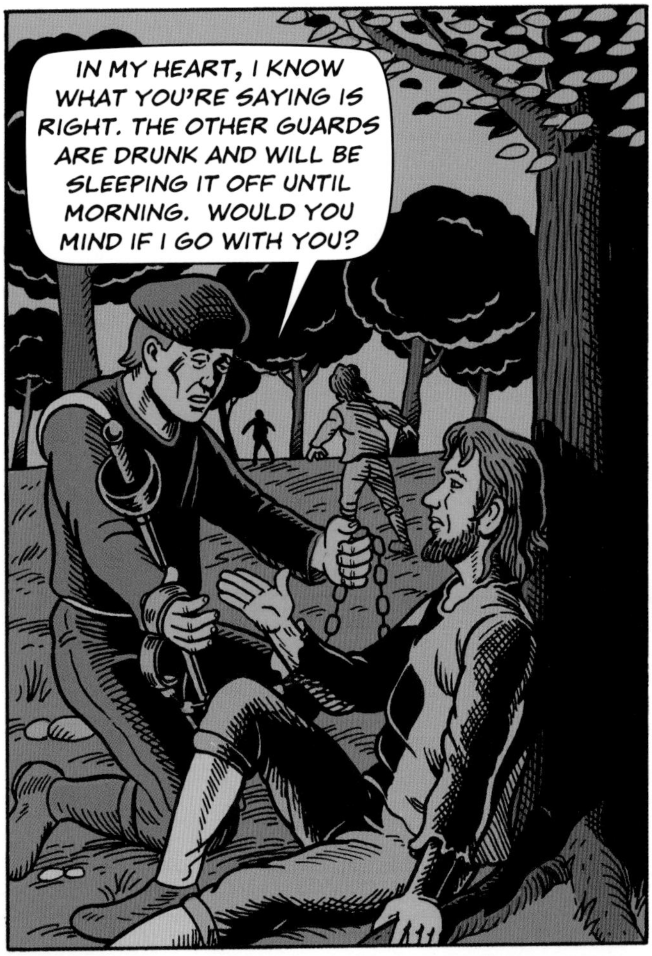
IN MY HEART, I KNOW WHAT YOU'RE SAYING IS RIGHT. THE OTHER GUARDS ARE DRUNK AND WILL BE SLEEPING IT OFF UNTIL MORNING. WOULD YOU MIND IF I GO WITH YOU?

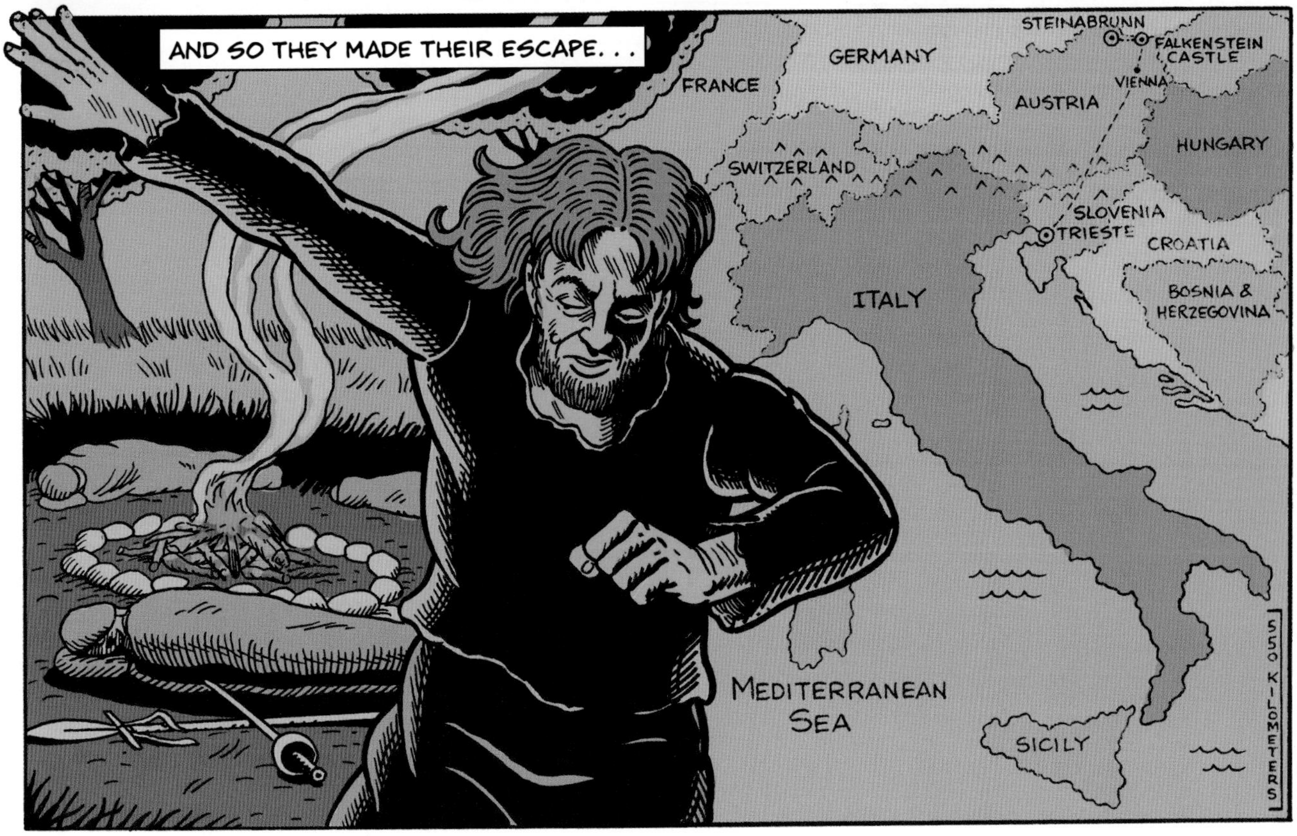
AND SO THEY MADE THEIR ESCAPE. . .
STEINABRUNN
FALKENSTEIN CASTLE
GERMANY
FRANCE
VIENNA
AUSTRIA
HUNGARY
SWITZERLAND
SLOVENIA
TRIESTE
CROATIA
BOSNIA & HERZEGOVINA
ITALY
MEDITERRANEAN SEA
SICILY
550 KILOMETERS

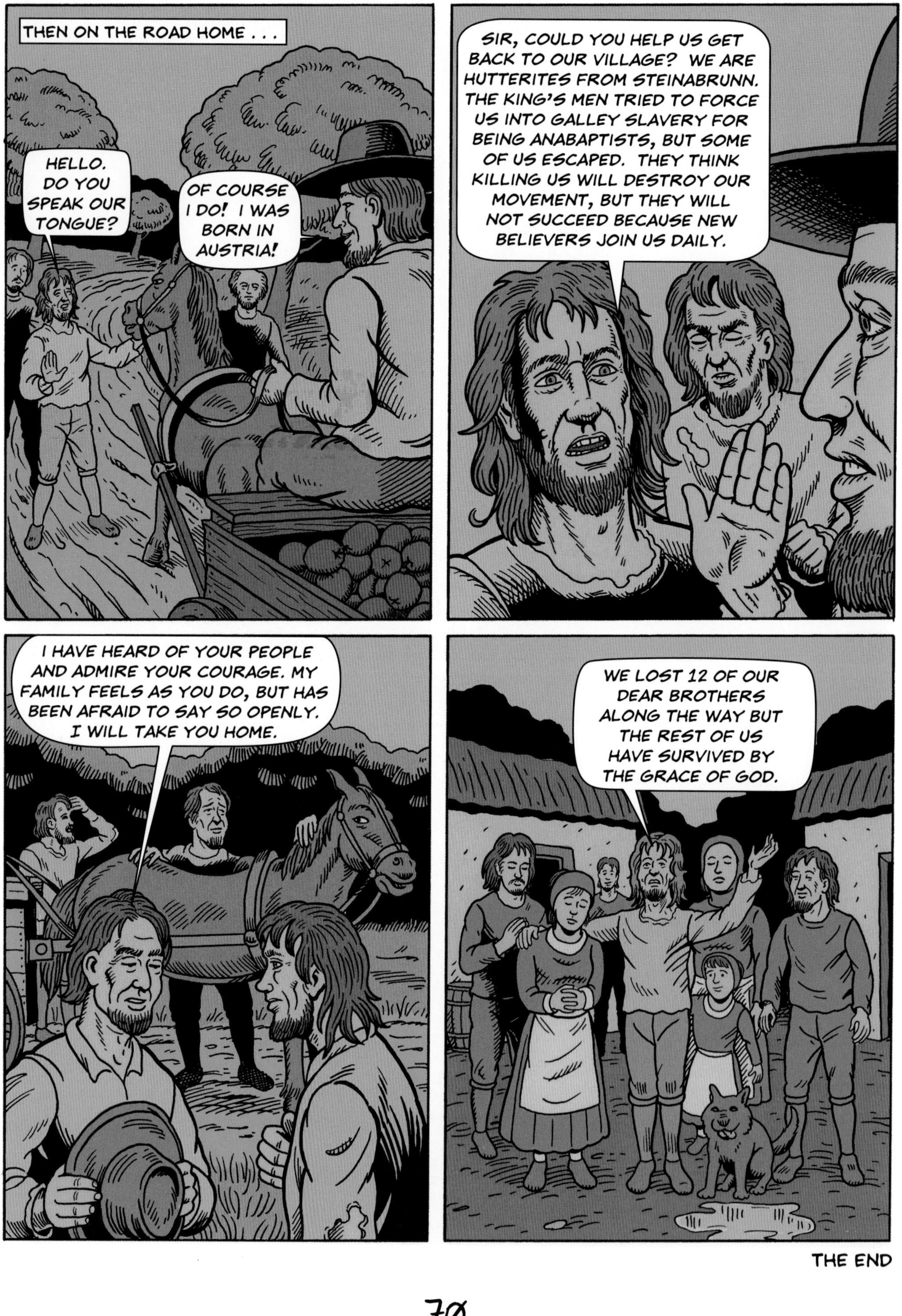
THEN ON THE ROAD HOME . . .
HELLO. DO YOU SPEAK OUR TONGUE?
OF COURSE I DO! I WAS BORN IN AUSTRIA!
SIR, COULD YOU HELP US GET BACK TO OUR VILLAGE? WE ARE HUTTERITES FROM STEINABRUNN. THE KING'S MEN TRIED TO FORCE US INTO GALLEY SLAVERY FOR BEING ANABAPTISTS, BUT SOME OF US ESCAPED. THEY THINK KILLING US WILL DESTROY OUR MOVEMENT, BUT THEY WILL NOT SUCCEED BECAUSE NEW BELIEVERS JOIN US DAILY.
I HAVE HEARD OF YOUR PEOPLE AND ADMIRE YOUR COURAGE. MY FAMILY FEELS AS YOU DO, BUT HAS BEEN AFRAID TO SAY SO OPENLY. I WILL TAKE YOU HOME.
WE LOST 12 OF OUR DEAR BROTHERS ALONG THE WAY BUT THE REST OF US HAVE SURVIVED BY THE GRACE OF GOD.

THE END

# THE STORY OF DIRK WILLEMS

STORY & ART BY GARY DUMM • COLOR BY LAURA DUMM

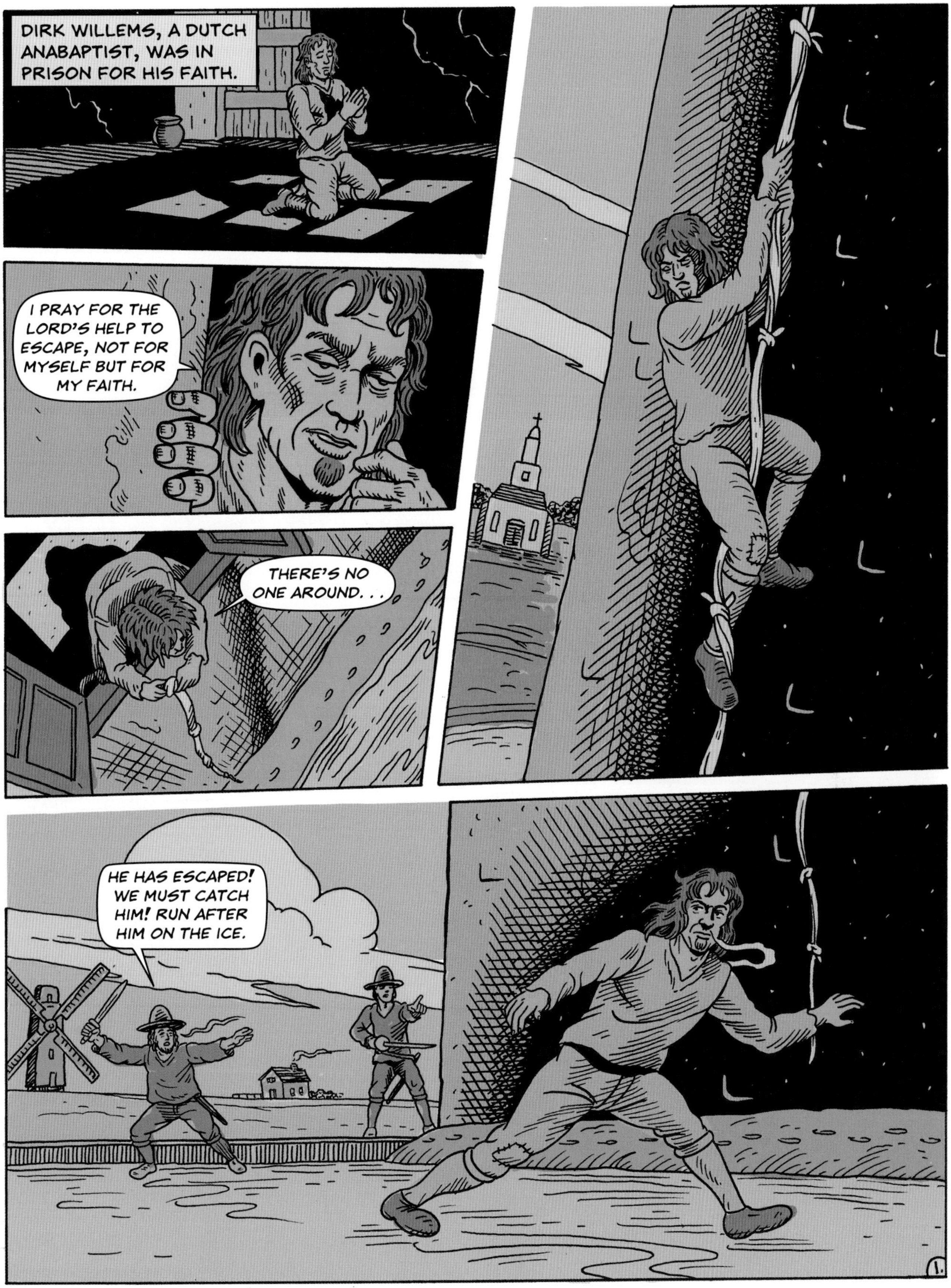

DIRK WILLEMS, A DUTCH ANABAPTIST, WAS IN PRISON FOR HIS FAITH.
I PRAY FOR THE LORD'S HELP TO ESCAPE, NOT FOR MYSELF BUT FOR MY FAITH.
THERE'S NO ONE AROUND. . .
HE HAS ESCAPED! WE MUST CATCH HIM! RUN AFTER HIM ON THE ICE.
1.

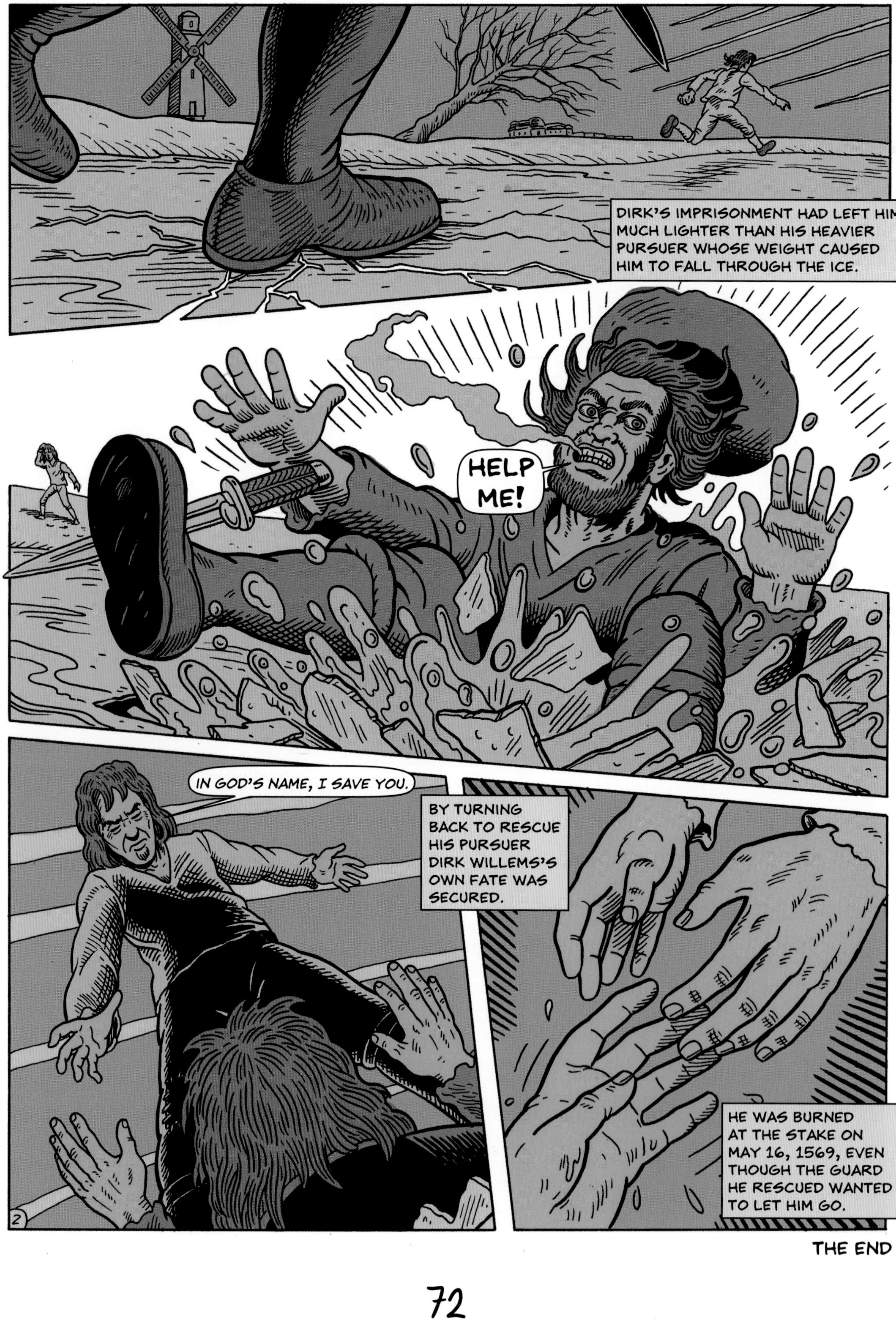
DIRK'S IMPRISONMENT HAD LEFT HIM MUCH LIGHTER THAN HIS HEAVIER PURSUER WHOSE WEIGHT CAUSED HIM TO FALL THROUGH THE ICE.
HELP ME!
IN GOD'S NAME, I SAVE YOU.
BY TURNING BACK TO RESCUE HIS PURSUER DIRK WILLEMS'S OWN FATE WAS SECURED.
HE WAS BURNED AT THE STAKE ON MAY 16, 1569, EVEN THOUGH THE GUARD HE RESCUED WANTED TO LET HIM GO.

THE END

# MYSTERY OF THE THATCH

SCRIPT: PAUL BUHLE • ART BY GARY DUMM • COLOR BY LAURA DUMM

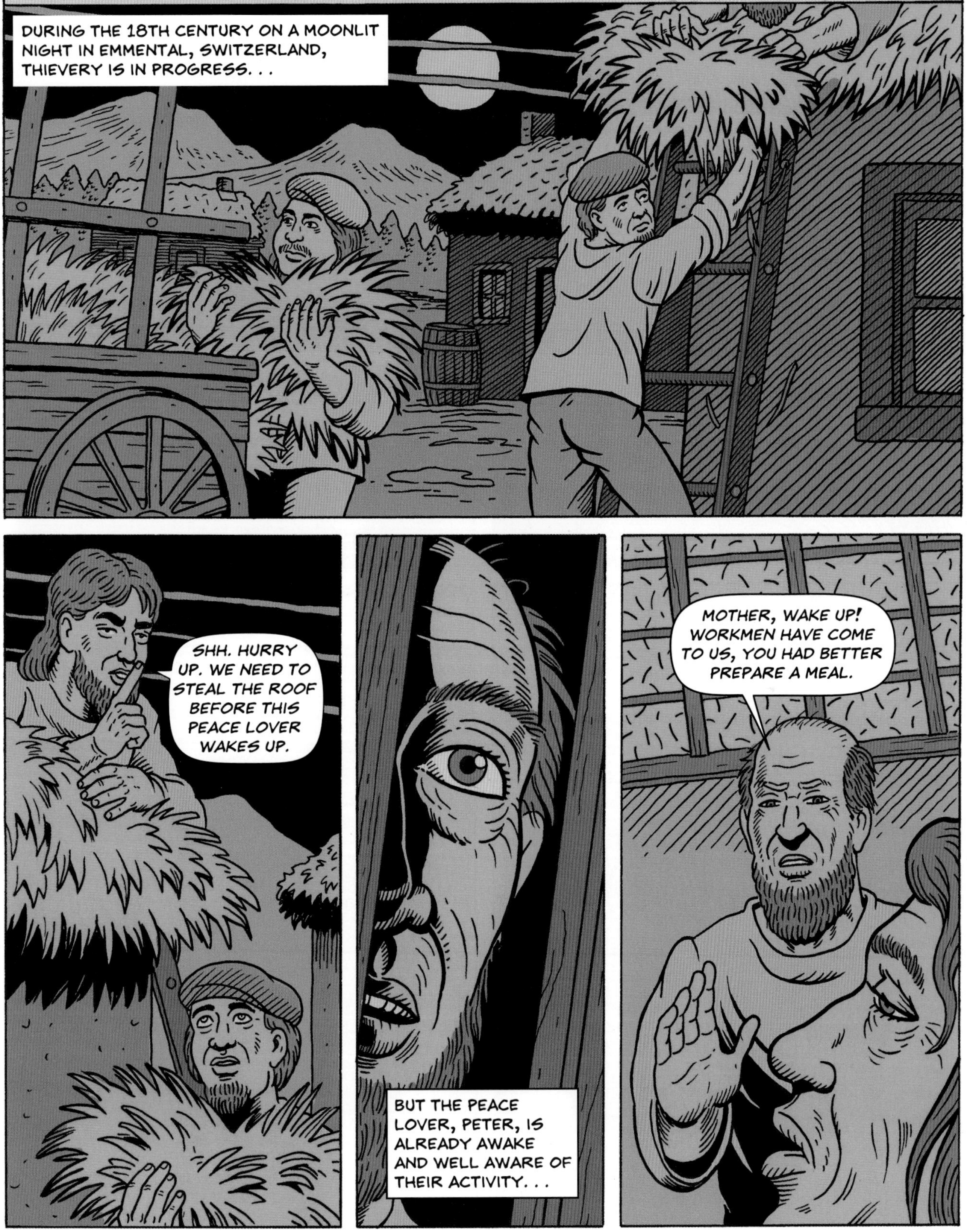

DURING THE 18TH CENTURY ON A MOONLIT NIGHT IN EMMENTAL, SWITZERLAND, THIEVERY IS IN PROGRESS. . .
SHH. HURRY UP. WE NEED TO STEAL THE ROOF BEFORE THIS PEACE LOVER WAKES UP.
BUT THE PEACE LOVER, PETER, IS ALREADY AWAKE AND WELL AWARE OF THEIR ACTIVITY. . .
MOTHER, WAKE UP! WORKMEN HAVE COME TO US, YOU HAD BETTER PREPARE A MEAL.

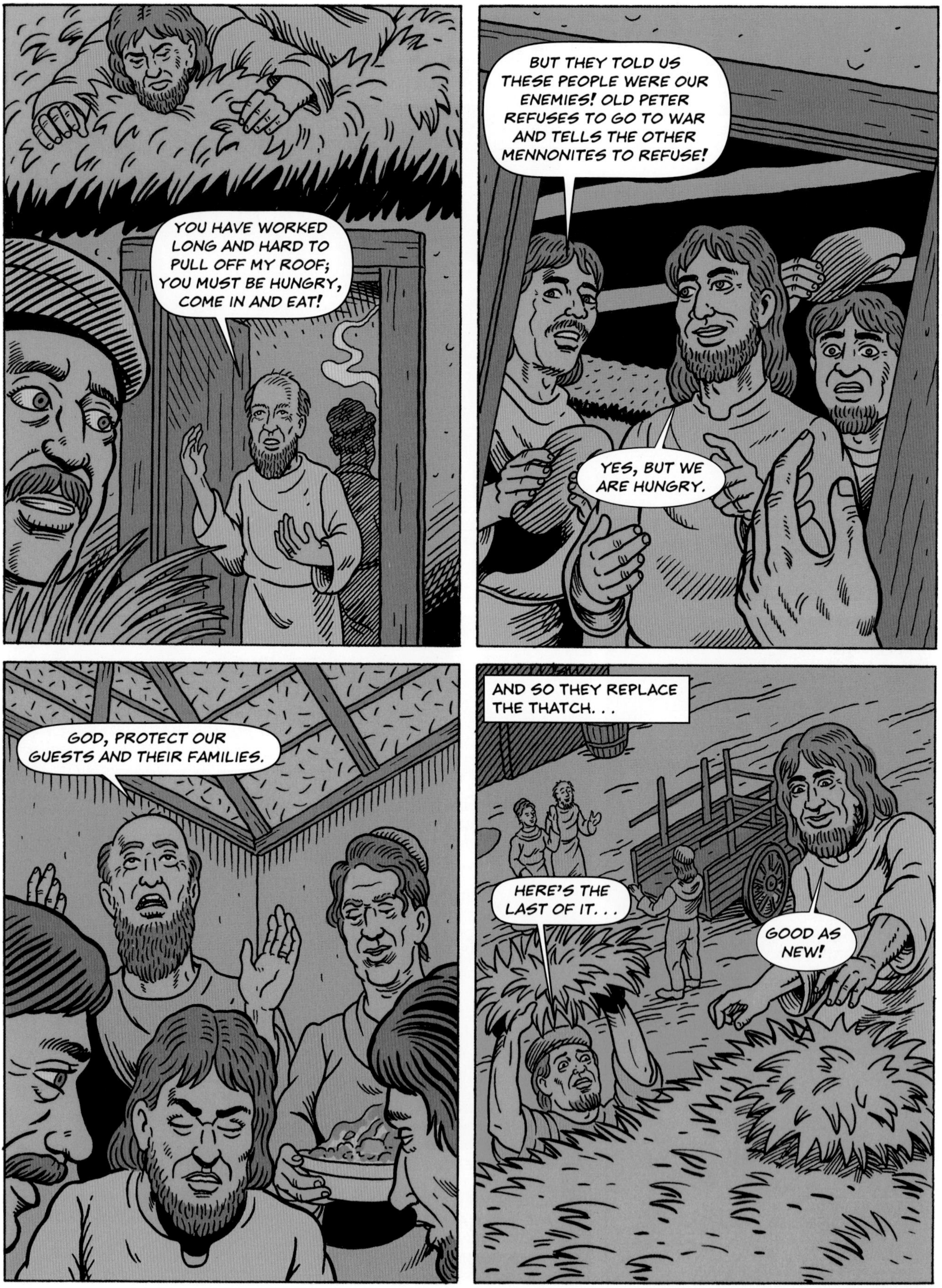
YOU HAVE WORKED LONG AND HARD TO PULL OFF MY ROOF; YOU MUST BE HUNGRY, COME IN AND EAT!
BUT THEY TOLD US THESE PEOPLE WERE OUR ENEMIES! OLD PETER REFUSES TO GO TO WAR AND TELLS THE OTHER MENNONITES TO REFUSE!
YES, BUT WE ARE HUNGRY.
GOD, PROTECT OUR GUESTS AND THEIR FAMILIES.
AND SO THEY REPLACE THE THATCH. . .
HERE'S THE LAST OF IT. . .
GOOD AS NEW!

THE END

# JACOB DECIDES

SCRIPT: PAUL BUHLE • ART BY GARY DUMM • COLOR BY LAURA DUMM

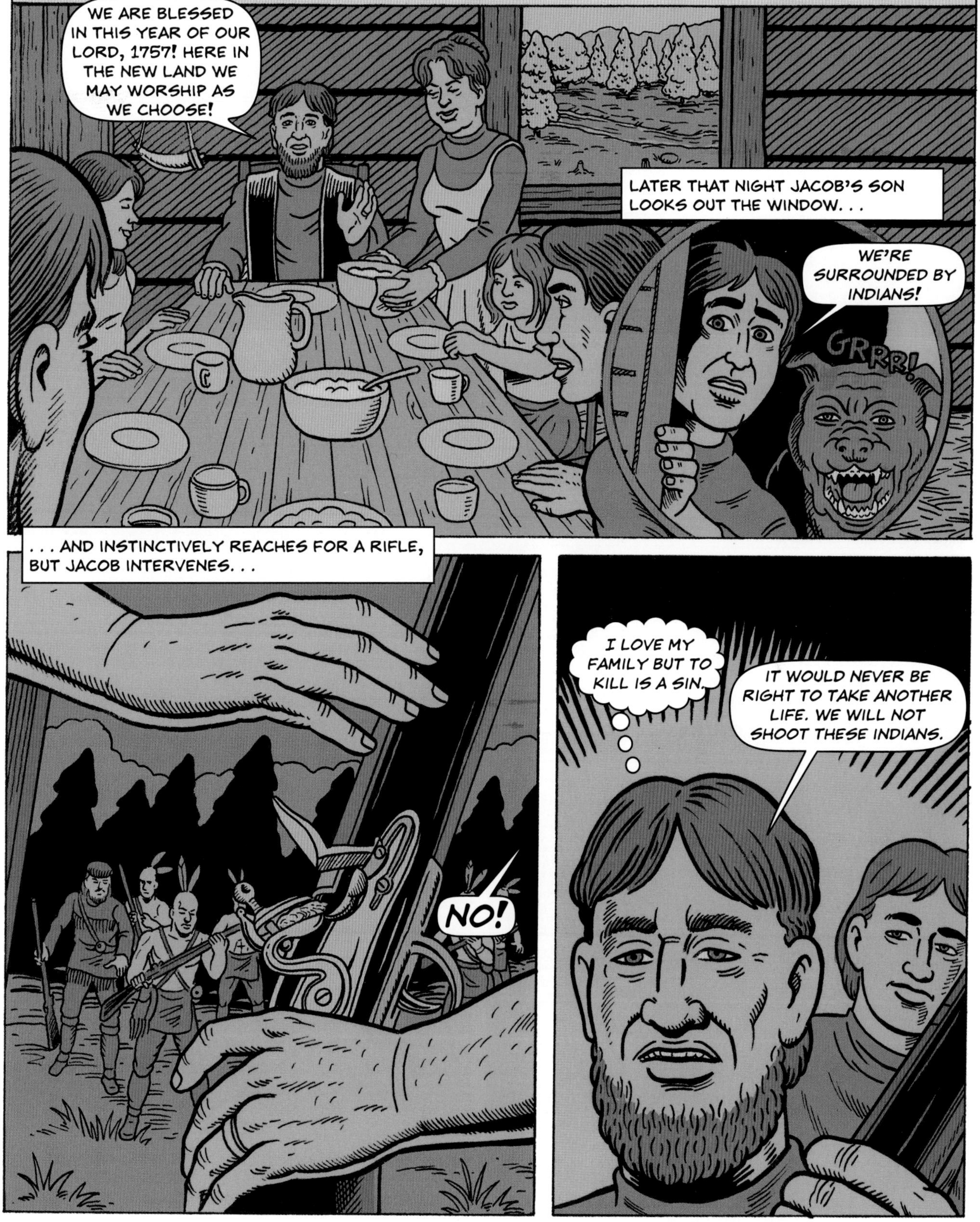

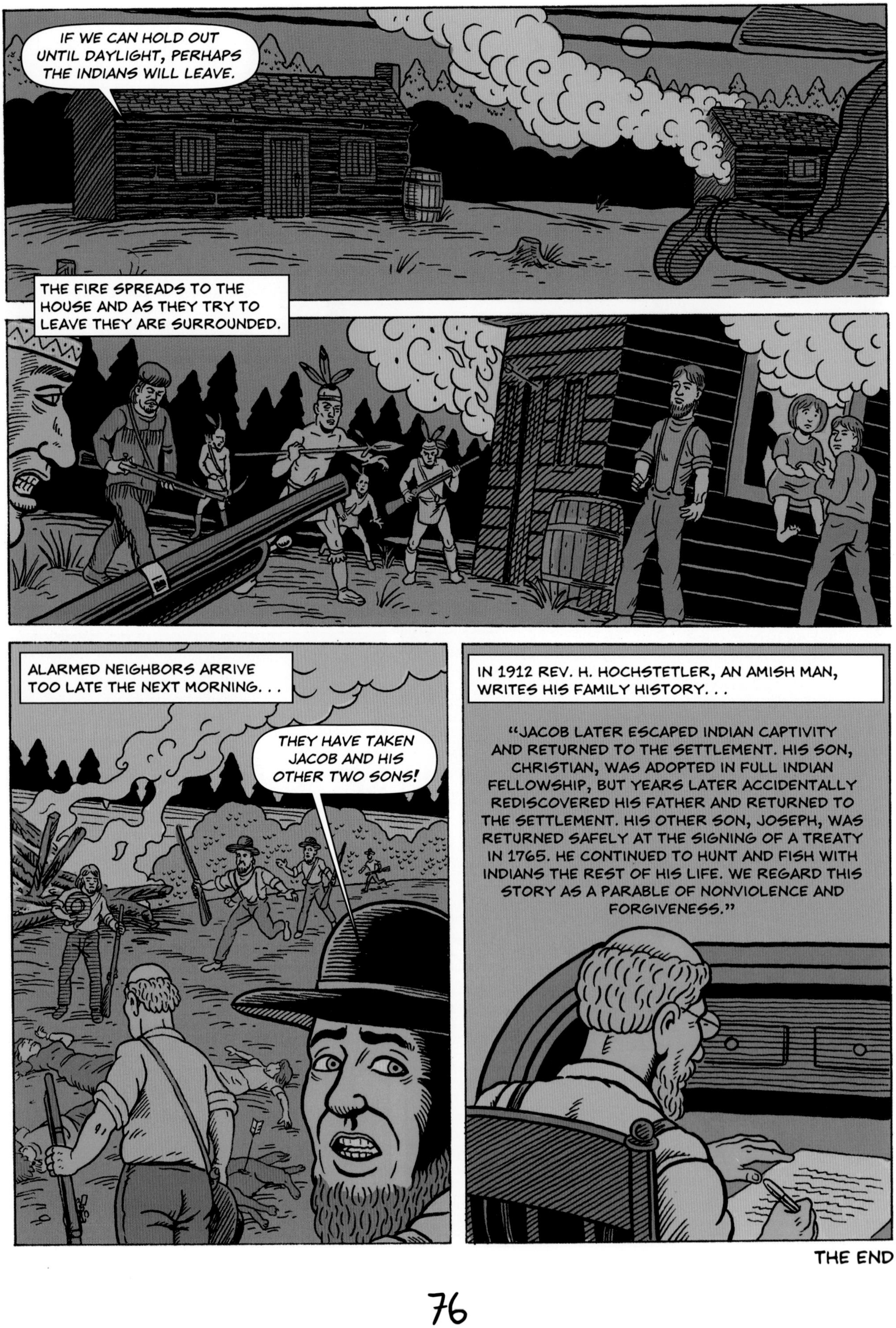
IF WE CAN HOLD OUT UNTIL DAYLIGHT, PERHAPS THE INDIANS WILL LEAVE.
THE FIRE SPREADS TO THE HOUSE AND AS THEY TRY TO LEAVE THEY ARE SURROUNDED.
ALARMED NEIGHBORS ARRIVE TOO LATE THE NEXT MORNING. . .
THEY HAVE TAKEN JACOB AND HIS OTHER TWO SONS!
IN 1912 REV. H. HOCHSTETLER, AN AMISH MAN, WRITES HIS FAMILY HISTORY. . .
"JACOB LATER ESCAPED INDIAN CAPTIVITY AND RETURNED TO THE SETTLEMENT. HIS SON, CHRISTIAN, WAS ADOPTED IN FULL INDIAN FELLOWSHIP, BUT YEARS LATER ACCIDENTALLY REDISCOVERED HIS FATHER AND RETURNED TO THE SETTLEMENT. HIS OTHER SON, JOSEPH, WAS RETURNED SAFELY AT THE SIGNING OF A TREATY IN 1765. HE CONTINUED TO HUNT AND FISH WITH INDIANS THE REST OF HIS LIFE. WE REGARD THIS STORY AS A PARABLE OF NONVIOLENCE AND FORGIVENESS."

THE END

# THE SOCIETY OF FRIENDS: JOHN WOOLMAN'S STORY

STORY BY PAUL BUHLE • ART BY GARY DUMM • COLOR BY LAURA DUMM

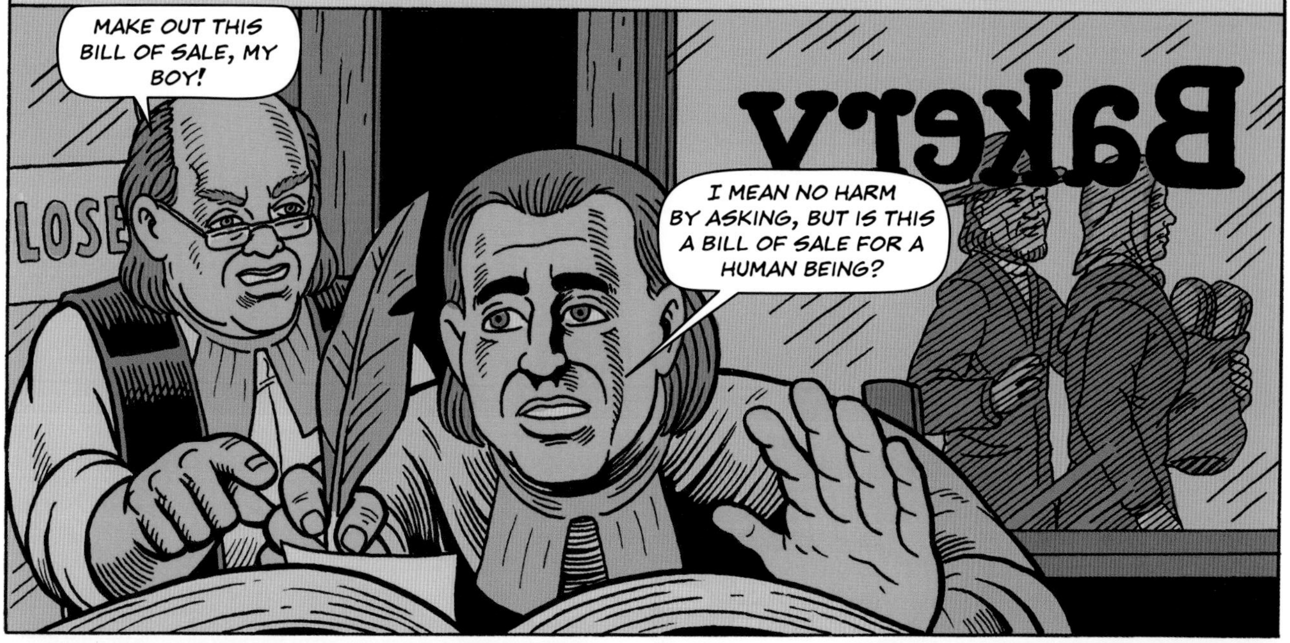
MAKE OUT THIS BILL OF SALE, MY BOY!
Bakery
LOSE
I MEAN NO HARM BY ASKING, BUT IS THIS A BILL OF SALE FOR A HUMAN BEING?

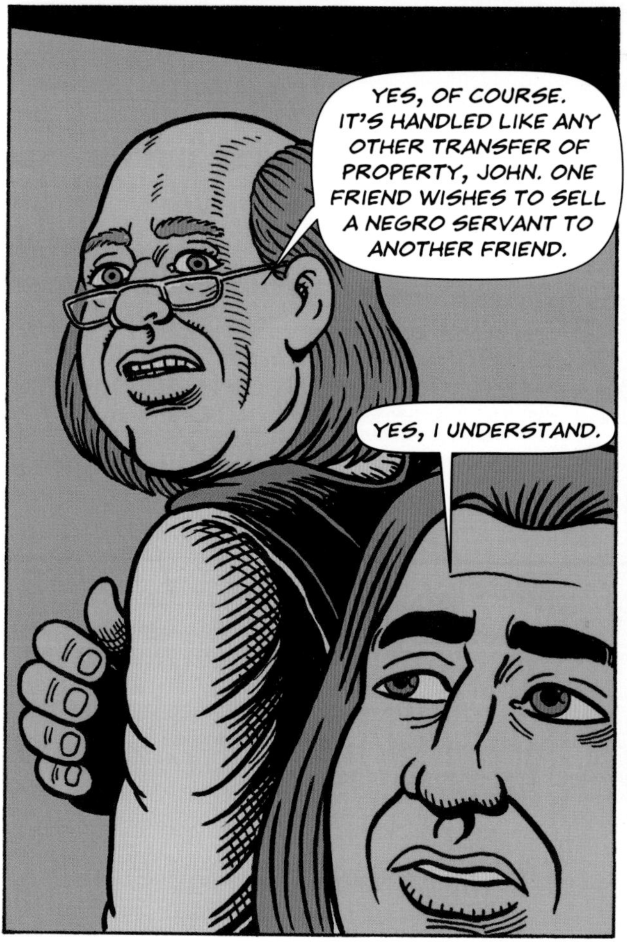
YES, OF COURSE. IT'S HANDLED LIKE ANY OTHER TRANSFER OF PROPERTY, JOHN. ONE FRIEND WISHES TO SELL A NEGRO SERVANT TO ANOTHER FRIEND.
YES, I UNDERSTAND.

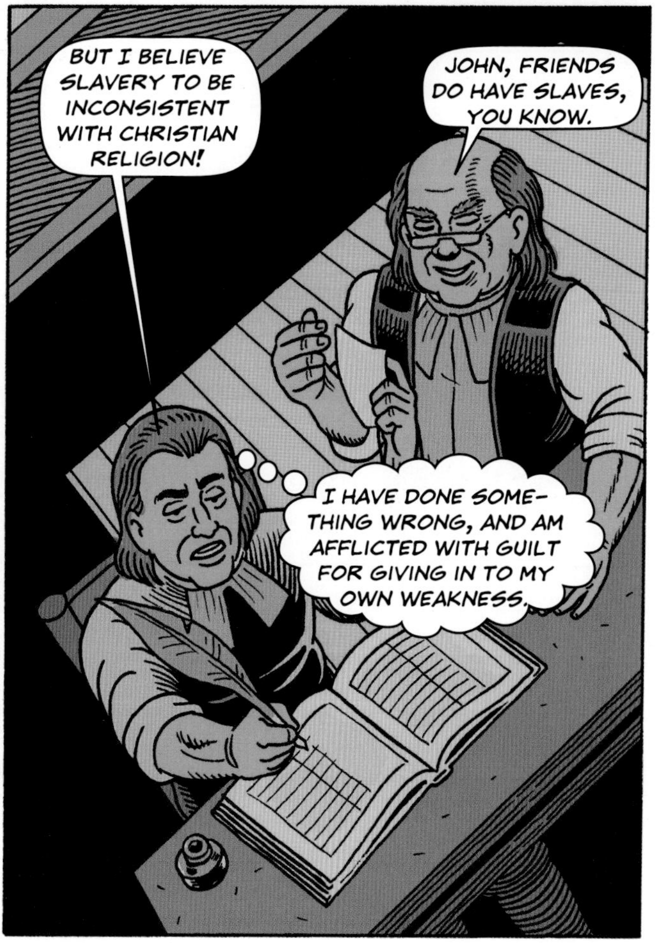
BUT I BELIEVE SLAVERY TO BE INCONSISTENT WITH CHRISTIAN RELIGION!
JOHN, FRIENDS DO HAVE SLAVES, YOU KNOW.
I HAVE DONE SOMETHING WRONG, AND AM AFFLICTED WITH GUILT FOR GIVING IN TO MY OWN WEAKNESS.

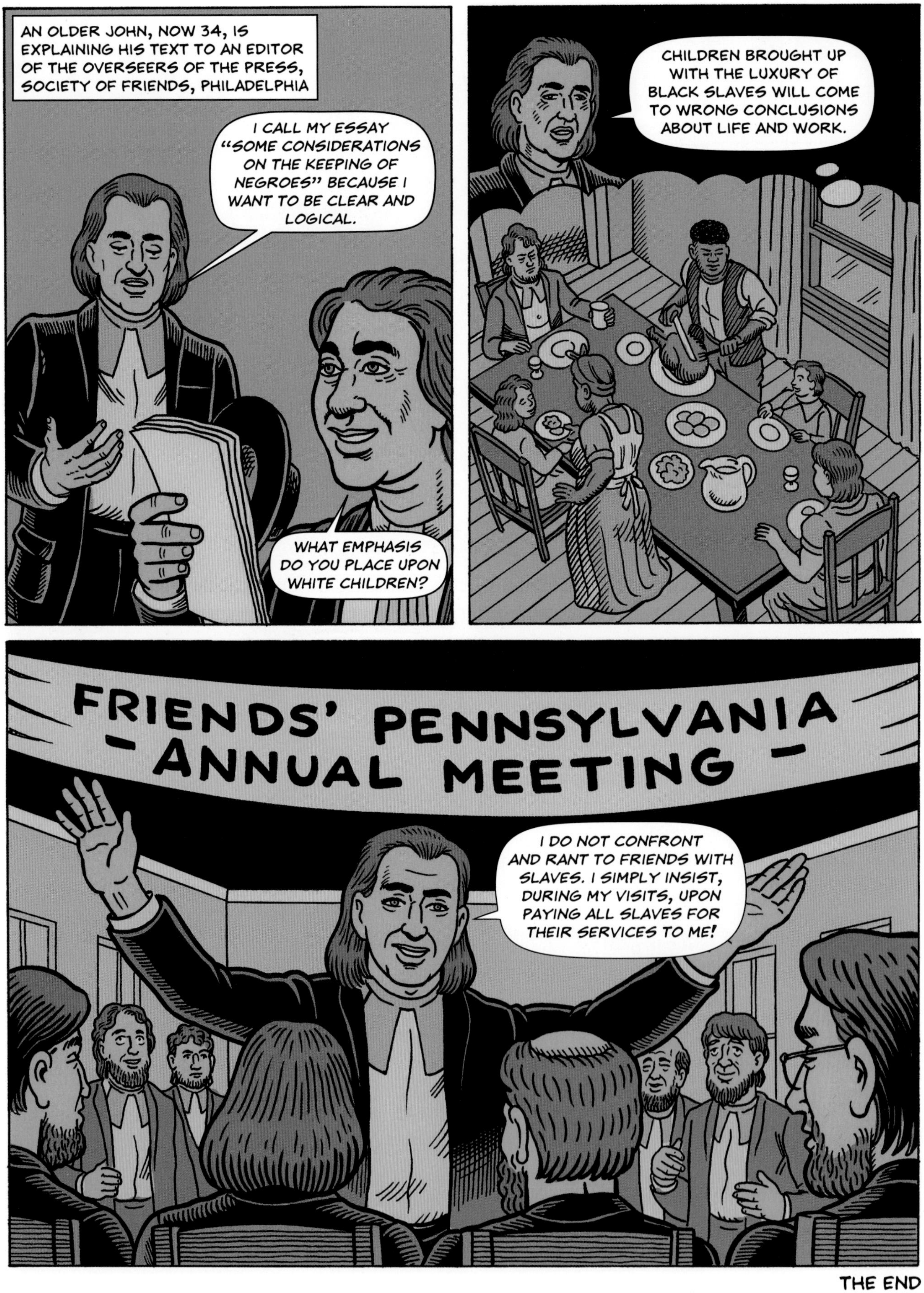
AN OLDER JOHN, NOW 34, IS EXPLAINING HIS TEXT TO AN EDITOR OF THE OVERSEERS OF THE PRESS, SOCIETY OF FRIENDS, PHILADELPHIA
I CALL MY ESSAY "SOME CONSIDERATIONS ON THE KEEPING OF NEGROES" BECAUSE I WANT TO BE CLEAR AND LOGICAL.
WHAT EMPHASIS DO YOU PLACE UPON WHITE CHILDREN?
CHILDREN BROUGHT UP WITH THE LUXURY OF BLACK SLAVES WILL COME TO WRONG CONCLUSIONS ABOUT LIFE AND WORK.
FRIENDS' PENNSYLVANIA - ANNUAL MEETING -
I DO NOT CONFRONT AND RANT TO FRIENDS WITH SLAVES. I SIMPLY INSIST, DURING MY VISITS, UPON PAYING ALL SLAVES FOR THEIR SERVICES TO ME!

THE END

# QUAKERS AND INDIANS

*STORY BY DAVE WAGNER • ART BY GARY DUMM • COLOR BY LAURA DUMM*

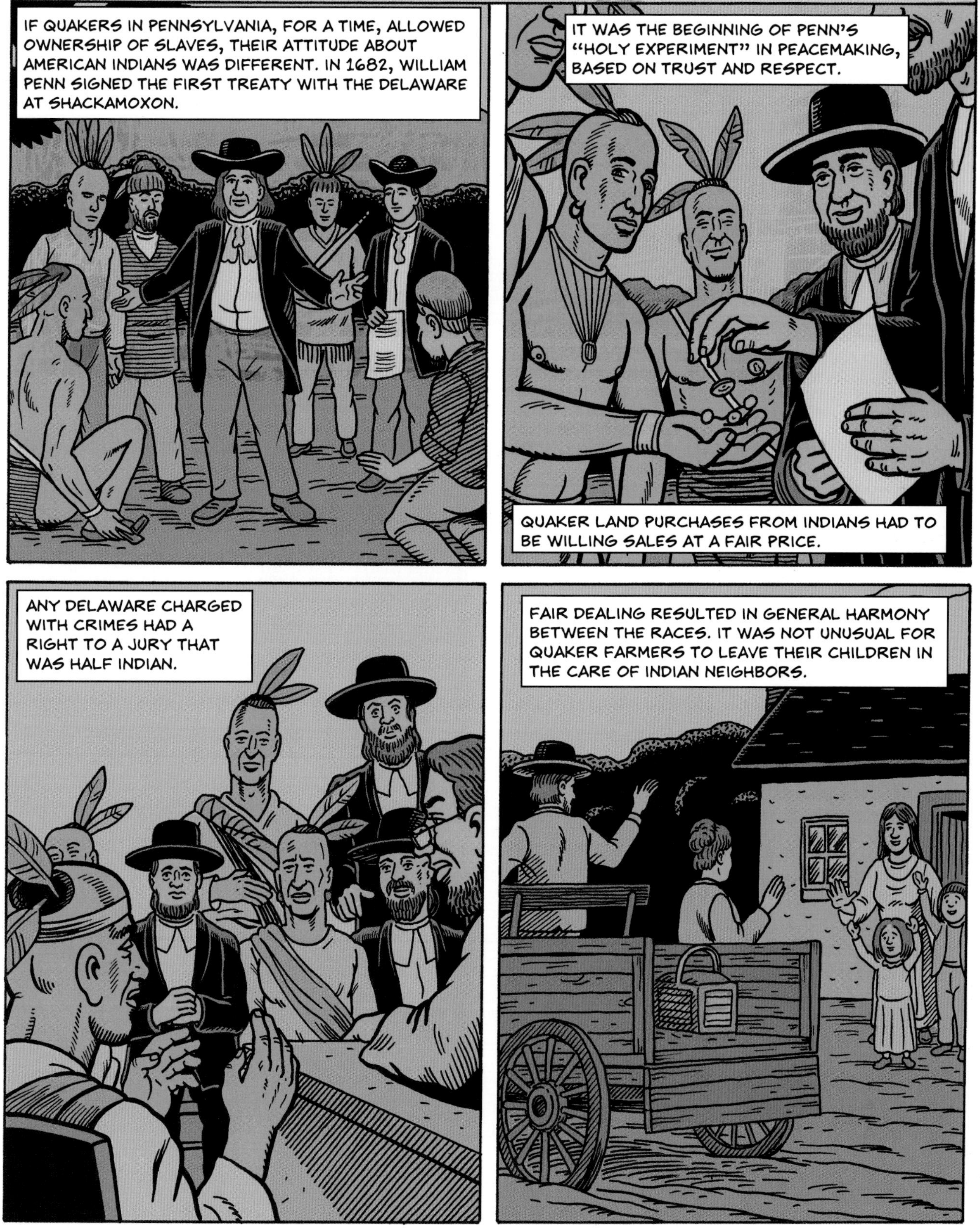
IF QUAKERS IN PENNSYLVANIA, FOR A TIME, ALLOWED OWNERSHIP OF SLAVES, THEIR ATTITUDE ABOUT AMERICAN INDIANS WAS DIFFERENT. IN 1682, WILLIAM PENN SIGNED THE FIRST TREATY WITH THE DELAWARE AT SHACKAMOXON.
IT WAS THE BEGINNING OF PENN'S "HOLY EXPERIMENT" IN PEACEMAKING, BASED ON TRUST AND RESPECT.
QUAKER LAND PURCHASES FROM INDIANS HAD TO BE WILLING SALES AT A FAIR PRICE.
ANY DELAWARE CHARGED WITH CRIMES HAD A RIGHT TO A JURY THAT WAS HALF INDIAN.
FAIR DEALING RESULTED IN GENERAL HARMONY BETWEEN THE RACES. IT WAS NOT UNUSUAL FOR QUAKER FARMERS TO LEAVE THEIR CHILDREN IN THE CARE OF INDIAN NEIGHBORS.

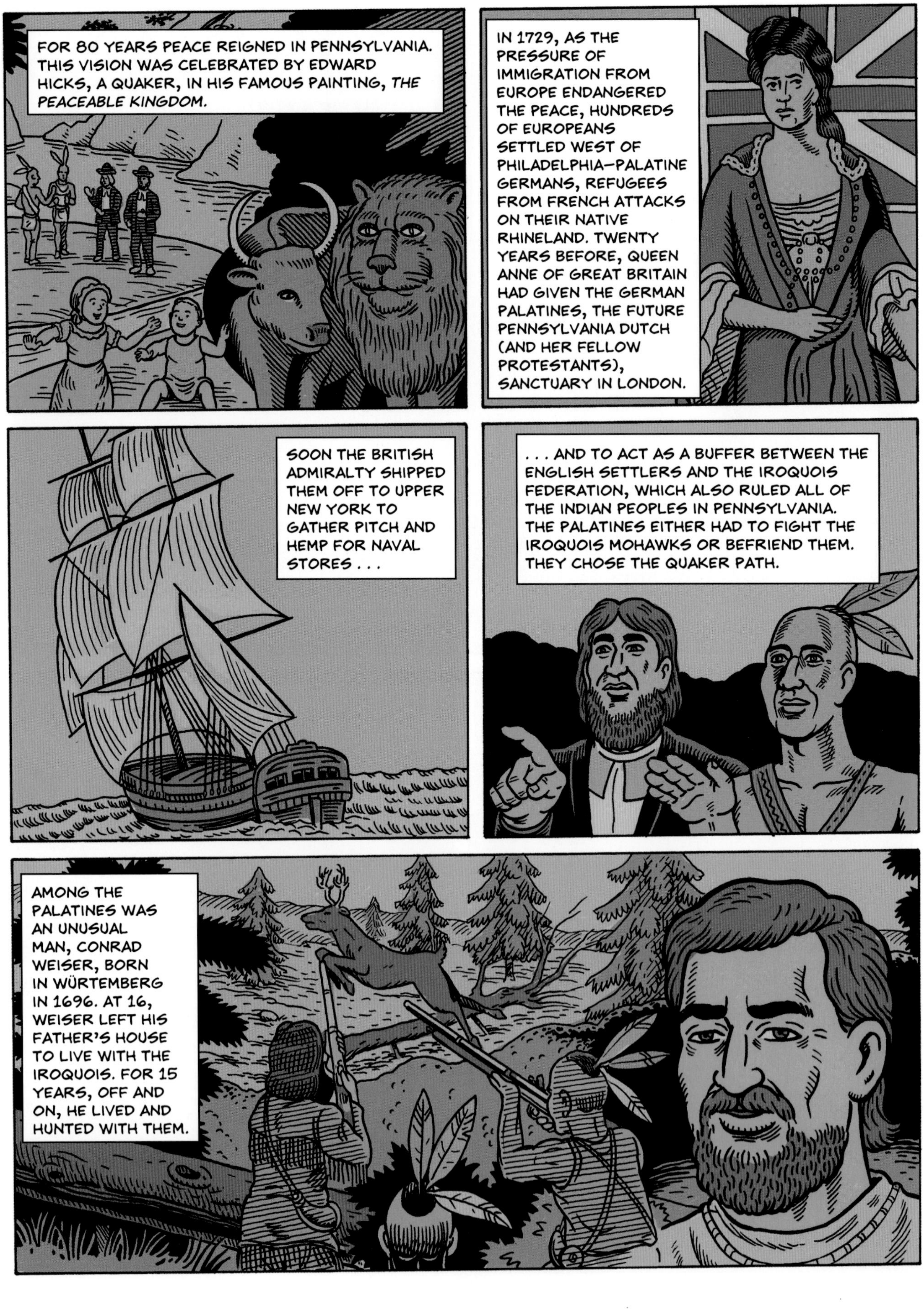
FOR 80 YEARS PEACE REIGNED IN PENNSYLVANIA. THIS VISION WAS CELEBRATED BY EDWARD HICKS, A QUAKER, IN HIS FAMOUS PAINTING, *THE PEACEABLE KINGDOM.*
IN 1729, AS THE PRESSURE OF IMMIGRATION FROM EUROPE ENDANGERED THE PEACE, HUNDREDS OF EUROPEANS SETTLED WEST OF PHILADELPHIA—PALATINE GERMANS, REFUGEES FROM FRENCH ATTACKS ON THEIR NATIVE RHINELAND. TWENTY YEARS BEFORE, QUEEN ANNE OF GREAT BRITAIN HAD GIVEN THE GERMAN PALATINES, THE FUTURE PENNSYLVANIA DUTCH (AND HER FELLOW PROTESTANTS), SANCTUARY IN LONDON.
SOON THE BRITISH ADMIRALTY SHIPPED THEM OFF TO UPPER NEW YORK TO GATHER PITCH AND HEMP FOR NAVAL STORES . . .
. . . AND TO ACT AS A BUFFER BETWEEN THE ENGLISH SETTLERS AND THE IROQUOIS FEDERATION, WHICH ALSO RULED ALL OF THE INDIAN PEOPLES IN PENNSYLVANIA. THE PALATINES EITHER HAD TO FIGHT THE IROQUOIS MOHAWKS OR BEFRIEND THEM. THEY CHOSE THE QUAKER PATH.
AMONG THE PALATINES WAS AN UNUSUAL MAN, CONRAD WEISER, BORN IN WÜRTEMBERG IN 1696. AT 16, WEISER LEFT HIS FATHER'S HOUSE TO LIVE WITH THE IROQUOIS. FOR 15 YEARS, OFF AND ON, HE LIVED AND HUNTED WITH THEM.

IN 1729 THE PALATINES, TO ESCAPE THE DRUDGERY AND SICKNESS OF THE PITCH PLANTATIONS IN NEW YORK, FLED SOUTH ALONG THE SUSQUEHANNA RIVER TO THE TULPEHOCKEN VALLEY IN PENNSYLVANIA. THEY WERE IMPOVERISHED SQUATTERS.

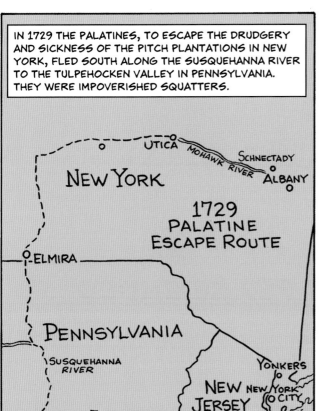

NEW YORK

UTICA  MOHAWK RIVER  SCHNECTADY
                      ALBANY

1729
PALATINE
ESCAPE ROUTE

ELMIRA

PENNSYLVANIA

SUSQUEHANNA RIVER

SHAMOKIN    TULPEHOCKEN
              WOLMENSDORF

YONKERS
NEW YORK CITY
NEW JERSEY
TRENTON

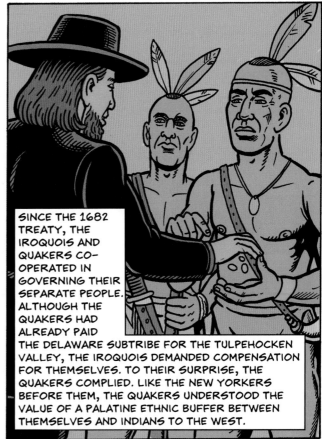

SINCE THE 1682 TREATY, THE IROQUOIS AND QUAKERS CO-OPERATED IN GOVERNING THEIR SEPARATE PEOPLE. ALTHOUGH THE QUAKERS HAD ALREADY PAID THE DELAWARE SUBTRIBE FOR THE TULPEHOCKEN VALLEY, THE IROQUOIS DEMANDED COMPENSATION FOR THEMSELVES. TO THEIR SURPRISE, THE QUAKERS COMPLIED. LIKE THE NEW YORKERS BEFORE THEM, THE QUAKERS UNDERSTOOD THE VALUE OF A PALATINE ETHNIC BUFFER BETWEEN THEMSELVES AND INDIANS TO THE WEST.

BY 1730, INLAND TRIBES RESENTED THE INTRUSION OF RUM TRADERS AND LAND SPECULATORS AND BLAMED THE QUAKERS FOR FAILING TO CONTROL THEM.

THE QUAKERS ASKED THE IROQUOIS TO ENTER INTO A FORMAL TREATY TO HELP CONTROL THE BORDER AREAS.

THE IROQUOIS SENT THE RESPECTED ONEIDA DIPLOMAT, SHIKELLAMY, TO PHILADELPHIA. HE WALKED THE 250 MILES SOUTH TO FORMALIZE AN ALLIANCE, AND AS HE PASSED THROUGH TULPEHOCKEN HE INVITED CONRAD WEISER TO JOIN HIM AS AN INTERPRETER.

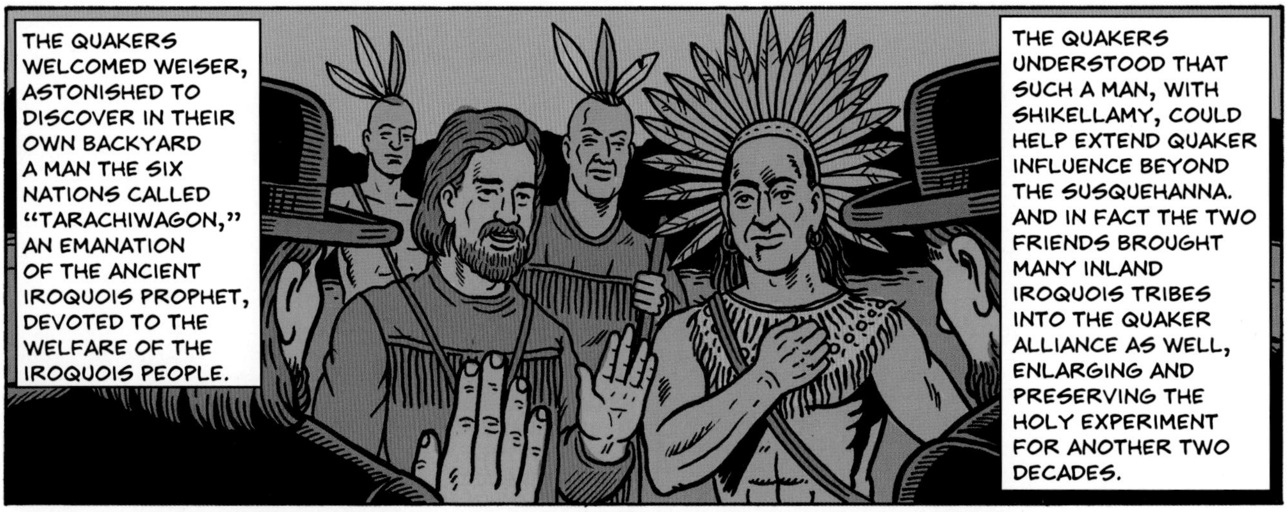
THE QUAKERS WELCOMED WEISER, ASTONISHED TO DISCOVER IN THEIR OWN BACKYARD A MAN THE SIX NATIONS CALLED "TARACHIWAGON," AN EMANATION OF THE ANCIENT IROQUOIS PROPHET, DEVOTED TO THE WELFARE OF THE IROQUOIS PEOPLE.
THE QUAKERS UNDERSTOOD THAT SUCH A MAN, WITH SHIKELLAMY, COULD HELP EXTEND QUAKER INFLUENCE BEYOND THE SUSQUEHANNA. AND IN FACT THE TWO FRIENDS BROUGHT MANY INLAND IROQUOIS TRIBES INTO THE QUAKER ALLIANCE AS WELL, ENLARGING AND PRESERVING THE HOLY EXPERIMENT FOR ANOTHER TWO DECADES.

# HOW THE GREAT PEACE ENDED

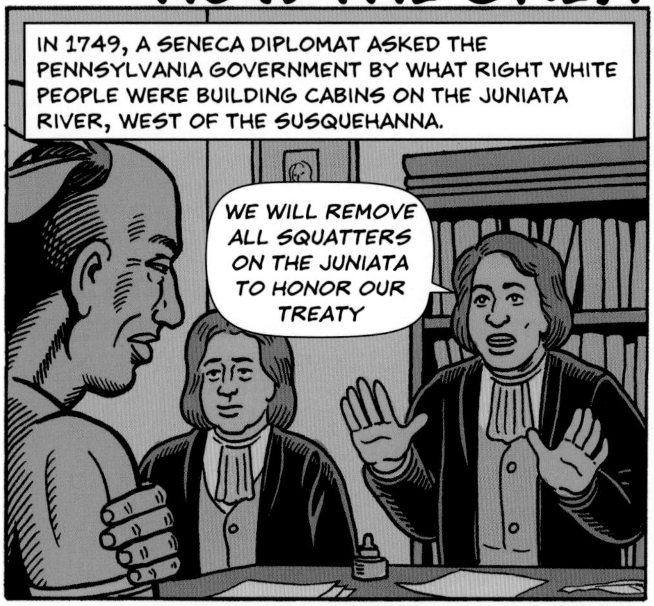
IN 1749, A SENECA DIPLOMAT ASKED THE PENNSYLVANIA GOVERNMENT BY WHAT RIGHT WHITE PEOPLE WERE BUILDING CABINS ON THE JUNIATA RIVER, WEST OF THE SUSQUEHANNA.
WE WILL REMOVE ALL SQUATTERS ON THE JUNIATA TO HONOR OUR TREATY

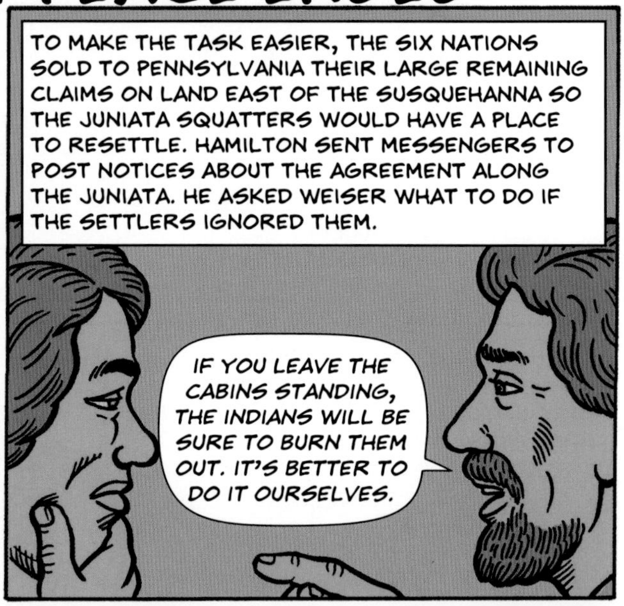
TO MAKE THE TASK EASIER, THE SIX NATIONS SOLD TO PENNSYLVANIA THEIR LARGE REMAINING CLAIMS ON LAND EAST OF THE SUSQUEHANNA SO THE JUNIATA SQUATTERS WOULD HAVE A PLACE TO RESETTLE. HAMILTON SENT MESSENGERS TO POST NOTICES ABOUT THE AGREEMENT ALONG THE JUNIATA. HE ASKED WEISER WHAT TO DO IF THE SETTLERS IGNORED THEM.
IF YOU LEAVE THE CABINS STANDING, THE INDIANS WILL BE SURE TO BURN THEM OUT. IT'S BETTER TO DO IT OURSELVES.

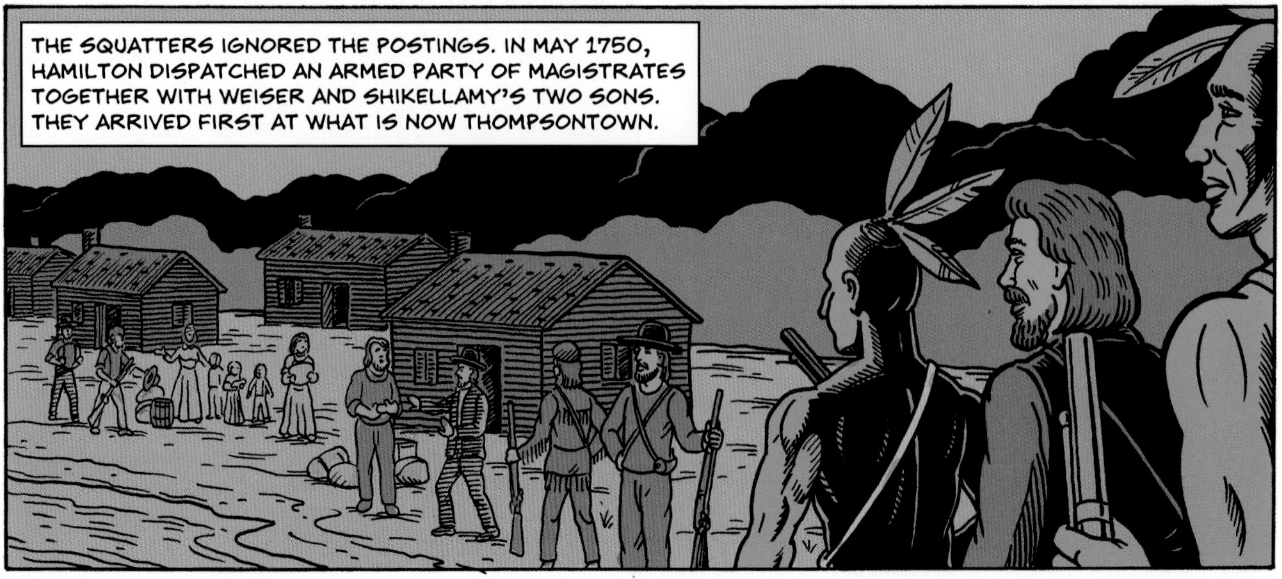
THE SQUATTERS IGNORED THE POSTINGS. IN MAY 1750, HAMILTON DISPATCHED AN ARMED PARTY OF MAGISTRATES TOGETHER WITH WEISER AND SHIKELLAMY'S TWO SONS. THEY ARRIVED FIRST AT WHAT IS NOW THOMPSONTOWN.

AT LITTLE JUNIATA, THE PARTY FOUND A CAMP OF 11 FAMILIES WHO WATCHED IN ANGER AND DISBELIEF AS THEIR CABINS WERE TORCHED.

OCCUPANTS OF ANOTHER CABIN FLED DURING THE NIGHT, LEAVING THEIR POSSESSIONS, ALL OF WHICH WERE BURNED BY THE MAGISTRATES.

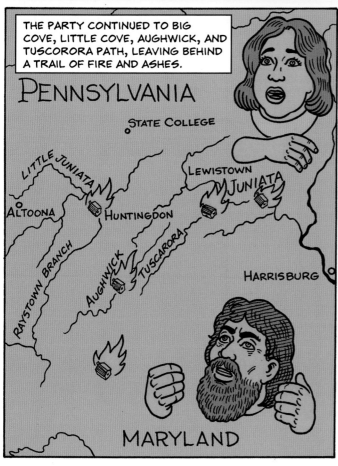

THE PARTY CONTINUED TO BIG COVE, LITTLE COVE, AUGHWICK, AND TUSCORORA PATH, LEAVING BEHIND A TRAIL OF FIRE AND ASHES.

PENNSYLVANIA

STATE COLLEGE

LITTLE JUNIATA

LEWISTOWN

JUNIATA

ALTOONA  HUNTINGDON

RAYSTOWN BRANCH

AUGHWICK

TUSCARORA

HARRISBURG

MARYLAND

WHEN THE GOVERNOR'S MISSION WAS ONLY HALF FINISHED . . .

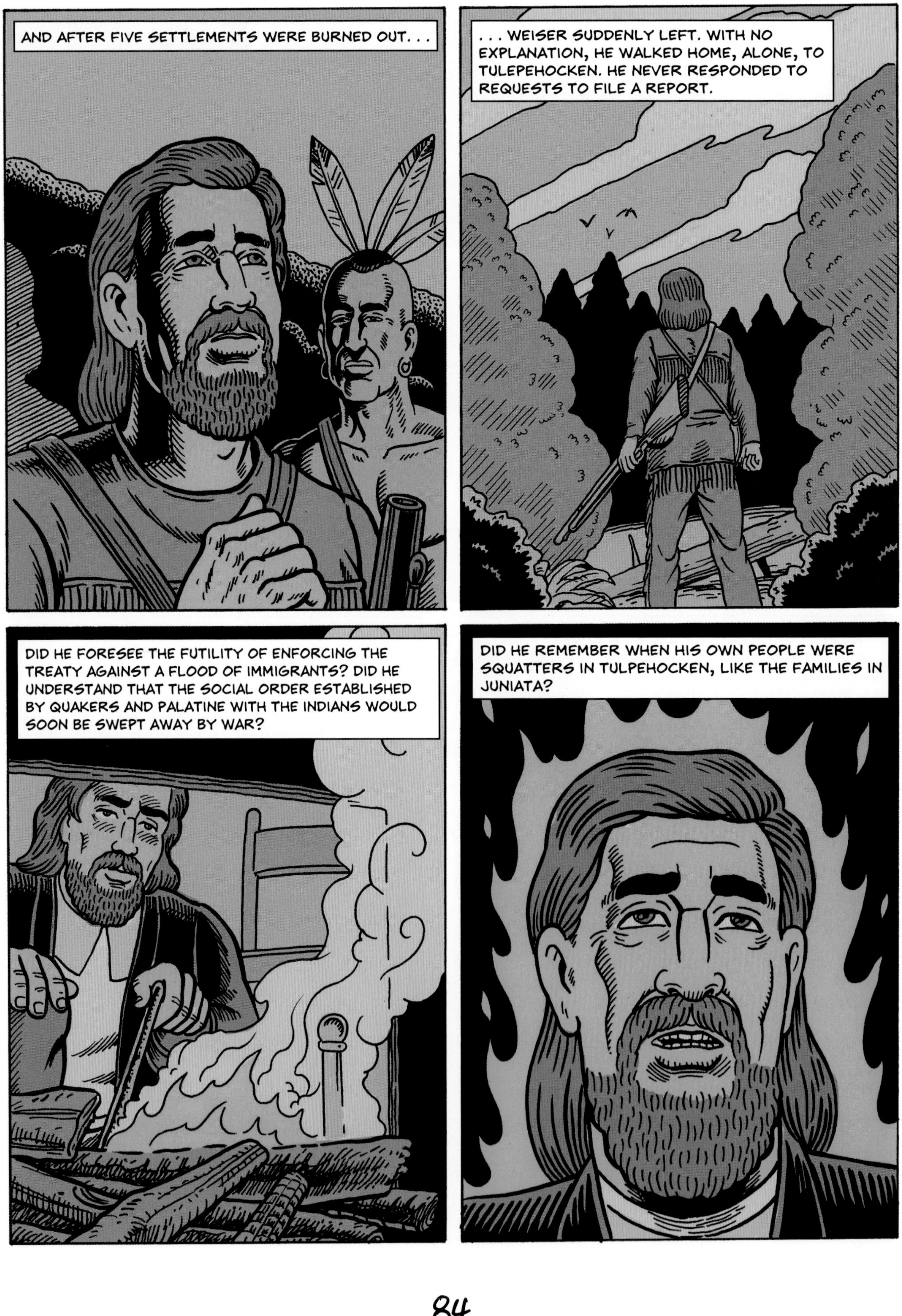
AND AFTER FIVE SETTLEMENTS WERE BURNED OUT. . .
. . . WEISER SUDDENLY LEFT. WITH NO EXPLANATION, HE WALKED HOME, ALONE, TO TULEPEHOCKEN. HE NEVER RESPONDED TO REQUESTS TO FILE A REPORT.
DID HE FORESEE THE FUTILITY OF ENFORCING THE TREATY AGAINST A FLOOD OF IMMIGRANTS? DID HE UNDERSTAND THAT THE SOCIAL ORDER ESTABLISHED BY QUAKERS AND PALATINE WITH THE INDIANS WOULD SOON BE SWEPT AWAY BY WAR?
DID HE REMEMBER WHEN HIS OWN PEOPLE WERE SQUATTERS IN TULPEHOCKEN, LIKE THE FAMILIES IN JUNIATA?

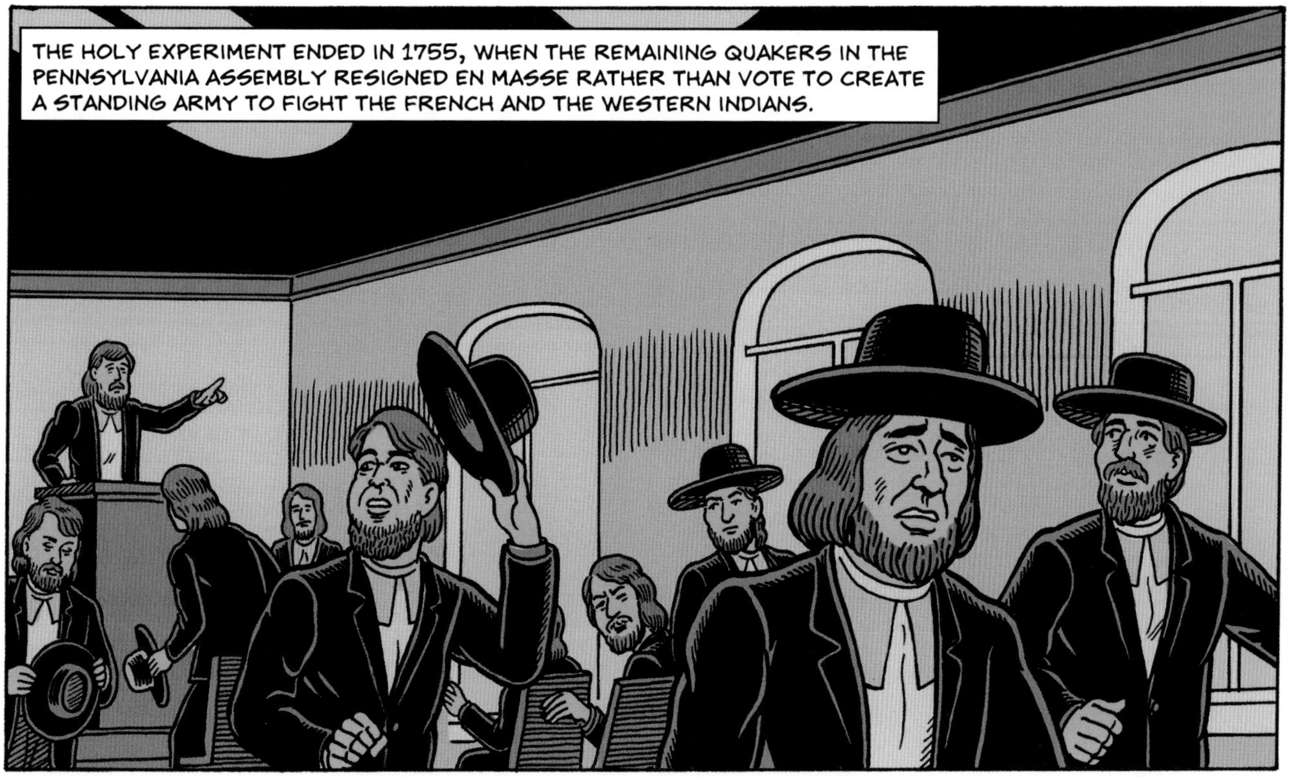
THE HOLY EXPERIMENT ENDED IN 1755, WHEN THE REMAINING QUAKERS IN THE PENNSYLVANIA ASSEMBLY RESIGNED EN MASSE RATHER THAN VOTE TO CREATE A STANDING ARMY TO FIGHT THE FRENCH AND THE WESTERN INDIANS.

# WHAT WAS LOST

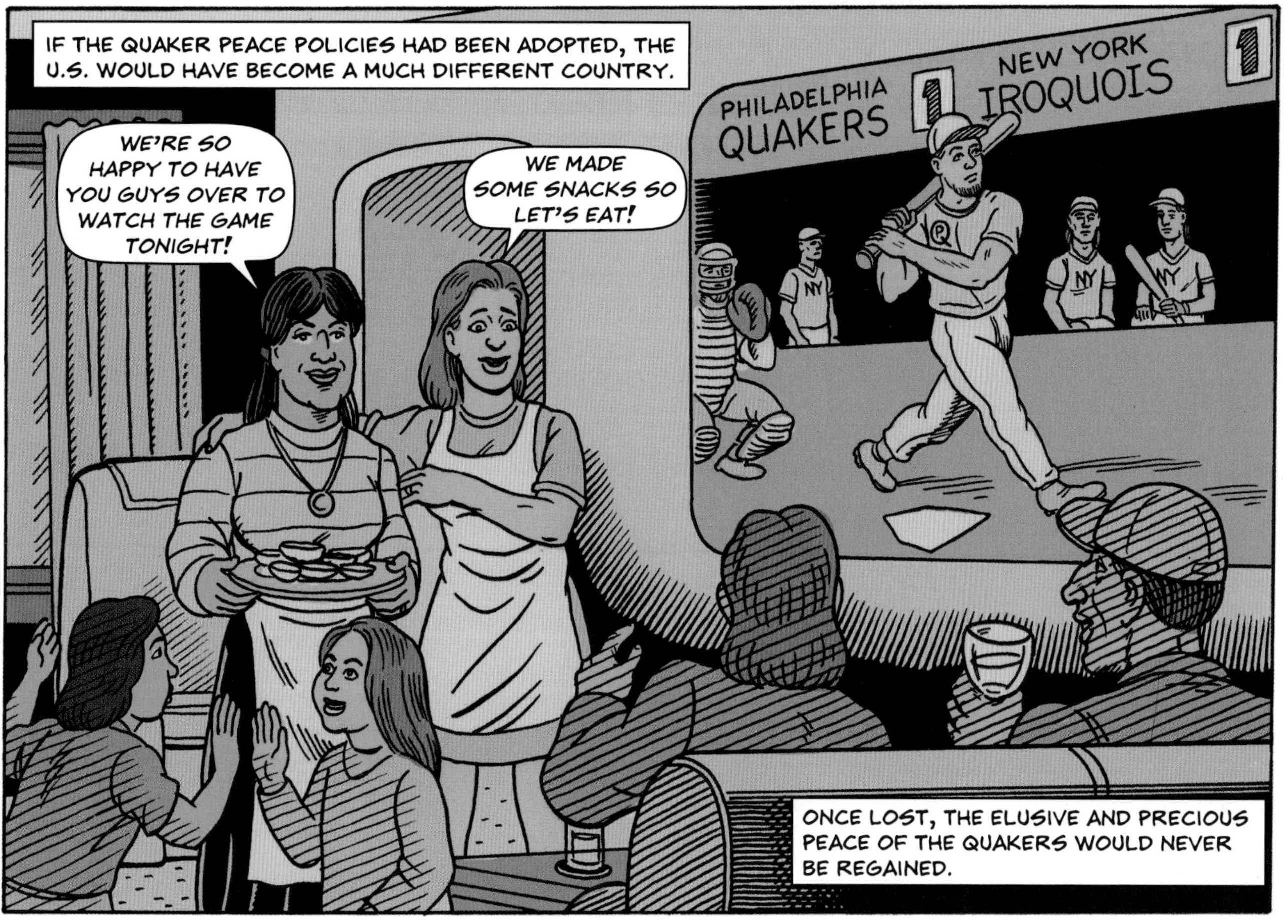
IF THE QUAKER PEACE POLICIES HAD BEEN ADOPTED, THE U.S. WOULD HAVE BECOME A MUCH DIFFERENT COUNTRY.
PHILADELPHIA QUAKERS 1
NEW YORK IROQUOIS 1
WE'RE SO HAPPY TO HAVE YOU GUYS OVER TO WATCH THE GAME TONIGHT!
WE MADE SOME SNACKS SO LET'S EAT!
NY
ONCE LOST, THE ELUSIVE AND PRECIOUS PEACE OF THE QUAKERS WOULD NEVER BE REGAINED.

THE END

# Angelina Grimke, Christian Abolitionist

SCRIPT: PAUL BUHLE • ART BY GARY DUMM • COLOR BY LAURA DUMM

ANGELINA CAME FROM A WEALTHY SOUTHERN BACKGROUND, BUT. . .

I AM HAVING DOUBTS ABOUT CHRISTIANITY AND SLAVERY.

LATER, AS A QUAKER CONVERT LIVING IN PHILADELPHIA, SHE WROTE HER FAMOUS PAMPHLET, "AN APPEAL TO THE CHRISTIAN WOMEN OF THE SOUTH" (1836).

. . .THAT SLAVERY IS CONTRARY TO THE FIRST CHARTER OF HUMAN RIGHTS BESTOWED UPON MAN IN THE BIBLE, THAT SLAVERY NEVER EXISTED UNDER HEBREW BIBLICAL LAW; AND THAT SLAVERY IS CONTRARY TO THE TEACHINGS OF JESUS AND THE APOSTLES.

IN 1839 ANGELINA, ALONG WITH HER HUSBAND, THEODORE WELD, AND HER SISTER, SARAH, WROTE AND EDITED AMERICAN SLAVERY AS IT IS: TESTIMONY OF A THOUSAND WITNESSES. THIS LED THOUSANDS OF READERS TO LEARN ABOUT THE CRUELTIES OF SLAVERY FOR THE FIRST TIME. HARRIET BEECHER STOWE'S UNCLE TOM'S CABIN IS SAID TO HAVE BEEN BASED UPON THE MATERIALS IN THIS VOLUME.

AMERICAN SLAVERY AS IT IS: TESTIMONY OF A THOUSAND WITNESSES

THE END

# Radical Resistance

By Nick Thorkelson

# THERE AM I AMONG THEM:
## FAITH-BASED MOVEMENTS IN MODERN TIMES

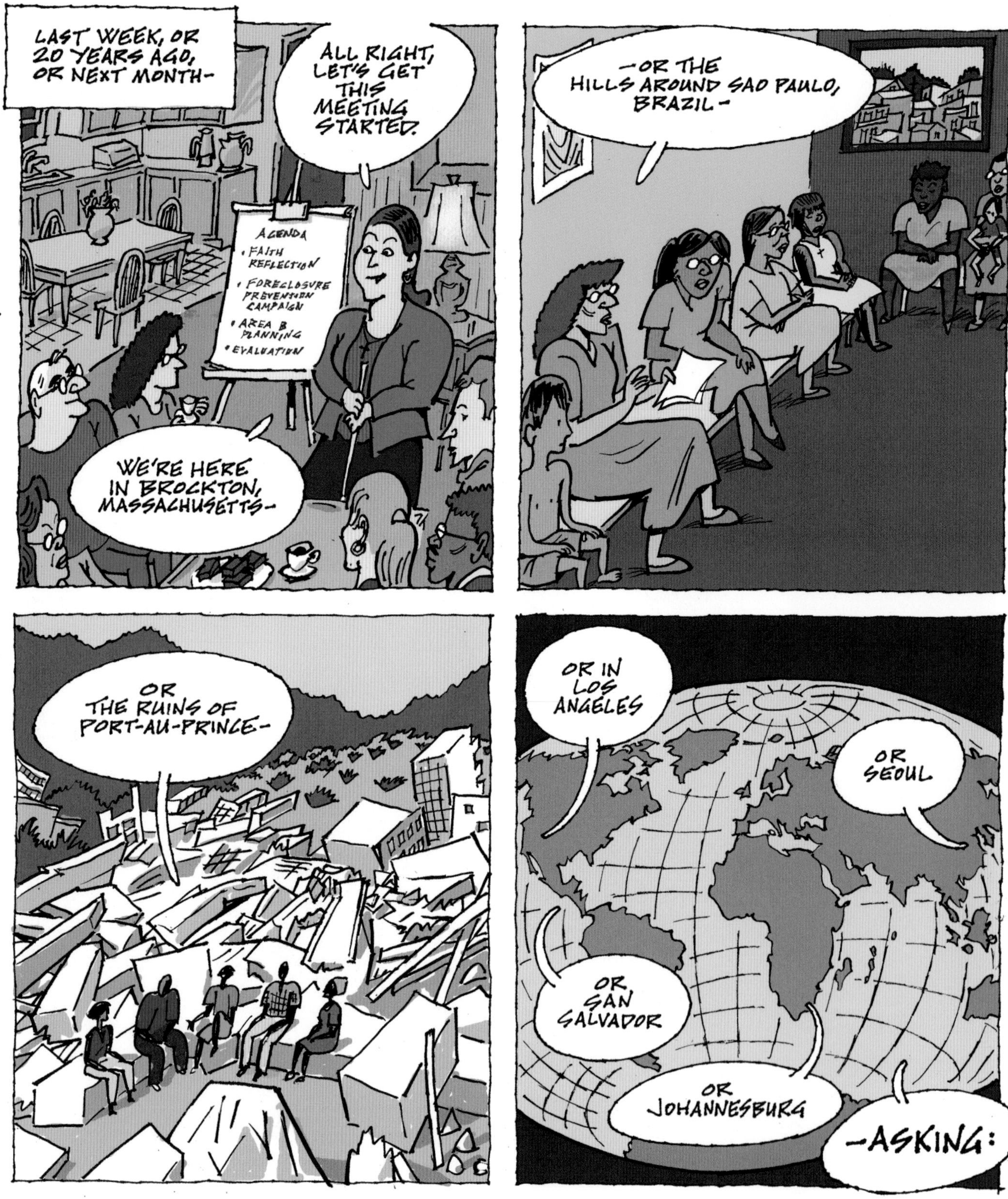
LAST WEEK, OR 20 YEARS AGO, OR NEXT MONTH-
ALL RIGHT, LET'S GET THIS MEETING STARTED.
AGENDA
• FAITH REFLECTION
• FORECLOSURE PREVENTION CAMPAIGN
• AREA B PLANNING
• EVALUATION
WE'RE HERE IN BROCKTON, MASSACHUSETTS-
-OR THE HILLS AROUND SAO PAULO, BRAZIL-
OR THE RUINS OF PORT-AU-PRINCE-
OR IN LOS ANGELES
OR SEOUL
OR, SAN SALVADOR
OR JOHANNESBURG
-ASKING:

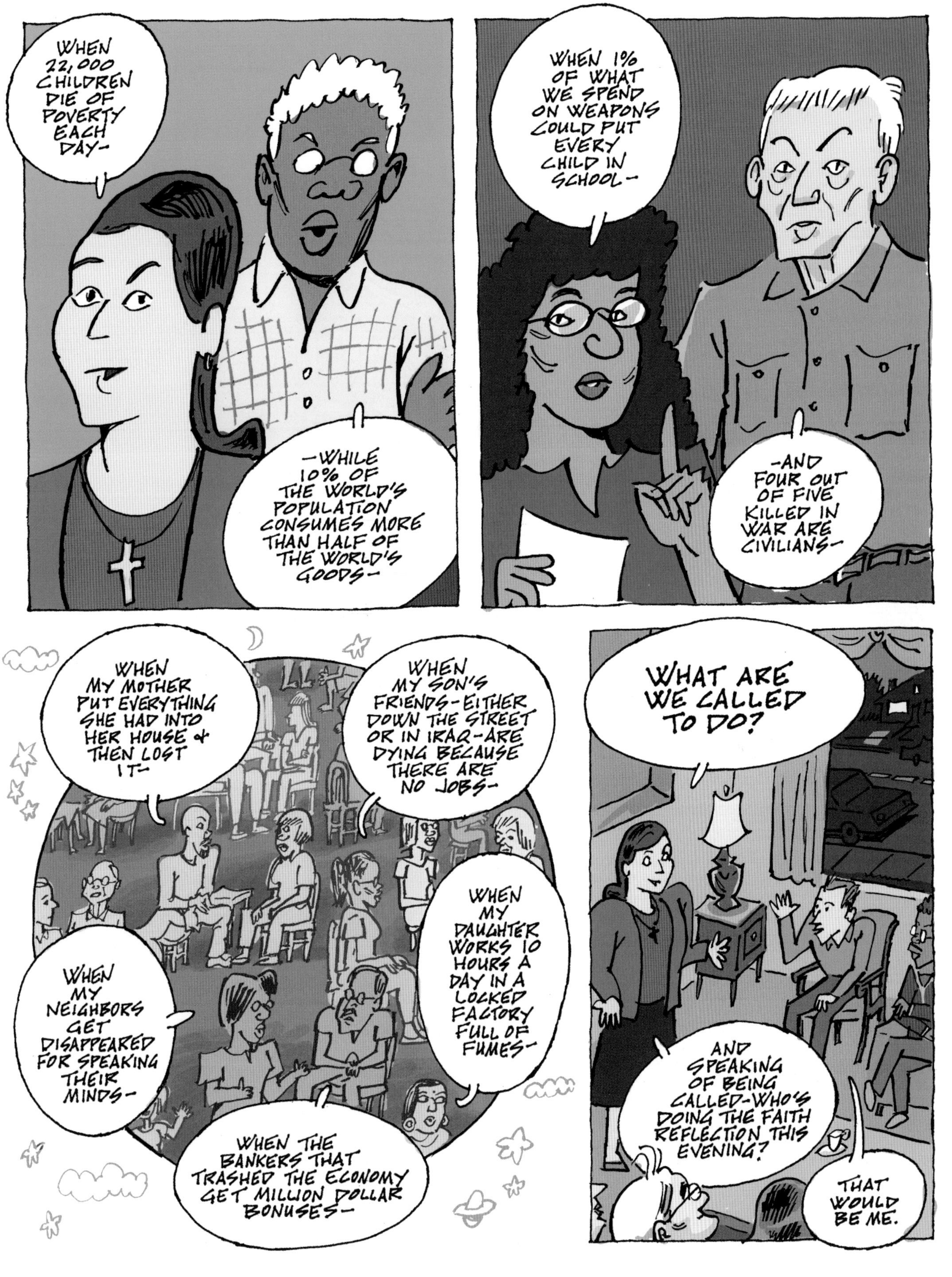
WHEN 22,000 CHILDREN DIE OF POVERTY EACH DAY-
-WHILE 10% OF THE WORLD'S POPULATION CONSUMES MORE THAN HALF OF THE WORLD'S GOODS-
WHEN 1% OF WHAT WE SPEND ON WEAPONS COULD PUT EVERY CHILD IN SCHOOL-
-AND FOUR OUT OF FIVE KILLED IN WAR ARE CIVILIANS-
WHEN MY MOTHER PUT EVERYTHING SHE HAD INTO HER HOUSE & THEN LOST IT-
WHEN MY SON'S FRIENDS-EITHER DOWN THE STREET OR IN IRAQ-ARE DYING BECAUSE THERE ARE NO JOBS-
WHEN MY DAUGHTER WORKS 10 HOURS A DAY IN A LOCKED FACTORY FULL OF FUMES-
WHEN MY NEIGHBORS GET DISAPPEARED FOR SPEAKING THEIR MINDS-
WHEN THE BANKERS THAT TRASHED THE ECONOMY GET MILLION DOLLAR BONUSES-
WHAT ARE WE CALLED TO DO?
AND SPEAKING OF BEING CALLED-WHO'S DOING THE FAITH REFLECTION THIS EVENING?
THAT WOULD BE ME.

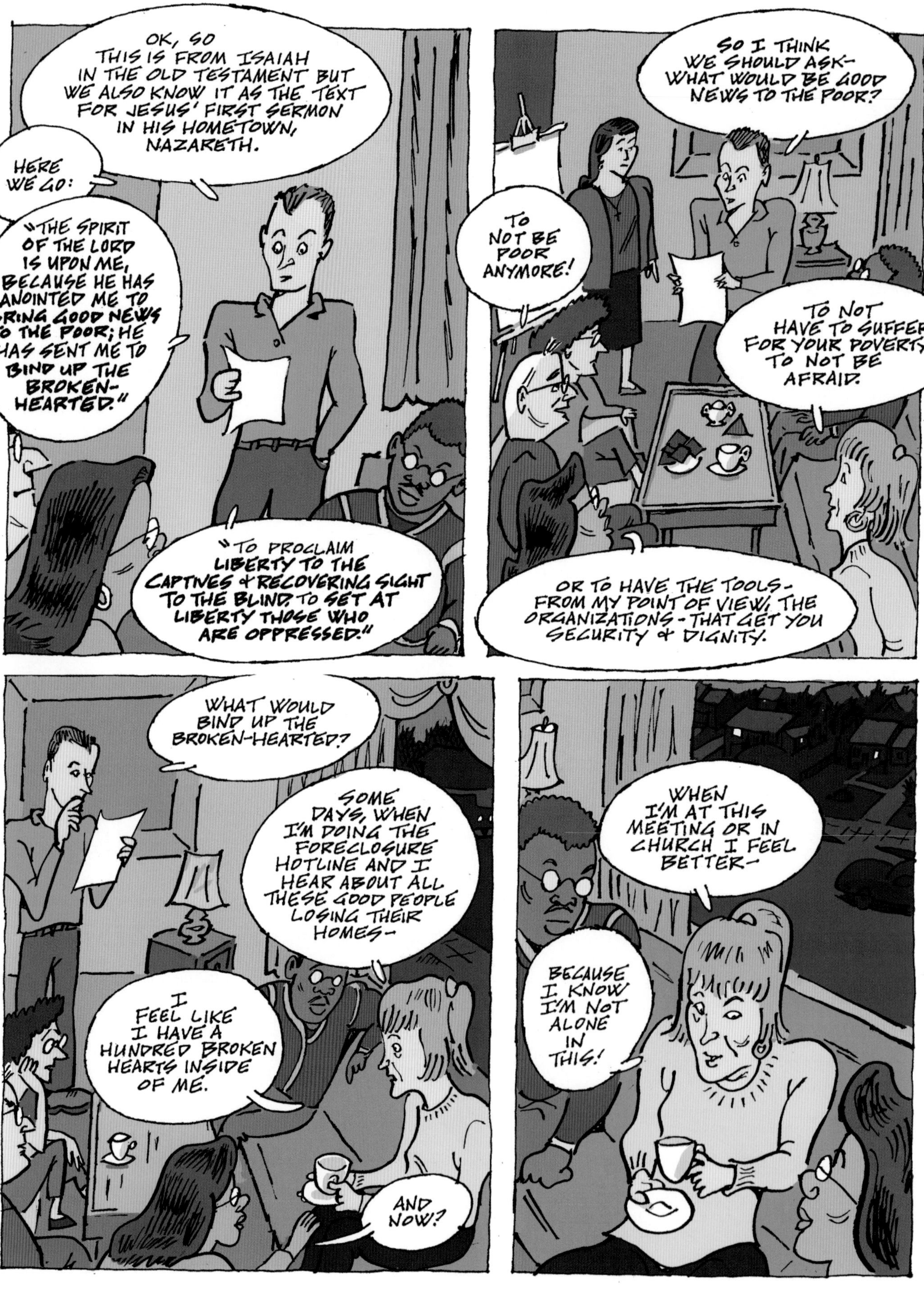
OK, SO THIS IS FROM ISAIAH IN THE OLD TESTAMENT BUT WE ALSO KNOW IT AS THE TEXT FOR JESUS' FIRST SERMON IN HIS HOMETOWN, NAZARETH.
HERE WE GO:
"THE SPIRIT OF THE LORD IS UPON ME, BECAUSE HE HAS ANOINTED ME TO BRING GOOD NEWS TO THE POOR; HE HAS SENT ME TO BIND UP THE BROKEN-HEARTED."
"TO PROCLAIM LIBERTY TO THE CAPTIVES & RECOVERING SIGHT TO THE BLIND, TO SET AT LIBERTY THOSE WHO ARE OPPRESSED."
SO I THINK WE SHOULD ASK- WHAT WOULD BE GOOD NEWS TO THE POOR?
TO NOT BE POOR ANYMORE!
TO NOT HAVE TO SUFFER FOR YOUR POVERTY, TO NOT BE AFRAID.
OR TO HAVE THE TOOLS- FROM MY POINT OF VIEW, THE ORGANIZATIONS - THAT GET YOU SECURITY & DIGNITY.
WHAT WOULD BIND UP THE BROKEN-HEARTED?
SOME DAYS, WHEN I'M DOING THE FORECLOSURE HOTLINE AND I HEAR ABOUT ALL THESE GOOD PEOPLE LOSING THEIR HOMES-
I FEEL LIKE I HAVE A HUNDRED BROKEN HEARTS INSIDE OF ME.
AND NOW?
WHEN I'M AT THIS MEETING OR IN CHURCH I FEEL BETTER-
BECAUSE I KNOW I'M NOT ALONE IN THIS!

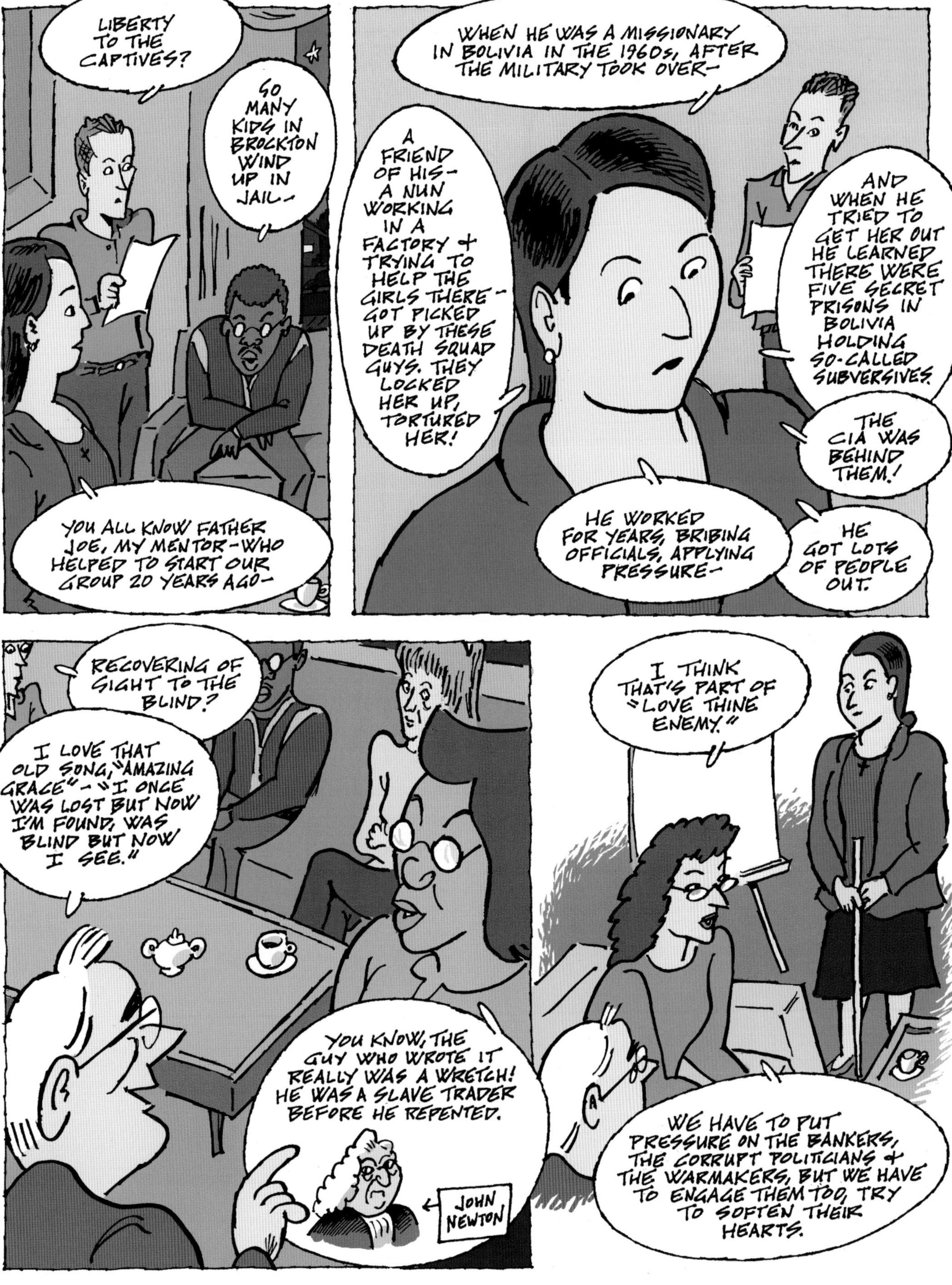
LIBERTY TO THE CAPTIVES?
SO MANY KIDS IN BROCKTON WIND UP IN JAIL–
YOU ALL KNOW FATHER JOE, MY MENTOR–WHO HELPED TO START OUR GROUP 20 YEARS AGO–
WHEN HE WAS A MISSIONARY IN BOLIVIA IN THE 1960s, AFTER THE MILITARY TOOK OVER–
A FRIEND OF HIS–A NUN WORKING IN A FACTORY & TRYING TO HELP THE GIRLS THERE–GOT PICKED UP BY THESE DEATH SQUAD GUYS. THEY LOCKED HER UP, TORTURED HER!
AND WHEN HE TRIED TO GET HER OUT HE LEARNED THERE WERE FIVE SECRET PRISONS IN BOLIVIA HOLDING SO-CALLED SUBVERSIVES.
THE CIA WAS BEHIND THEM!
HE WORKED FOR YEARS, BRIBING OFFICIALS, APPLYING PRESSURE–
HE GOT LOTS OF PEOPLE OUT.
RECOVERING OF SIGHT TO THE BLIND?
I LOVE THAT OLD SONG, "AMAZING GRACE"–"I ONCE WAS LOST BUT NOW I'M FOUND, WAS BLIND BUT NOW I SEE."
YOU KNOW, THE GUY WHO WROTE IT REALLY WAS A WRETCH! HE WAS A SLAVE TRADER BEFORE HE REPENTED.
JOHN NEWTON
I THINK THAT'S PART OF "LOVE THINE ENEMY."
WE HAVE TO PUT PRESSURE ON THE BANKERS, THE CORRUPT POLITICIANS & THE WARMAKERS, BUT WE HAVE TO ENGAGE THEM TOO, TRY TO SOFTEN THEIR HEARTS.

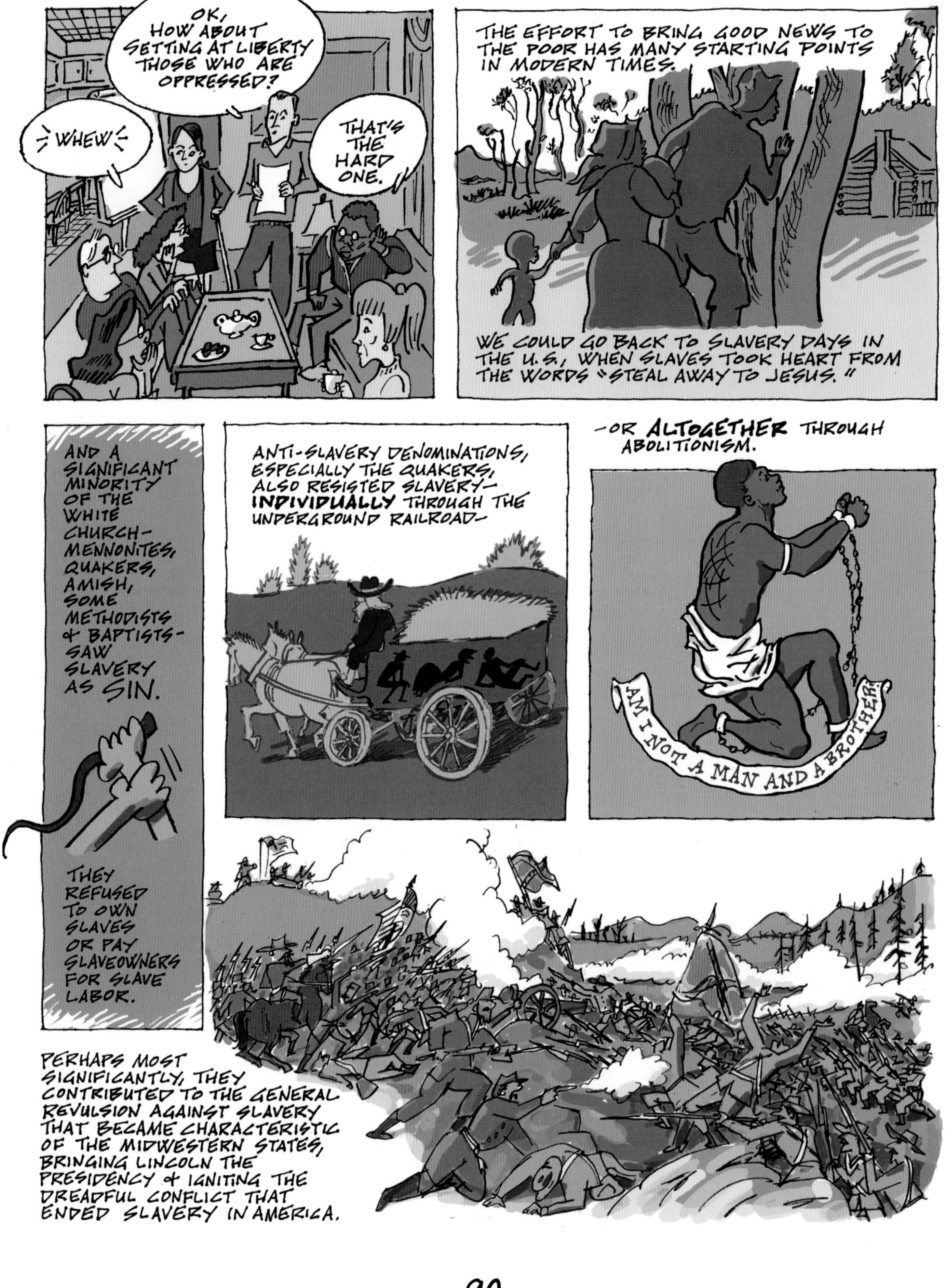

OK, HOW ABOUT SETTING AT LIBERTY THOSE WHO ARE OPPRESSED?
WHEW
THAT'S THE HARD ONE.
THE EFFORT TO BRING GOOD NEWS TO THE POOR HAS MANY STARTING POINTS IN MODERN TIMES.
WE COULD GO BACK TO SLAVERY DAYS IN THE U.S., WHEN SLAVES TOOK HEART FROM THE WORDS "STEAL AWAY TO JESUS."
AND A SIGNIFICANT MINORITY OF THE WHITE CHURCH— MENNONITES, QUAKERS, AMISH, SOME METHODISTS & BAPTISTS— SAW SLAVERY AS SIN.
THEY REFUSED TO OWN SLAVES OR PAY SLAVEOWNERS FOR SLAVE LABOR.
ANTI-SLAVERY DENOMINATIONS, ESPECIALLY THE QUAKERS, ALSO RESISTED SLAVERY— INDIVIDUALLY THROUGH THE UNDERGROUND RAILROAD—
—OR ALTOGETHER THROUGH ABOLITIONISM.
AM I NOT A MAN AND A BROTHER?
PERHAPS MOST SIGNIFICANTLY, THEY CONTRIBUTED TO THE GENERAL REVULSION AGAINST SLAVERY THAT BECAME CHARACTERISTIC OF THE MIDWESTERN STATES, BRINGING LINCOLN THE PRESIDENCY & IGNITING THE DREADFUL CONFLICT THAT ENDED SLAVERY IN AMERICA.

# STEAL AWAY: ABOLITIONISM & BLACK FREEDOM

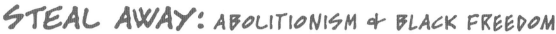

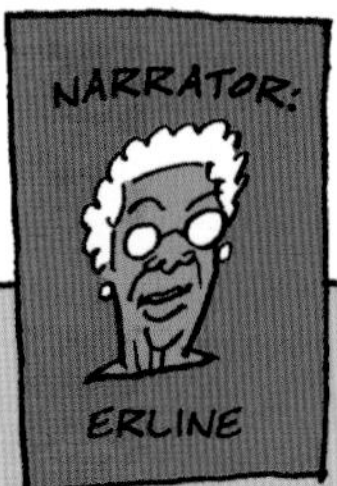
NARRATOR:
ERLINE

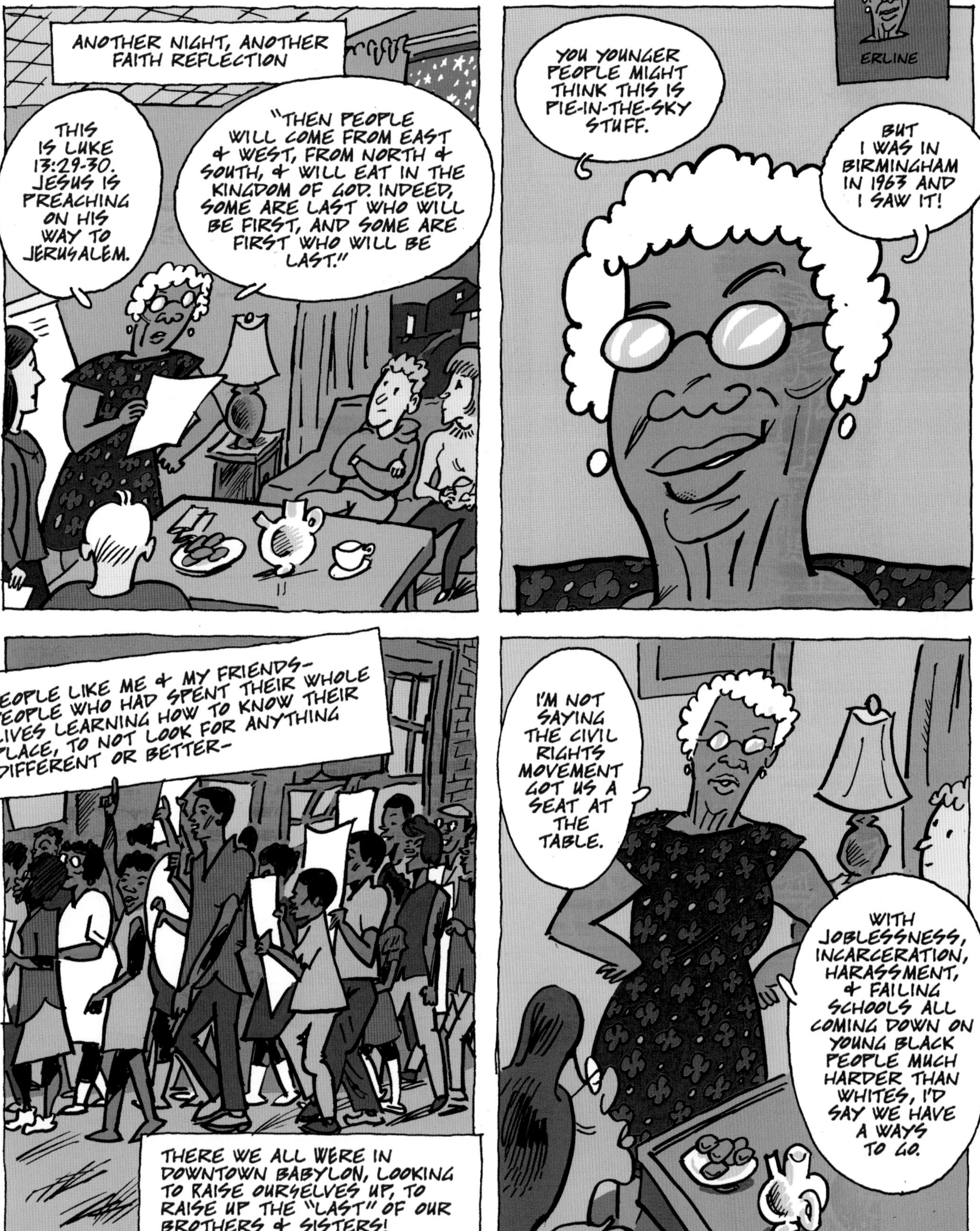
ANOTHER NIGHT, ANOTHER FAITH REFLECTION
THIS IS LUKE 13:29-30. JESUS IS PREACHING ON HIS WAY TO JERUSALEM.
"THEN PEOPLE WILL COME FROM EAST & WEST, FROM NORTH & SOUTH, & WILL EAT IN THE KINGDOM OF GOD. INDEED, SOME ARE LAST WHO WILL BE FIRST, AND SOME ARE FIRST WHO WILL BE LAST."
YOU YOUNGER PEOPLE MIGHT THINK THIS IS PIE-IN-THE-SKY STUFF.
BUT I WAS IN BIRMINGHAM IN 1963 AND I SAW IT!
PEOPLE LIKE ME & MY FRIENDS- PEOPLE WHO HAD SPENT THEIR WHOLE LIVES LEARNING HOW TO KNOW THEIR PLACE, TO NOT LOOK FOR ANYTHING DIFFERENT OR BETTER-
THERE WE ALL WERE IN DOWNTOWN BABYLON, LOOKING TO RAISE OURSELVES UP, TO RAISE UP THE "LAST" OF OUR BROTHERS & SISTERS!
I'M NOT SAYING THE CIVIL RIGHTS MOVEMENT GOT US A SEAT AT THE TABLE.
WITH JOBLESSNESS, INCARCERATION, HARASSMENT, & FAILING SCHOOLS ALL COMING DOWN ON YOUNG BLACK PEOPLE MUCH HARDER THAN WHITES, I'D SAY WE HAVE A WAYS TO GO.

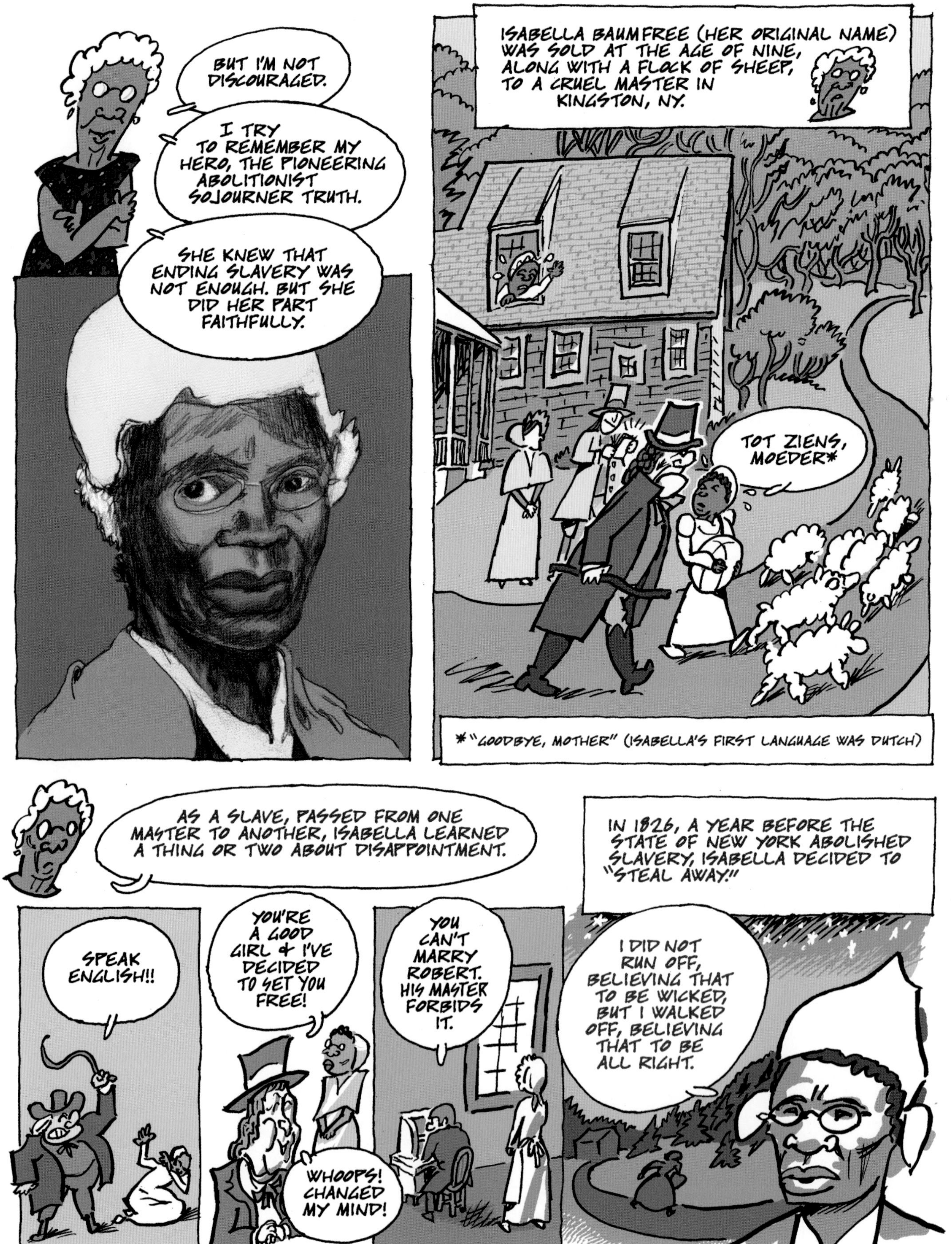
BUT I'M NOT DISCOURAGED.
I TRY TO REMEMBER MY HERO, THE PIONEERING ABOLITIONIST SOJOURNER TRUTH.
SHE KNEW THAT ENDING SLAVERY WAS NOT ENOUGH. BUT SHE DID HER PART FAITHFULLY.
ISABELLA BAUMFREE (HER ORIGINAL NAME) WAS SOLD AT THE AGE OF NINE, ALONG WITH A FLOCK OF SHEEP, TO A CRUEL MASTER IN KINGSTON, NY.
TOT ZIENS, MOEDER*
*"GOODBYE, MOTHER" (ISABELLA'S FIRST LANGUAGE WAS DUTCH)
AS A SLAVE, PASSED FROM ONE MASTER TO ANOTHER, ISABELLA LEARNED A THING OR TWO ABOUT DISAPPOINTMENT.
SPEAK ENGLISH!!
YOU'RE A GOOD GIRL & I'VE DECIDED TO SET YOU FREE!
WHOOPS! CHANGED MY MIND!
YOU CAN'T MARRY ROBERT. HIS MASTER FORBIDS IT.
IN 1826, A YEAR BEFORE THE STATE OF NEW YORK ABOLISHED SLAVERY, ISABELLA DECIDED TO "STEAL AWAY."
I DID NOT RUN OFF, BELIEVING THAT TO BE WICKED, BUT I WALKED OFF, BELIEVING THAT TO BE ALL RIGHT.

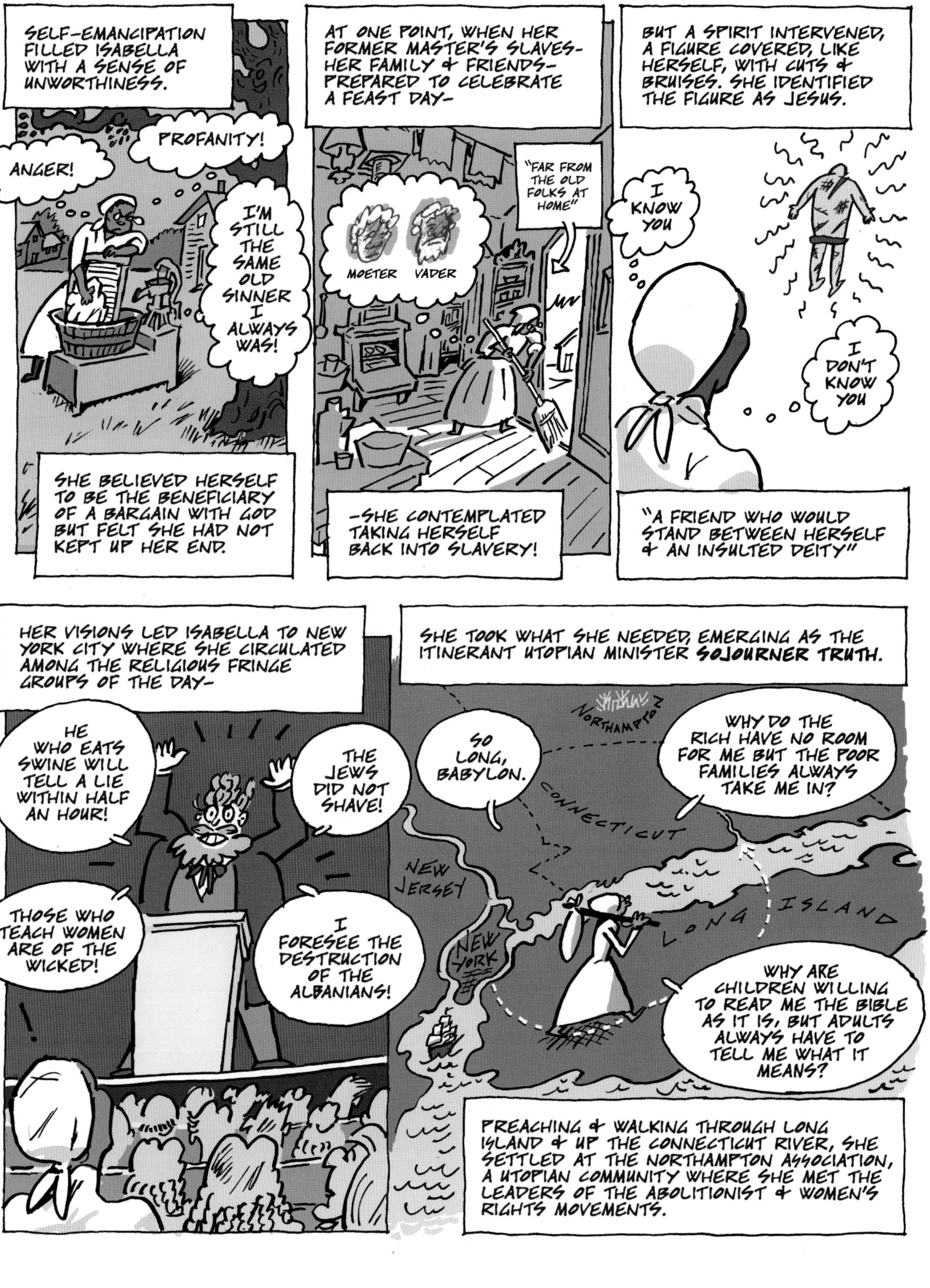

SELF-EMANCIPATION FILLED ISABELLA WITH A SENSE OF UNWORTHINESS.
ANGER!
PROFANITY!
I'M STILL THE SAME OLD SINNER I ALWAYS WAS!
SHE BELIEVED HERSELF TO BE THE BENEFICIARY OF A BARGAIN WITH GOD BUT FELT SHE HAD NOT KEPT UP HER END.
AT ONE POINT, WHEN HER FORMER MASTER'S SLAVES- HER FAMILY & FRIENDS- PREPARED TO CELEBRATE A FEAST DAY-
MOETER
VADER
"FAR FROM THE OLD FOLKS AT HOME"
-SHE CONTEMPLATED TAKING HERSELF BACK INTO SLAVERY!
BUT A SPIRIT INTERVENED, A FIGURE COVERED, LIKE HERSELF, WITH CUTS & BRUISES. SHE IDENTIFIED THE FIGURE AS JESUS.
I KNOW YOU
I DON'T KNOW YOU
"A FRIEND WHO WOULD STAND BETWEEN HERSELF & AN INSULTED DEITY"
HER VISIONS LED ISABELLA TO NEW YORK CITY WHERE SHE CIRCULATED AMONG THE RELIGIOUS FRINGE GROUPS OF THE DAY-
HE WHO EATS SWINE WILL TELL A LIE WITHIN HALF AN HOUR!
THE JEWS DID NOT SHAVE!
THOSE WHO TEACH WOMEN ARE OF THE WICKED!
I FORESEE THE DESTRUCTION OF THE ALBANIANS!
SHE TOOK WHAT SHE NEEDED, EMERGING AS THE ITINERANT UTOPIAN MINISTER SOJOURNER TRUTH.
NORTHAMPTON
SO LONG, BABYLON.
CONNECTICUT
WHY DO THE RICH HAVE NO ROOM FOR ME BUT THE POOR FAMILIES ALWAYS TAKE ME IN?
NEW JERSEY
NEW YORK
LONG ISLAND
WHY ARE CHILDREN WILLING TO READ ME THE BIBLE AS IT IS, BUT ADULTS ALWAYS HAVE TO TELL ME WHAT IT MEANS?
PREACHING & WALKING THROUGH LONG ISLAND & UP THE CONNECTICUT RIVER, SHE SETTLED AT THE NORTHAMPTON ASSOCIATION, A UTOPIAN COMMUNITY WHERE SHE MET THE LEADERS OF THE ABOLITIONIST & WOMEN'S RIGHTS MOVEMENTS.

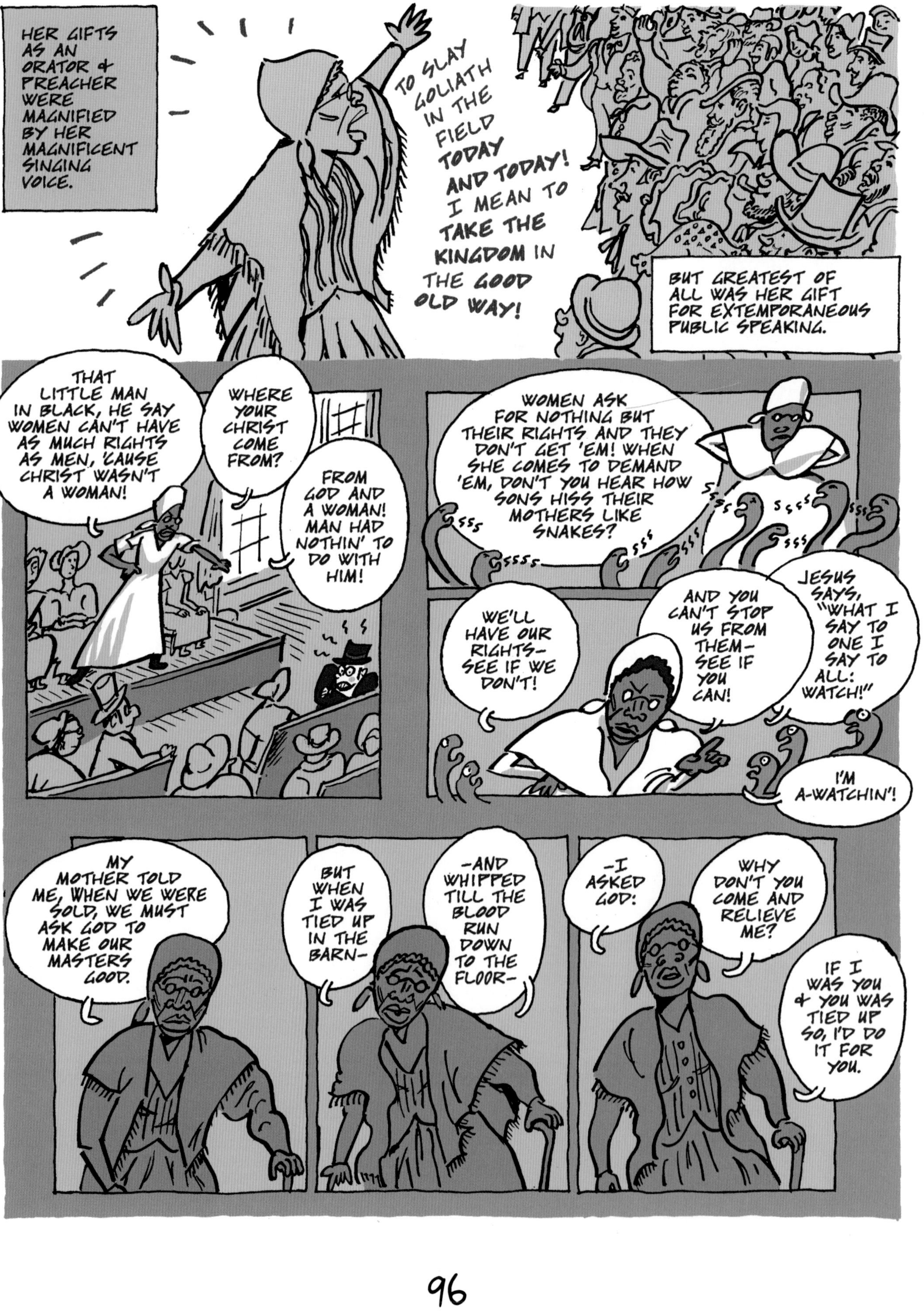

HER GIFTS AS AN ORATOR & PREACHER WERE MAGNIFIED BY HER MAGNIFICENT SINGING VOICE.
TO SLAY GOLIATH IN THE FIELD TODAY AND TODAY! I MEAN TO TAKE THE KINGDOM IN THE GOOD OLD WAY!
BUT GREATEST OF ALL WAS HER GIFT FOR EXTEMPORANEOUS PUBLIC SPEAKING.
THAT LITTLE MAN IN BLACK, HE SAY WOMEN CAN'T HAVE AS MUCH RIGHTS AS MEN, 'CAUSE CHRIST WASN'T A WOMAN!
WHERE YOUR CHRIST COME FROM?
FROM GOD AND A WOMAN! MAN HAD NOTHIN' TO DO WITH HIM!
WOMEN ASK FOR NOTHING BUT THEIR RIGHTS AND THEY DON'T GET 'EM! WHEN SHE COMES TO DEMAND 'EM, DON'T YOU HEAR HOW SONS HISS THEIR MOTHERS LIKE SNAKES?
SSS
SSSSS
SSS
SSS
SSSS
SSS
SSS
WE'LL HAVE OUR RIGHTS- SEE IF WE DON'T!
AND YOU CAN'T STOP US FROM THEM- SEE IF YOU CAN!
JESUS SAYS, "WHAT I SAY TO ONE I SAY TO ALL: WATCH!"
I'M A-WATCHIN'!
MY MOTHER TOLD ME, WHEN WE WERE SOLD, WE MUST ASK GOD TO MAKE OUR MASTERS GOOD.
BUT WHEN I WAS TIED UP IN THE BARN-
-AND WHIPPED TILL THE BLOOD RUN DOWN TO THE FLOOR-
-I ASKED GOD:
WHY DON'T YOU COME AND RELIEVE ME?
IF I WAS YOU & YOU WAS TIED UP SO, I'D DO IT FOR YOU.

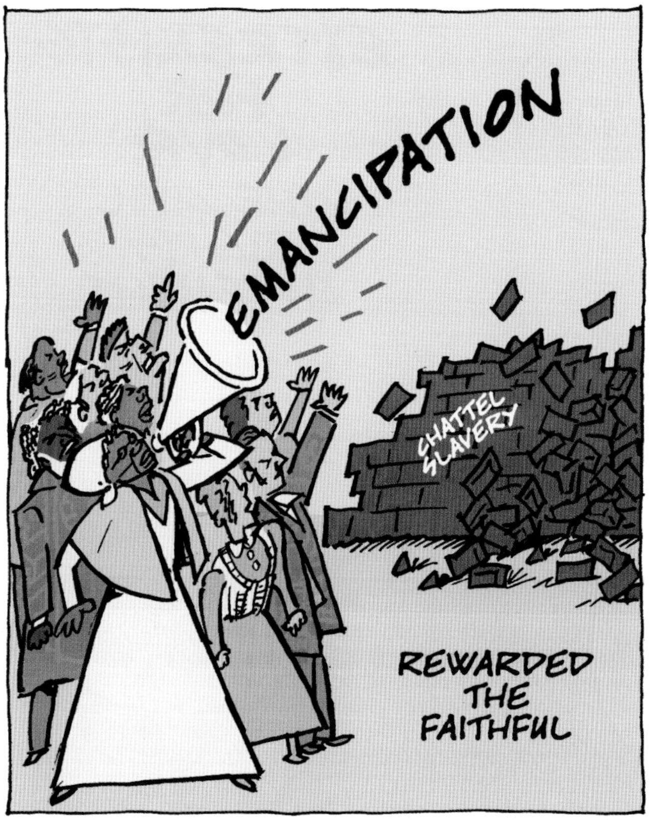
EMANCIPATION
CHATTEL SLAVERY
REWARDED THE FAITHFUL

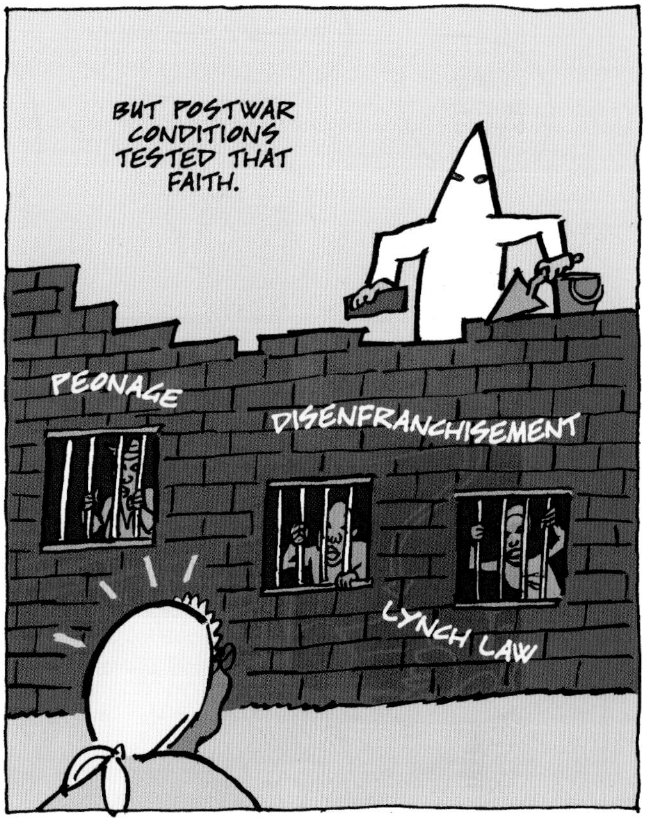
BUT POSTWAR CONDITIONS TESTED THAT FAITH.
PEONAGE
DISENFRANCHISEMENT
LYNCH LAW

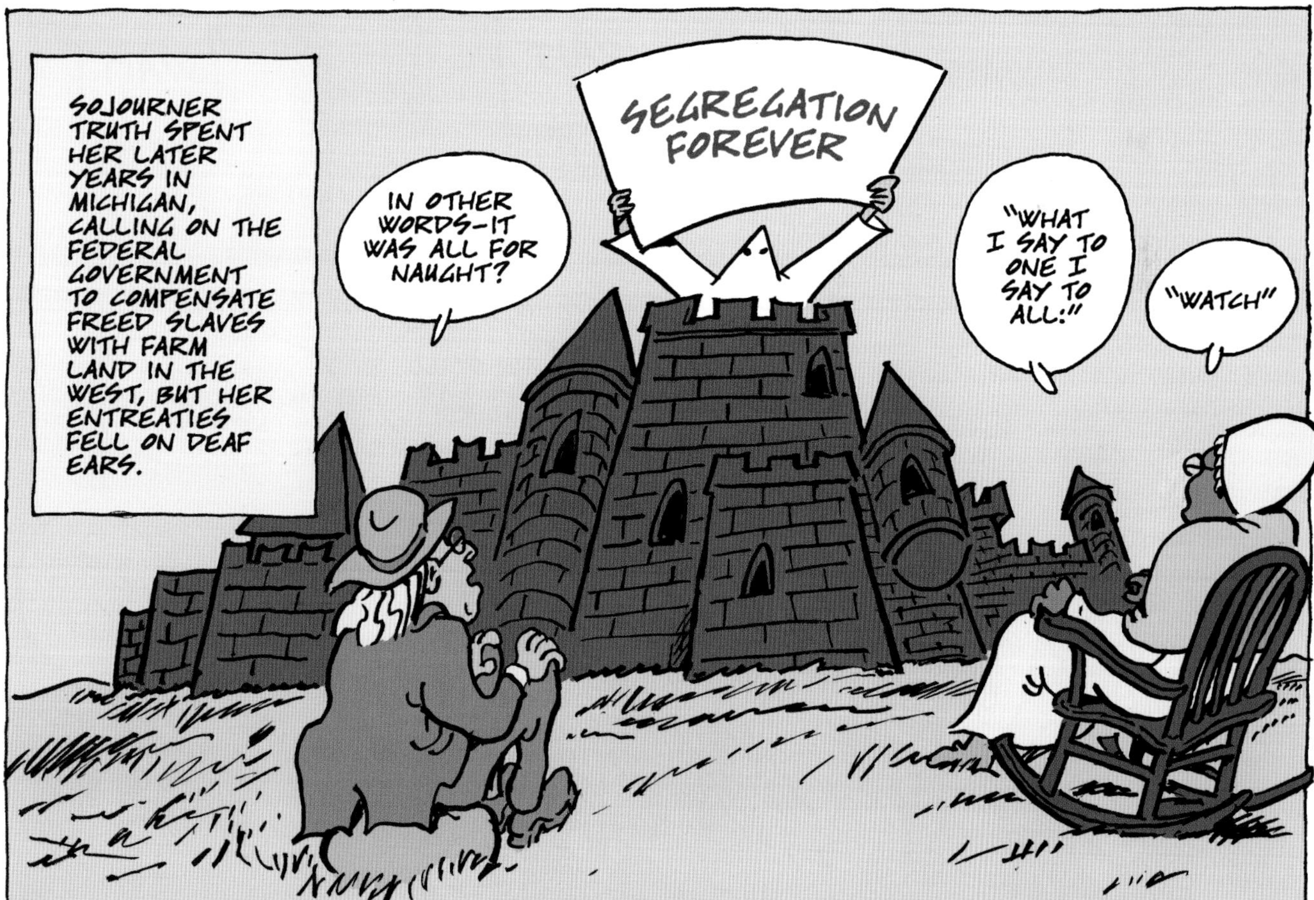
SOJOURNER TRUTH SPENT HER LATER YEARS IN MICHIGAN, CALLING ON THE FEDERAL GOVERNMENT TO COMPENSATE FREED SLAVES WITH FARM LAND IN THE WEST, BUT HER ENTREATIES FELL ON DEAF EARS.
SEGREGATION FOREVER
IN OTHER WORDS—IT WAS ALL FOR NAUGHT?
"WHAT I SAY TO ONE I SAY TO ALL:"
"WATCH"

# EXTREMISTS FOR LOVE: THE CIVIL RIGHTS MOVEMENT

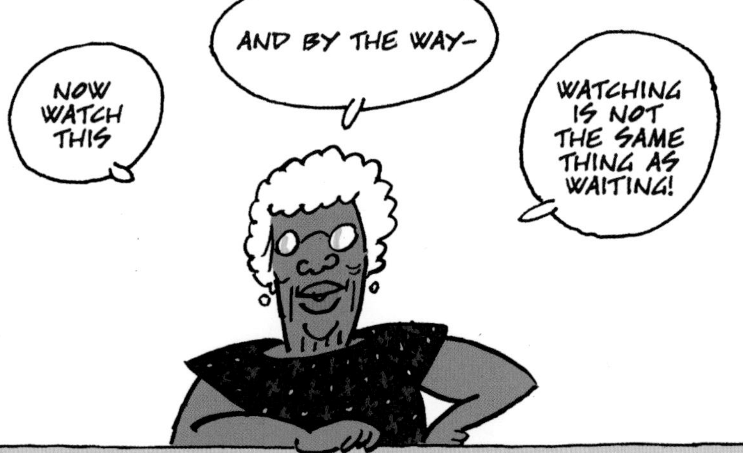

NOW WATCH THIS
AND BY THE WAY-
WATCHING IS NOT THE SAME THING AS WAITING!


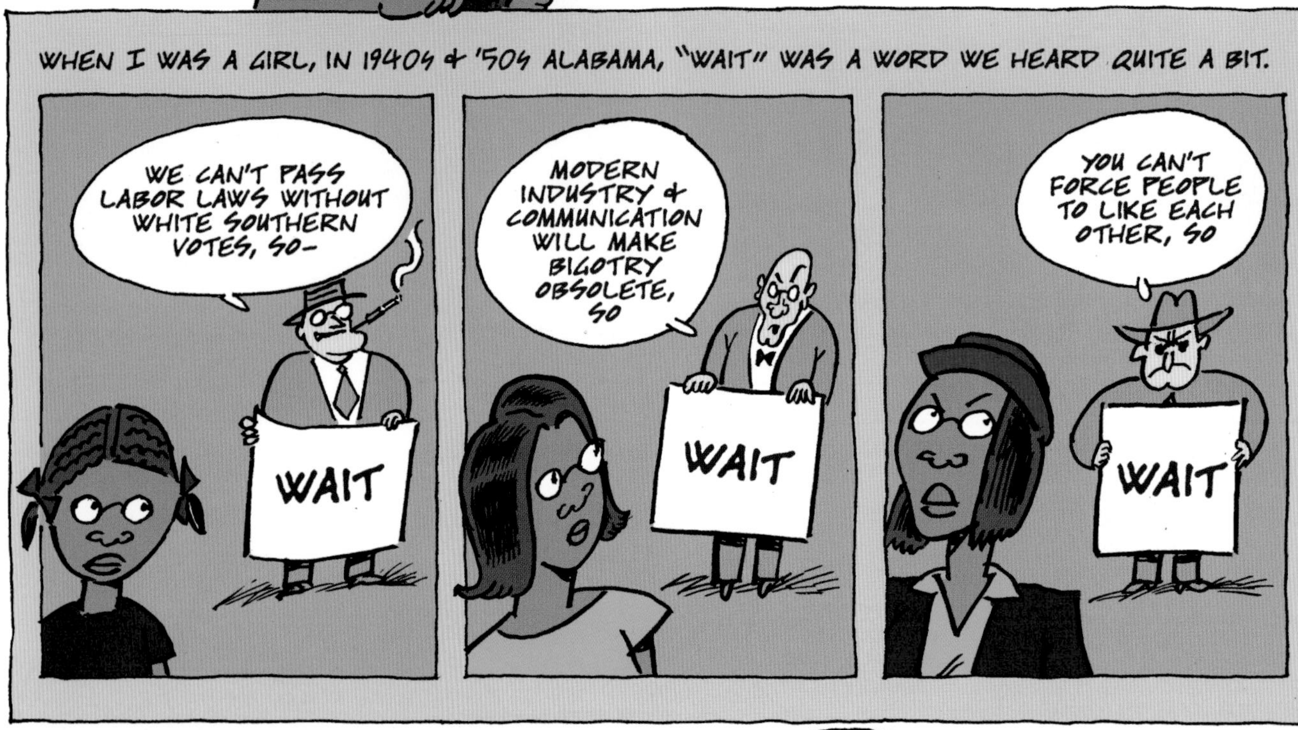

WHEN I WAS A GIRL, IN 1940s & '50s ALABAMA, "WAIT" WAS A WORD WE HEARD QUITE A BIT.
WE CAN'T PASS LABOR LAWS WITHOUT WHITE SOUTHERN VOTES, SO-
WAIT
MODERN INDUSTRY & COMMUNICATION WILL MAKE BIGOTRY OBSOLETE, SO
WAIT
YOU CAN'T FORCE PEOPLE TO LIKE EACH OTHER, SO
WAIT


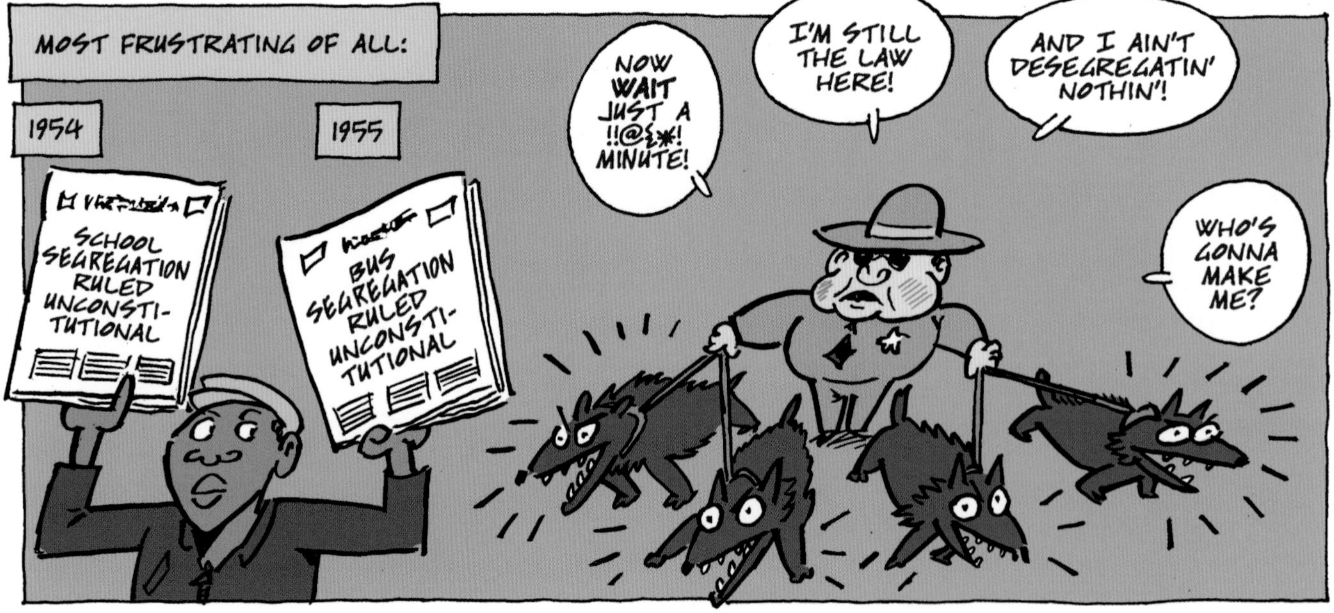

MOST FRUSTRATING OF ALL:
1954
SCHOOL SEGREGATION RULED UNCONSTI-TUTIONAL
1955
BUS SEGREGATION RULED UNCONSTI-TUTIONAL
NOW WAIT JUST A !!@{*! MINUTE!
I'M STILL THE LAW HERE!
AND I AIN'T DESEGREGATIN' NOTHIN'!
WHO'S GONNA MAKE ME?

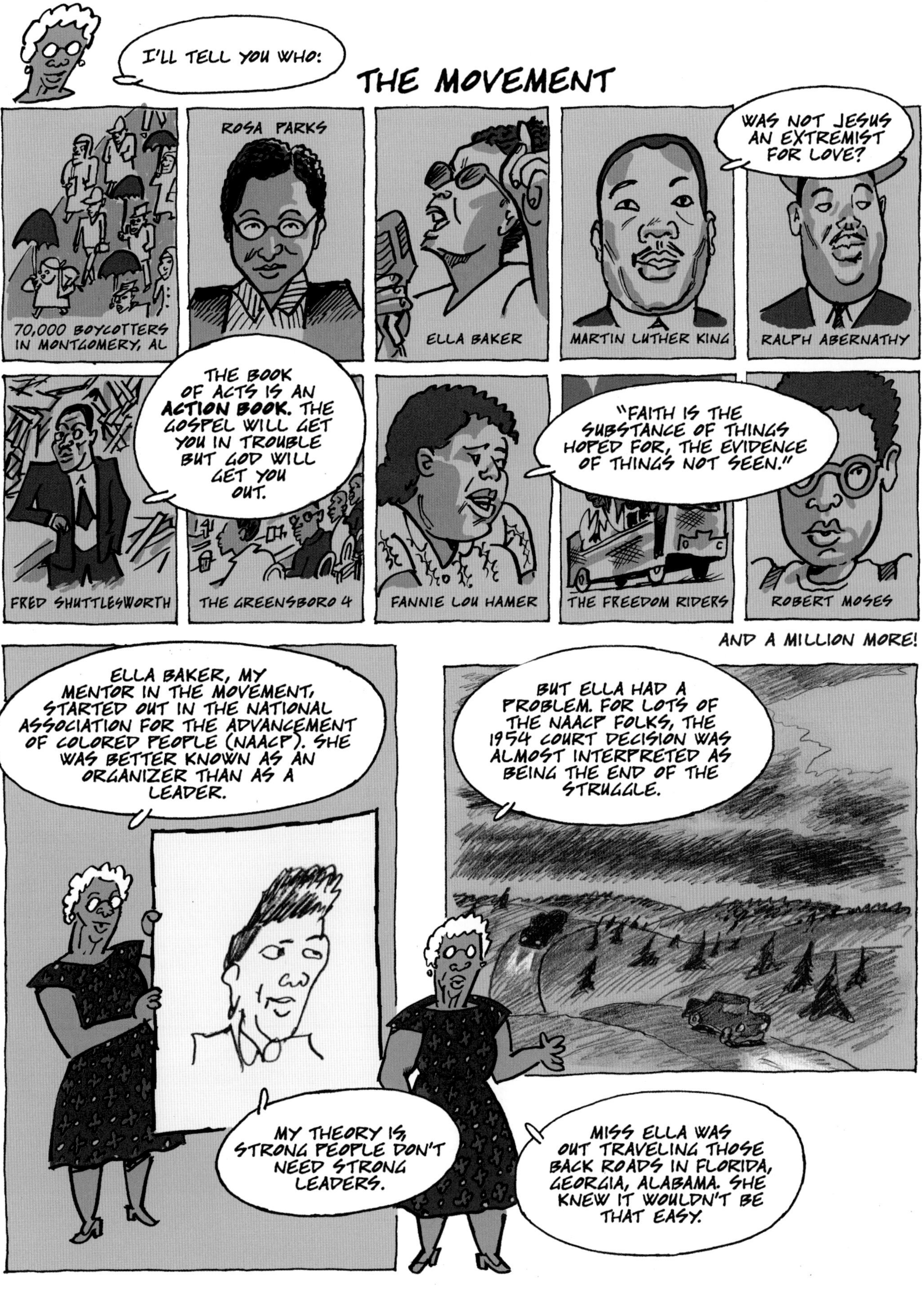
I'LL TELL YOU WHO:
THE MOVEMENT
70,000 BOYCOTTERS IN MONTGOMERY, AL
ROSA PARKS
ELLA BAKER
MARTIN LUTHER KING
WAS NOT JESUS AN EXTREMIST FOR LOVE?
RALPH ABERNATHY
FRED SHUTTLESWORTH
THE BOOK OF ACTS IS AN **ACTION BOOK.** THE GOSPEL WILL GET YOU IN TROUBLE BUT GOD WILL GET YOU OUT.
THE GREENSBORO 4
FANNIE LOU HAMER
"FAITH IS THE SUBSTANCE OF THINGS HOPED FOR, THE EVIDENCE OF THINGS NOT SEEN."
THE FREEDOM RIDERS
ROBERT MOSES
AND A MILLION MORE!
ELLA BAKER, MY MENTOR IN THE MOVEMENT, STARTED OUT IN THE NATIONAL ASSOCIATION FOR THE ADVANCEMENT OF COLORED PEOPLE (NAACP). SHE WAS BETTER KNOWN AS AN ORGANIZER THAN AS A LEADER.
BUT ELLA HAD A PROBLEM. FOR LOTS OF THE NAACP FOLKS, THE 1954 COURT DECISION WAS ALMOST INTERPRETED AS BEING THE END OF THE STRUGGLE.
MY THEORY IS, STRONG PEOPLE DON'T NEED STRONG LEADERS.
MISS ELLA WAS OUT TRAVELING THOSE BACK ROADS IN FLORIDA, GEORGIA, ALABAMA. SHE KNEW IT WOULDN'T BE THAT EASY.

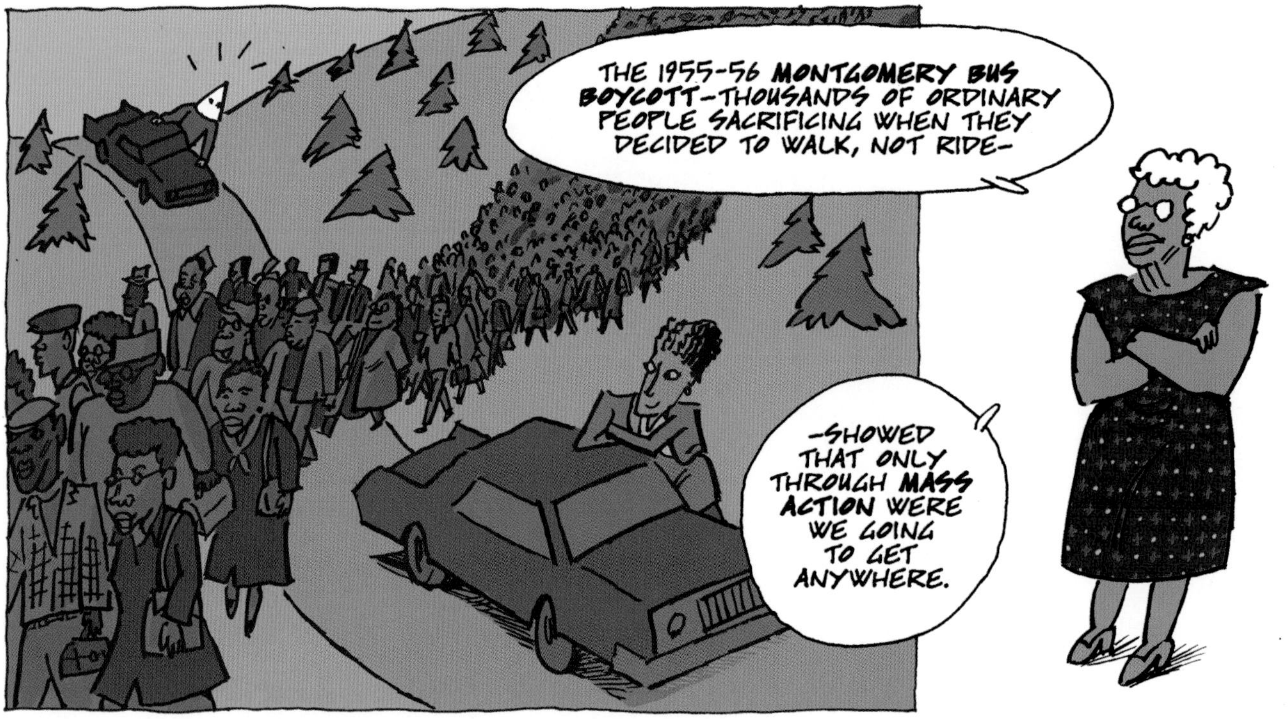

THE 1955-56 **MONTGOMERY BUS BOYCOTT**-THOUSANDS OF ORDINARY PEOPLE SACRIFICING WHEN THEY DECIDED TO WALK, NOT RIDE-
-SHOWED THAT ONLY THROUGH **MASS ACTION** WERE WE GOING TO GET ANYWHERE.


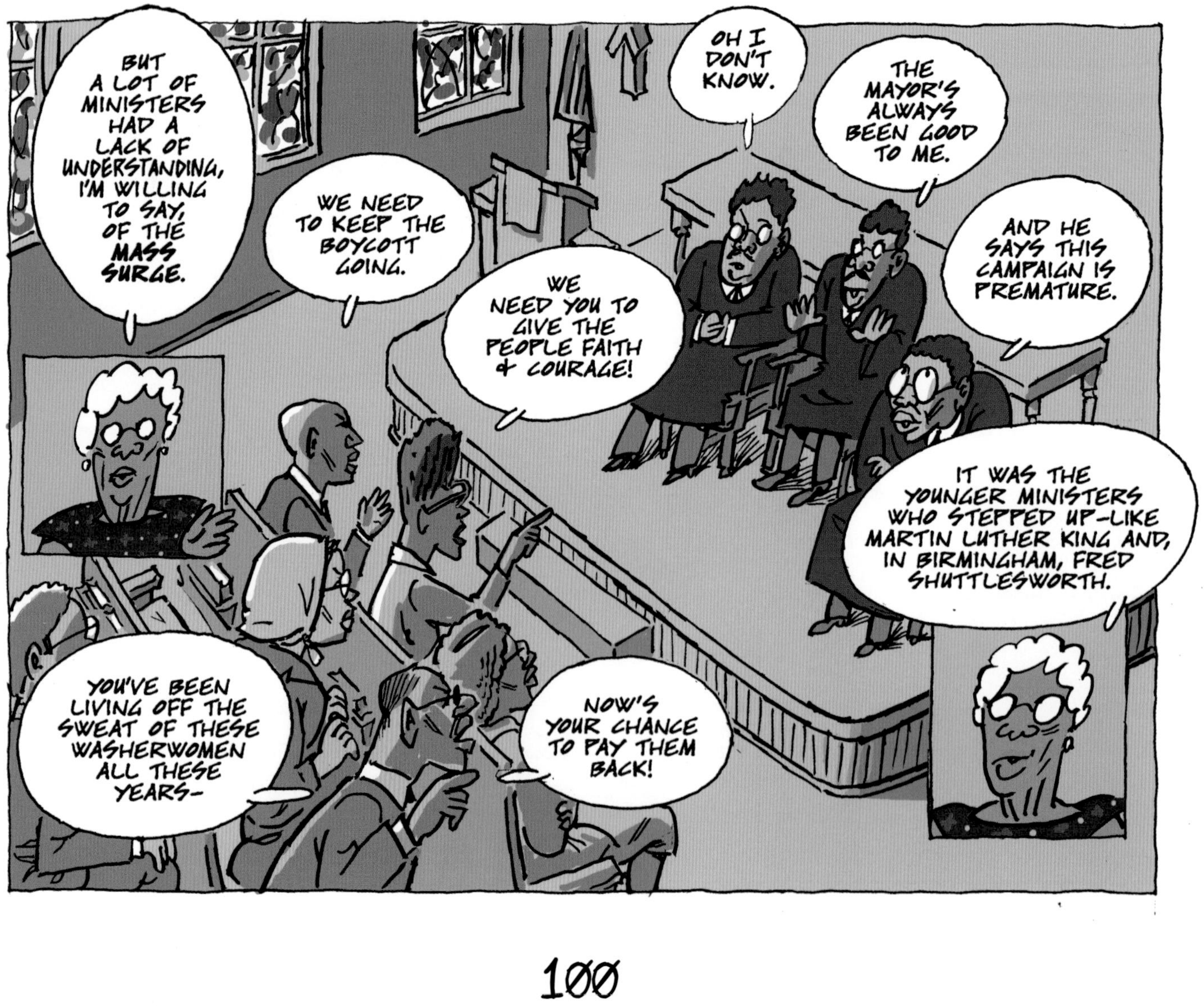

BUT A LOT OF MINISTERS HAD A LACK OF UNDERSTANDING, I'M WILLING TO SAY, OF THE **MASS SURGE.**
WE NEED TO KEEP THE BOYCOTT GOING.
WE NEED YOU TO GIVE THE PEOPLE FAITH & COURAGE!
OH I DON'T KNOW.
THE MAYOR'S ALWAYS BEEN GOOD TO ME.
AND HE SAYS THIS CAMPAIGN IS PREMATURE.
IT WAS THE YOUNGER MINISTERS WHO STEPPED UP-LIKE MARTIN LUTHER KING AND, IN BIRMINGHAM, FRED SHUTTLESWORTH.
YOU'VE BEEN LIVING OFF THE SWEAT OF THESE WASHERWOMEN ALL THESE YEARS-
NOW'S YOUR CHANCE TO PAY THEM BACK!

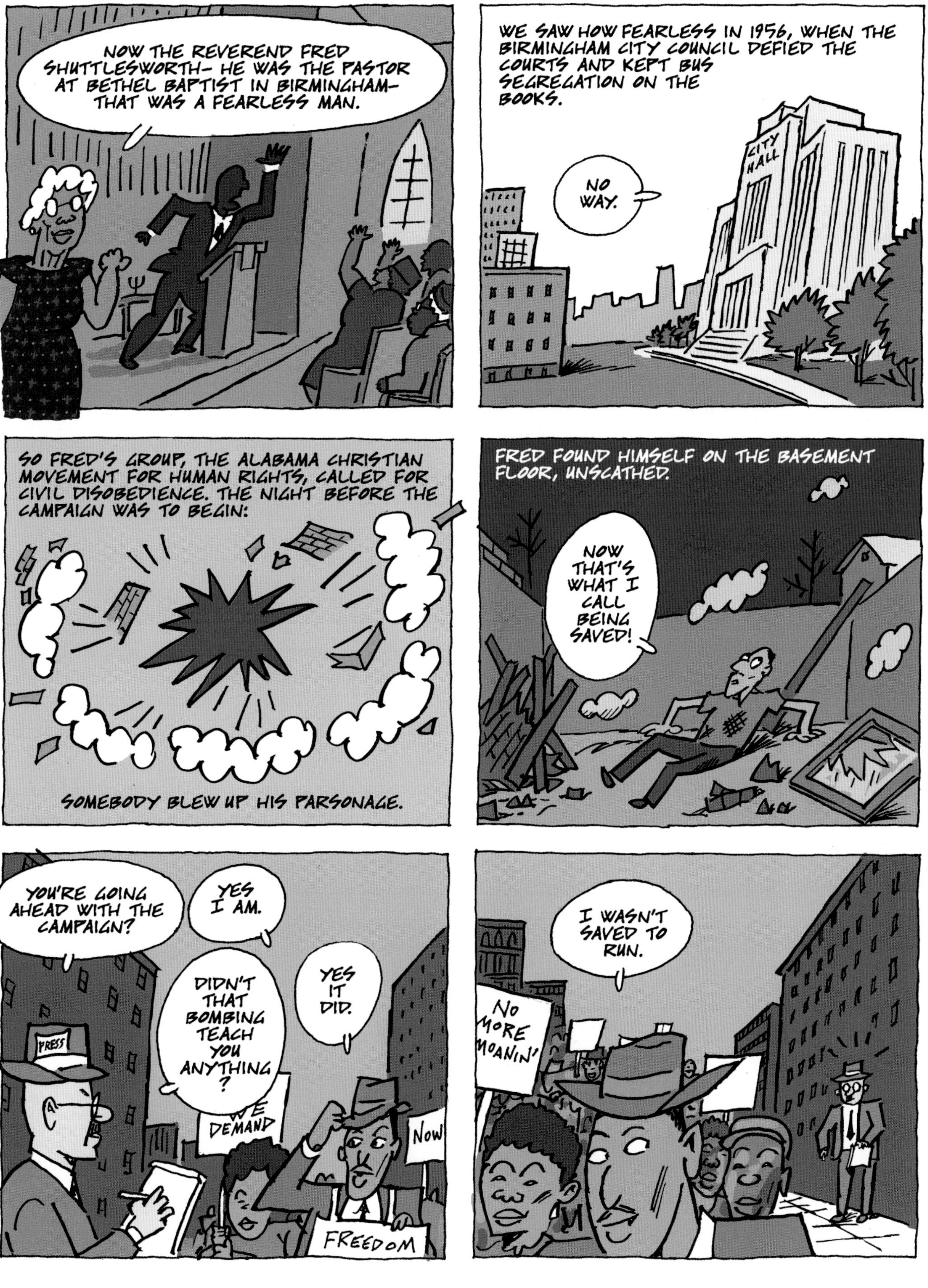
NOW THE REVEREND FRED SHUTTLESWORTH- HE WAS THE PASTOR AT BETHEL BAPTIST IN BIRMINGHAM- THAT WAS A FEARLESS MAN.
WE SAW HOW FEARLESS IN 1956, WHEN THE BIRMINGHAM CITY COUNCIL DEFIED THE COURTS AND KEPT BUS SEGREGATION ON THE BOOKS.
CITY HALL
NO WAY.
SO FRED'S GROUP, THE ALABAMA CHRISTIAN MOVEMENT FOR HUMAN RIGHTS, CALLED FOR CIVIL DISOBEDIENCE. THE NIGHT BEFORE THE CAMPAIGN WAS TO BEGIN:
SOMEBODY BLEW UP HIS PARSONAGE.
FRED FOUND HIMSELF ON THE BASEMENT FLOOR, UNSCATHED.
NOW THAT'S WHAT I CALL BEING SAVED!
YOU'RE GOING AHEAD WITH THE CAMPAIGN?
YES I AM.
DIDN'T THAT BOMBING TEACH YOU ANYTHING?
YES IT DID.
PRESS
WE DEMAND
NOW
FREEDOM
I WASN'T SAVED TO RUN.
NO MORE MOANIN'

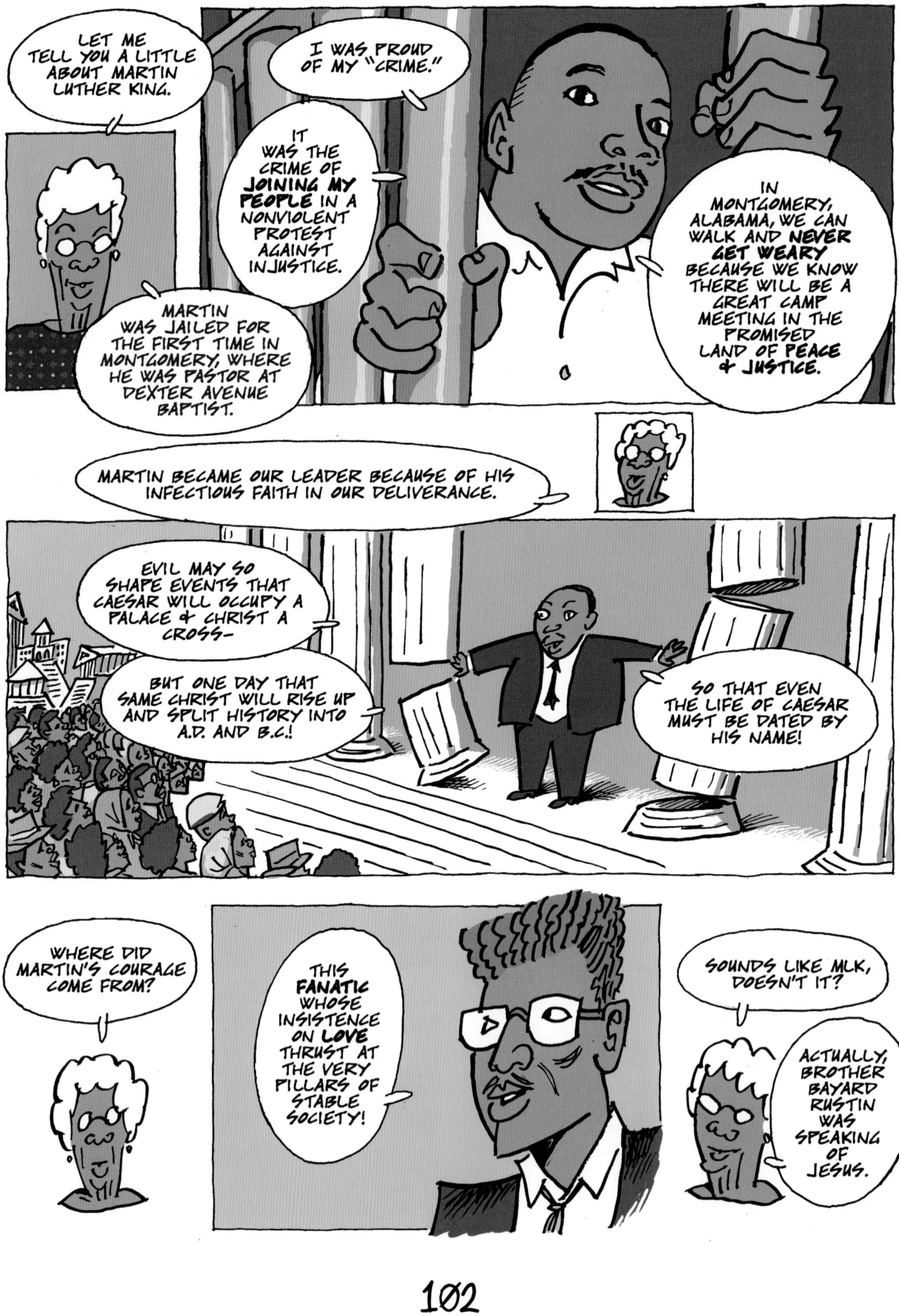
LET ME TELL YOU A LITTLE ABOUT MARTIN LUTHER KING.
MARTIN WAS JAILED FOR THE FIRST TIME IN MONTGOMERY, WHERE HE WAS PASTOR AT DEXTER AVENUE BAPTIST.
I WAS PROUD OF MY "CRIME."
IT WAS THE CRIME OF **JOINING MY PEOPLE** IN A NONVIOLENT PROTEST AGAINST INJUSTICE.
IN MONTGOMERY, ALABAMA, WE CAN WALK AND **NEVER GET WEARY** BECAUSE WE KNOW THERE WILL BE A GREAT CAMP MEETING IN THE PROMISED LAND OF **PEACE & JUSTICE.**
MARTIN BECAME OUR LEADER BECAUSE OF HIS INFECTIOUS FAITH IN OUR DELIVERANCE.
EVIL MAY SO SHAPE EVENTS THAT CAESAR WILL OCCUPY A PALACE & CHRIST A CROSS–
BUT ONE DAY THAT SAME CHRIST WILL RISE UP AND SPLIT HISTORY INTO A.D. AND B.C.!
SO THAT EVEN THE LIFE OF CAESAR MUST BE DATED BY HIS NAME!
WHERE DID MARTIN'S COURAGE COME FROM?
THIS **FANATIC** WHOSE INSISTENCE ON **LOVE** THRUST AT THE VERY PILLARS OF STABLE SOCIETY!
SOUNDS LIKE MLK, DOESN'T IT?
ACTUALLY, BROTHER BAYARD RUSTIN WAS SPEAKING OF JESUS.

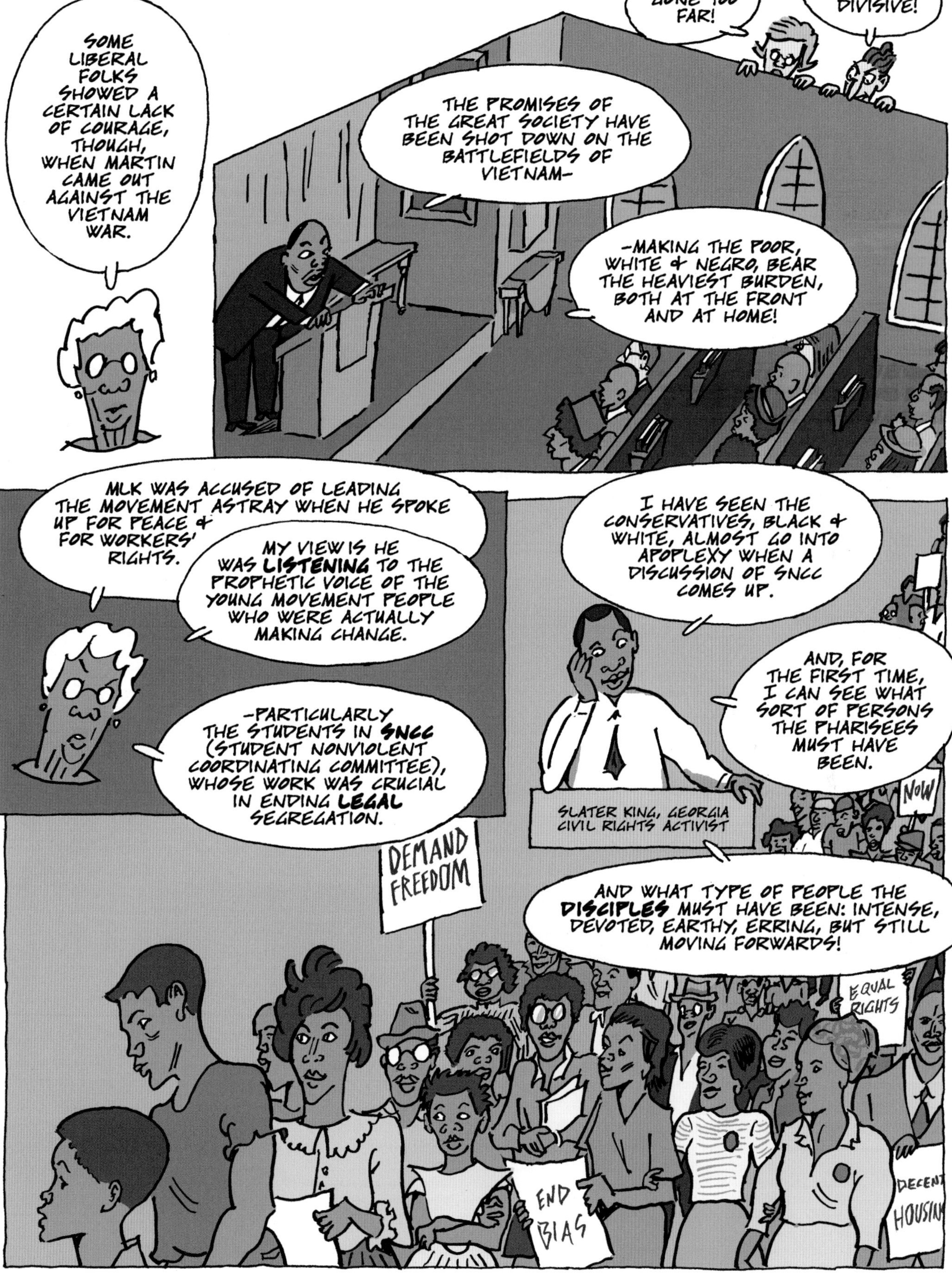
SOME LIBERAL FOLKS SHOWED A CERTAIN LACK OF COURAGE, THOUGH, WHEN MARTIN CAME OUT AGAINST THE VIETNAM WAR.
THE PROMISES OF THE GREAT SOCIETY HAVE BEEN SHOT DOWN ON THE BATTLEFIELDS OF VIETNAM-
HE'S GONE TOO FAR!
THIS IS SO DIVISIVE!
-MAKING THE POOR, WHITE & NEGRO, BEAR THE HEAVIEST BURDEN, BOTH AT THE FRONT AND AT HOME!
MLK WAS ACCUSED OF LEADING THE MOVEMENT ASTRAY WHEN HE SPOKE UP FOR PEACE & FOR WORKERS' RIGHTS.
MY VIEW IS HE WAS **LISTENING** TO THE PROPHETIC VOICE OF THE YOUNG MOVEMENT PEOPLE WHO WERE ACTUALLY MAKING CHANGE.
-PARTICULARLY THE STUDENTS IN **SNCC** (STUDENT NONVIOLENT COORDINATING COMMITTEE), WHOSE WORK WAS CRUCIAL IN ENDING **LEGAL** SEGREGATION.
I HAVE SEEN THE CONSERVATIVES, BLACK & WHITE, ALMOST GO INTO APOPLEXY WHEN A DISCUSSION OF SNCC COMES UP.
AND, FOR THE FIRST TIME, I CAN SEE WHAT SORT OF PERSONS THE PHARISEES MUST HAVE BEEN.
SLATER KING, GEORGIA CIVIL RIGHTS ACTIVIST
AND WHAT TYPE OF PEOPLE THE **DISCIPLES** MUST HAVE BEEN: INTENSE, DEVOTED, EARTHY, ERRING, BUT STILL MOVING FORWARDS!
NOW
DEMAND FREEDOM
EQUAL RIGHTS
END BIAS
DECENT
HOUSIN

YOU NOTICE I SAID **LEGAL** SEGREGATION. WE STILL HAVE JIM CROW IN THIS COUNTRY! ONE FORM IT TAKES IS **MASS INCARCERATION**, DISPROPORTIONATELY DIRECTED AT YOUNG BLACK MEN (AND, INCREASINGLY, WOMEN).

THE REVEREND JEREMIAH WRIGHT (A PROPHETIC VOICE MUCH MALIGNED IN THE MAINSTREAM MEDIA BUT CHERISHED BY THE THOUSANDS OF BLACK CHURCHES ALLIED AGAINST MASS INCARCERATION) PUT IT THIS WAY:

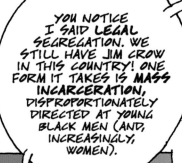

**JOSEPH** THE INMATE! HE'S THERE ON FALSE CHARGES, MANDATORY SENTENCING, ACCUSED OF RAPE—

AND, MORE IMPORTANTLY, VIOLATION OF ANOTHER MAN'S PROPERTY, FOR IN JOSEPH'S TIME WOMEN WERE THE PROPERTY OF THEIR HUSBANDS.

JOSEPH'S BIGGEST PROBLEM IS, HE DIDN'T STAY IN HIS PLACE.

MY NAMESAKE, **JEREMIAH** THE PROPHET, SHUT UP IN THE JOINT.

JEREMIAH WAS A THREAT TO **HOMELAND SECURITY**

AND YET, PRESIDENT ZEDEKIAH SNEAKED INTO HIS CELL AT NIGHT TO SAY →

IS THERE ANY WORD FROM THE LORD?

THE OTHER INMATE WAS NAMED JESUS, FALSE CHARGES, RAILROADED, SET UP.

**PAUL & SILAS**, THE INMATES, DISRUPTED THE ILLEGAL ECONOMY.

PAUL & SILAS LIED ON, BROUGHT BEFORE THE MAN—

—THE ROMANS WHO RAN THE PRISON SYSTEM.

(BUT THEN THE STORY SAYS THAT NOT EVERYBODY THAT WORKS FOR AN EVIL SYSTEM IS AN EVIL PERSON.)

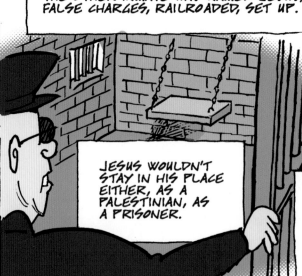

JESUS WOULDN'T STAY IN HIS PLACE EITHER, AS A PALESTINIAN, AS A PRISONER.

HE WOULDN'T EVEN STAY IN HIS PLACE WHEN THEY PUT HIM IN A TOMB!

# SWORDS INTO PLOWSHARES:
## SERVING THE POOR BY RESISTING WAR

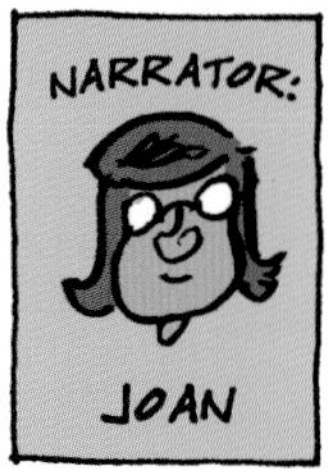
NARRATOR:
JOAN

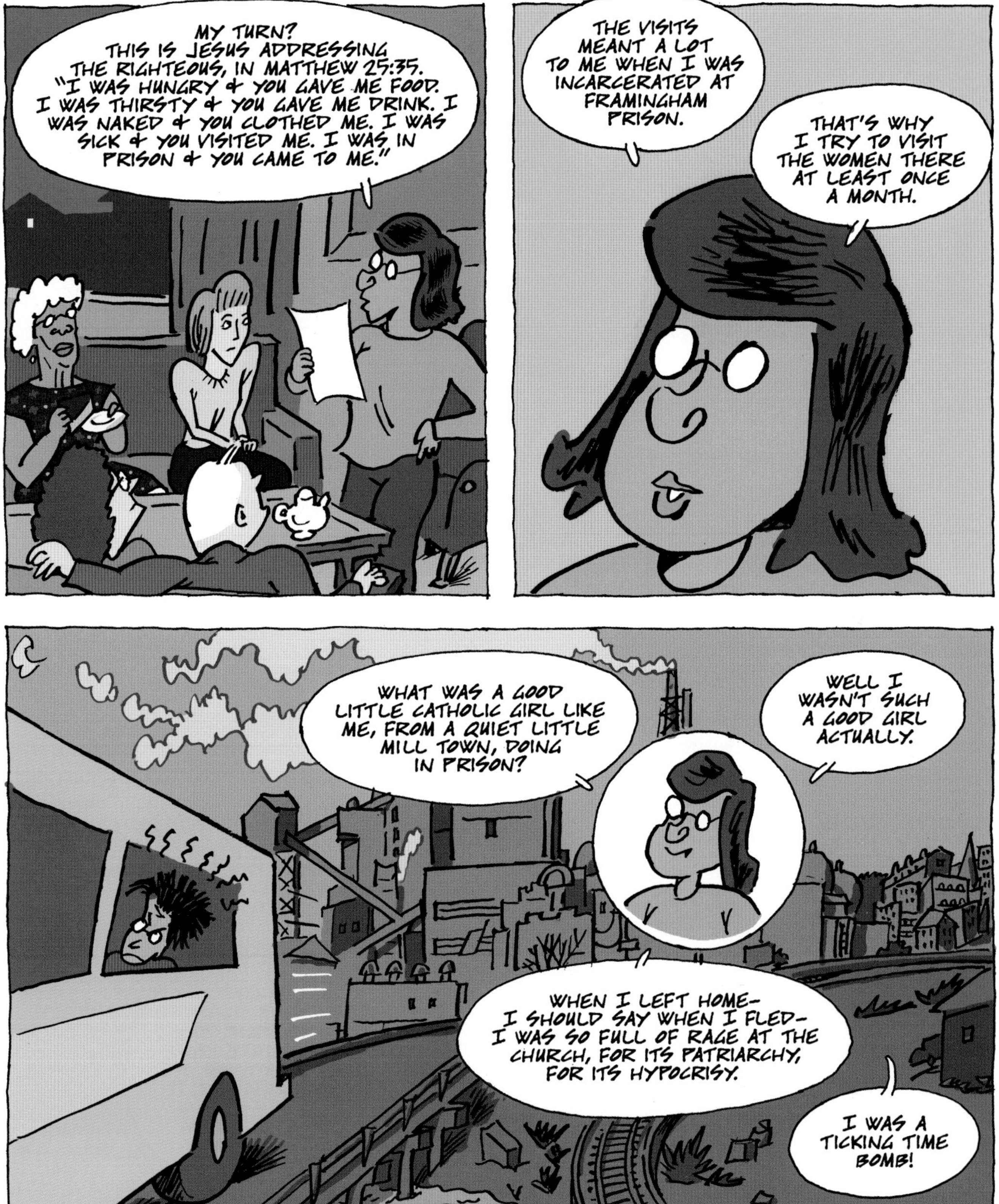
MY TURN? THIS IS JESUS ADDRESSING THE RIGHTEOUS, IN MATTHEW 25:35. "I WAS HUNGRY & YOU GAVE ME FOOD. I WAS THIRSTY & YOU GAVE ME DRINK. I WAS NAKED & YOU CLOTHED ME. I WAS SICK & YOU VISITED ME. I WAS IN PRISON & YOU CAME TO ME."
THE VISITS MEANT A LOT TO ME WHEN I WAS INCARCERATED AT FRAMINGHAM PRISON.
THAT'S WHY I TRY TO VISIT THE WOMEN THERE AT LEAST ONCE A MONTH.
WHAT WAS A GOOD LITTLE CATHOLIC GIRL LIKE ME, FROM A QUIET LITTLE MILL TOWN, DOING IN PRISON?
WELL I WASN'T SUCH A GOOD GIRL ACTUALLY.
WHEN I LEFT HOME- I SHOULD SAY WHEN I FLED- I WAS SO FULL OF RAGE AT THE CHURCH, FOR ITS PATRIARCHY, FOR ITS HYPOCRISY.
I WAS A TICKING TIME BOMB!

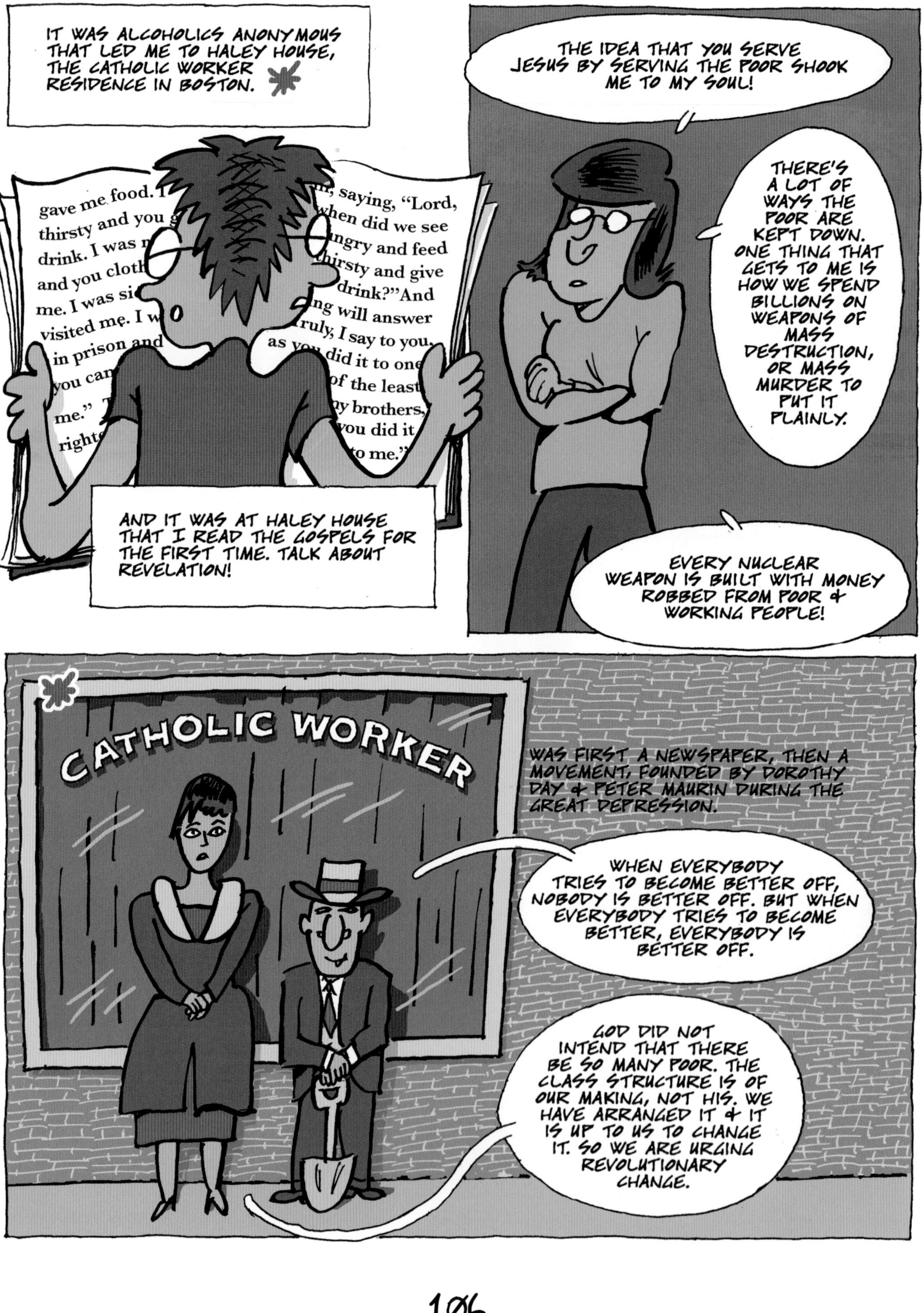

IT WAS ALCOHOLICS ANONYMOUS THAT LED ME TO HALEY HOUSE, THE CATHOLIC WORKER RESIDENCE IN BOSTON. ✱
AND IT WAS AT HALEY HOUSE THAT I READ THE GOSPELS FOR THE FIRST TIME. TALK ABOUT REVELATION!
THE IDEA THAT YOU SERVE JESUS BY SERVING THE POOR SHOOK ME TO MY SOUL!
THERE'S A LOT OF WAYS THE POOR ARE KEPT DOWN. ONE THING THAT GETS TO ME IS HOW WE SPEND BILLIONS ON WEAPONS OF MASS DESTRUCTION, OR MASS MURDER TO PUT IT PLAINLY.
EVERY NUCLEAR WEAPON IS BUILT WITH MONEY ROBBED FROM POOR & WORKING PEOPLE!
✱
CATHOLIC WORKER
WAS FIRST A NEWSPAPER, THEN A MOVEMENT, FOUNDED BY DOROTHY DAY & PETER MAURIN DURING THE GREAT DEPRESSION.
WHEN EVERYBODY TRIES TO BECOME BETTER OFF, NOBODY IS BETTER OFF. BUT WHEN EVERYBODY TRIES TO BECOME BETTER, EVERYBODY IS BETTER OFF.
GOD DID NOT INTEND THAT THERE BE SO MANY POOR. THE CLASS STRUCTURE IS OF OUR MAKING, NOT HIS. WE HAVE ARRANGED IT & IT IS UP TO US TO CHANGE IT. SO WE ARE URGING REVOLUTIONARY CHANGE.

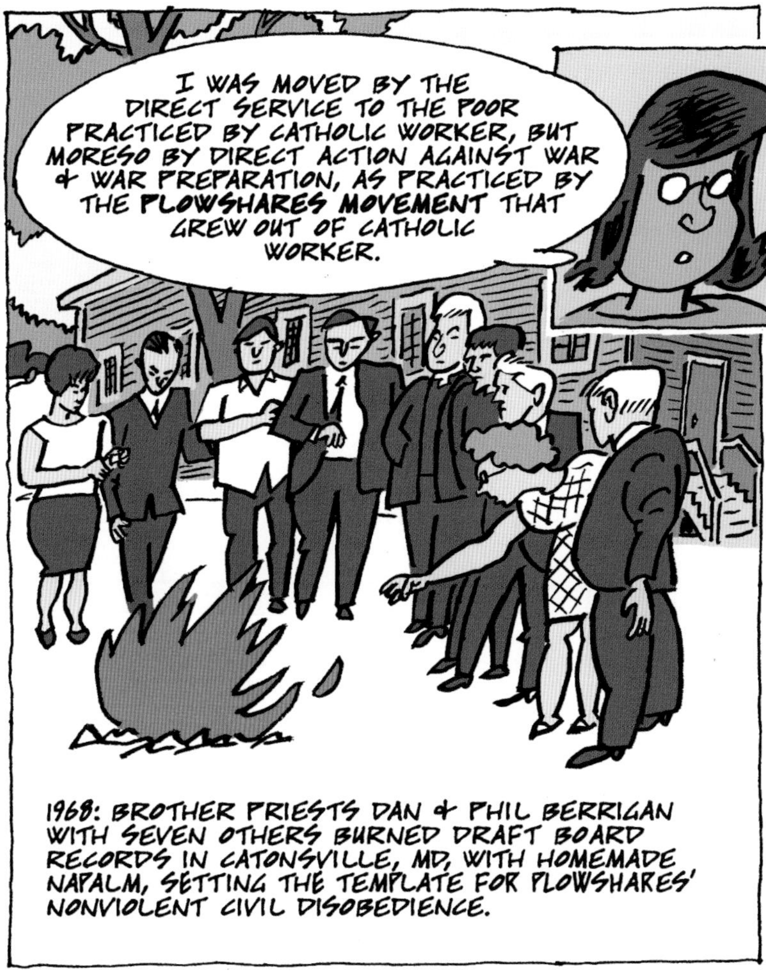
I WAS MOVED BY THE DIRECT SERVICE TO THE POOR PRACTICED BY CATHOLIC WORKER, BUT MORESO BY DIRECT ACTION AGAINST WAR & WAR PREPARATION, AS PRACTICED BY THE **PLOWSHARES MOVEMENT** THAT GREW OUT OF CATHOLIC WORKER.
1968: BROTHER PRIESTS DAN & PHIL BERRIGAN WITH SEVEN OTHERS BURNED DRAFT BOARD RECORDS IN CATONSVILLE, MD, WITH HOMEMADE NAPALM, SETTING THE TEMPLATE FOR PLOWSHARES' NONVIOLENT CIVIL DISOBEDIENCE.

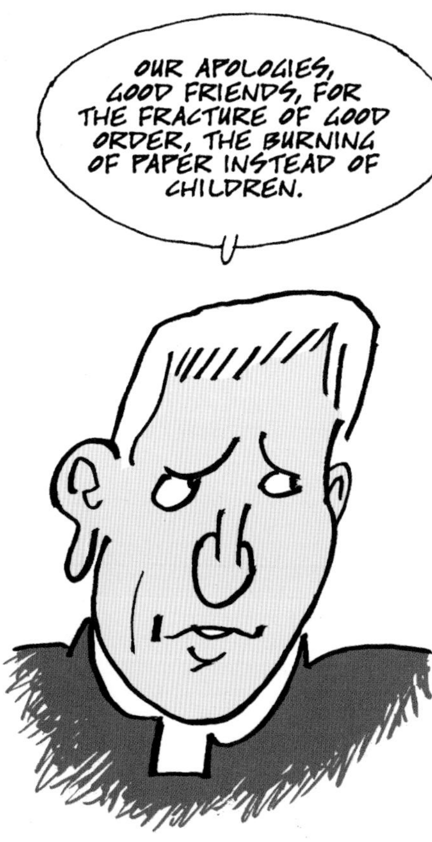
OUR APOLOGIES, GOOD FRIENDS, FOR THE FRACTURE OF GOOD ORDER, THE BURNING OF PAPER INSTEAD OF CHILDREN.

FR. DANIEL BERRIGAN'S STATEMENT AT THE TRIAL OF THE "CATONSVILLE NINE"

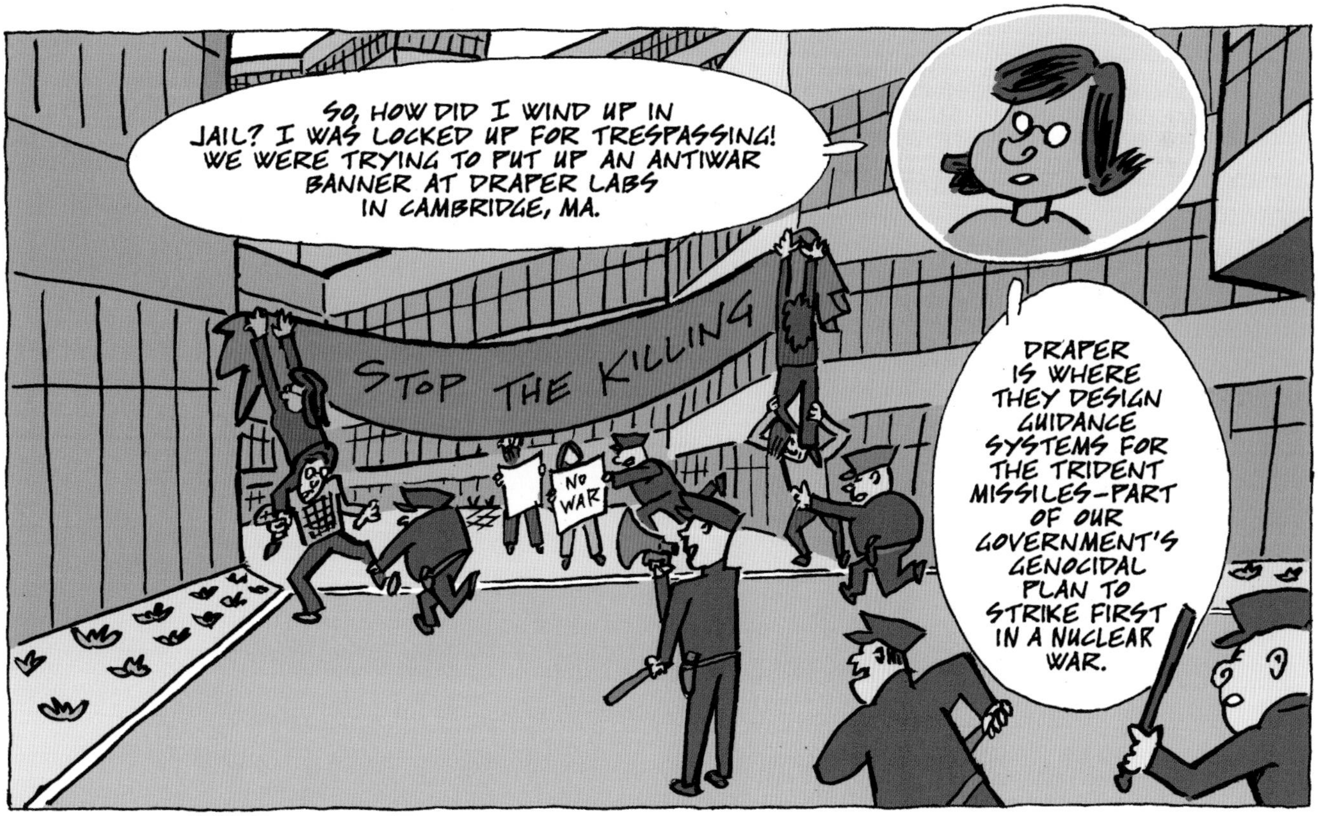
SO, HOW DID I WIND UP IN JAIL? I WAS LOCKED UP FOR TRESPASSING! WE WERE TRYING TO PUT UP AN ANTIWAR BANNER AT DRAPER LABS IN CAMBRIDGE, MA.
STOP THE KILLING
NO WAR
DRAPER IS WHERE THEY DESIGN GUIDANCE SYSTEMS FOR THE TRIDENT MISSILES—PART OF OUR GOVERNMENT'S GENOCIDAL PLAN TO STRIKE FIRST IN A NUCLEAR WAR.

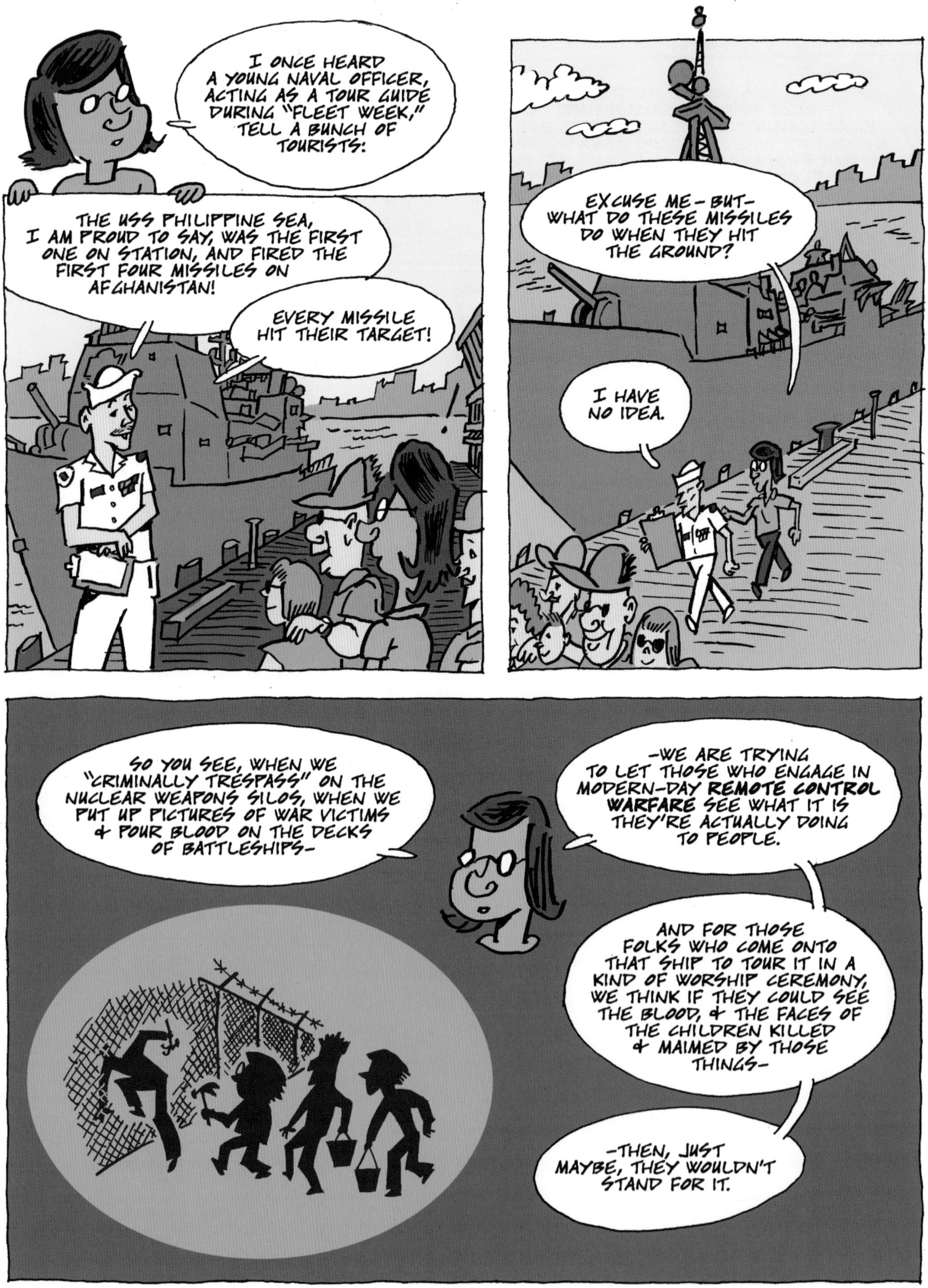

I ONCE HEARD A YOUNG NAVAL OFFICER, ACTING AS A TOUR GUIDE DURING "FLEET WEEK," TELL A BUNCH OF TOURISTS:
THE USS PHILIPPINE SEA, I AM PROUD TO SAY, WAS THE FIRST ONE ON STATION, AND FIRED THE FIRST FOUR MISSILES ON AFGHANISTAN!
EVERY MISSILE HIT THEIR TARGET!
EXCUSE ME- BUT- WHAT DO THESE MISSILES DO WHEN THEY HIT THE GROUND?
I HAVE NO IDEA.
SO YOU SEE, WHEN WE "CRIMINALLY TRESPASS" ON THE NUCLEAR WEAPONS SILOS, WHEN WE PUT UP PICTURES OF WAR VICTIMS & POUR BLOOD ON THE DECKS OF BATTLESHIPS-
-WE ARE TRYING TO LET THOSE WHO ENGAGE IN MODERN-DAY **REMOTE CONTROL WARFARE** SEE WHAT IT IS THEY'RE ACTUALLY DOING TO PEOPLE.
AND FOR THOSE FOLKS WHO COME ONTO THAT SHIP TO TOUR IT IN A KIND OF WORSHIP CEREMONY, WE THINK IF THEY COULD SEE THE BLOOD, & THE FACES OF THE CHILDREN KILLED & MAIMED BY THOSE THINGS-
-THEN, JUST MAYBE, THEY WOULDN'T STAND FOR IT.

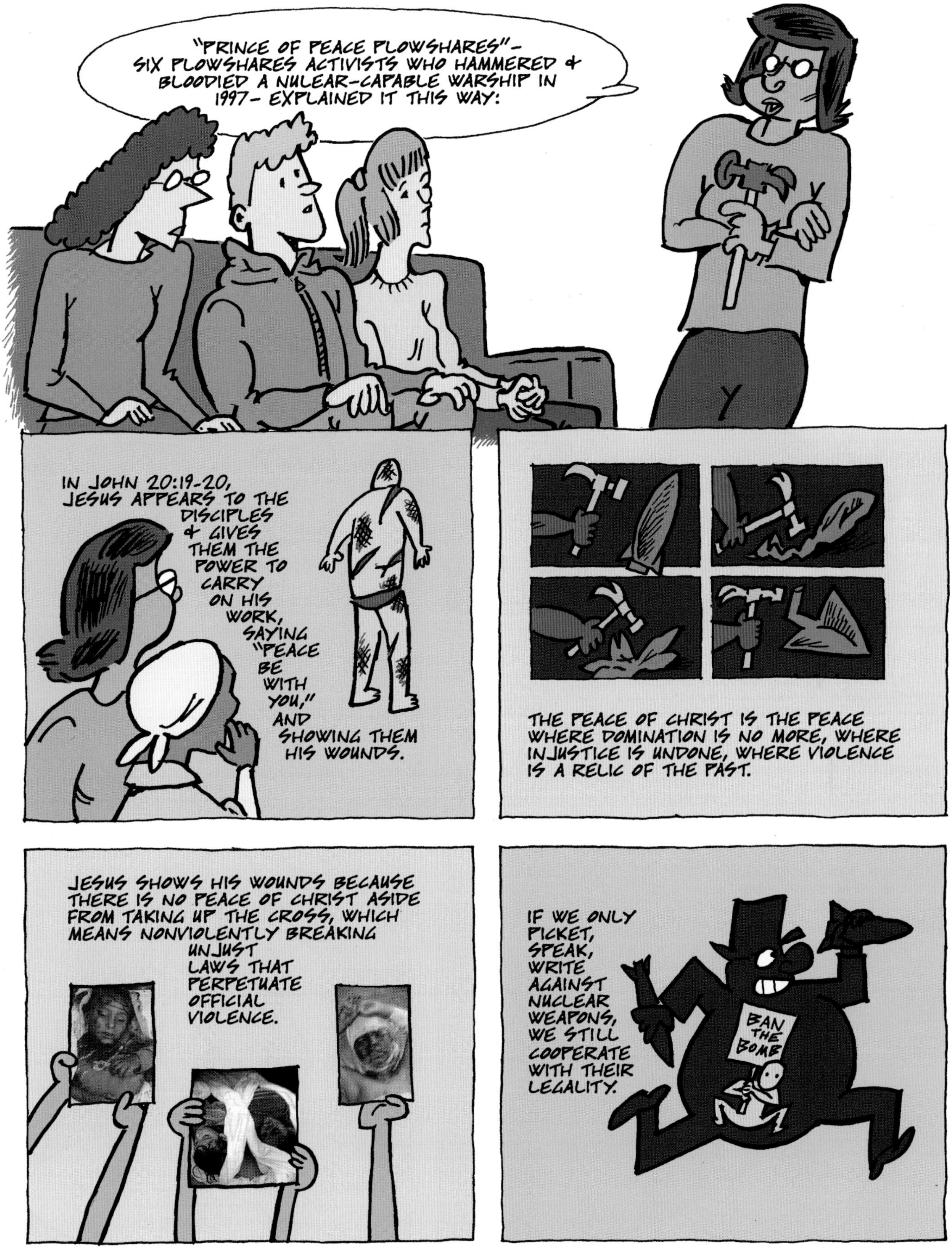
"PRINCE OF PEACE PLOWSHARES"– SIX PLOWSHARES ACTIVISTS WHO HAMMERED & BLOODIED A NULEAR-CAPABLE WARSHIP IN 1997– EXPLAINED IT THIS WAY:
IN JOHN 20:19-20, JESUS APPEARS TO THE DISCIPLES & GIVES THEM THE POWER TO CARRY ON HIS WORK, SAYING "PEACE BE WITH YOU," AND SHOWING THEM HIS WOUNDS.
THE PEACE OF CHRIST IS THE PEACE WHERE DOMINATION IS NO MORE, WHERE INJUSTICE IS UNDONE, WHERE VIOLENCE IS A RELIC OF THE PAST.
JESUS SHOWS HIS WOUNDS BECAUSE THERE IS NO PEACE OF CHRIST ASIDE FROM TAKING UP THE CROSS, WHICH MEANS NONVIOLENTLY BREAKING UNJUST LAWS THAT PERPETUATE OFFICIAL VIOLENCE.
IF WE ONLY PICKET, SPEAK, WRITE AGAINST NUCLEAR WEAPONS, WE STILL COOPERATE WITH THEIR LEGALITY.
BAN THE BOMB

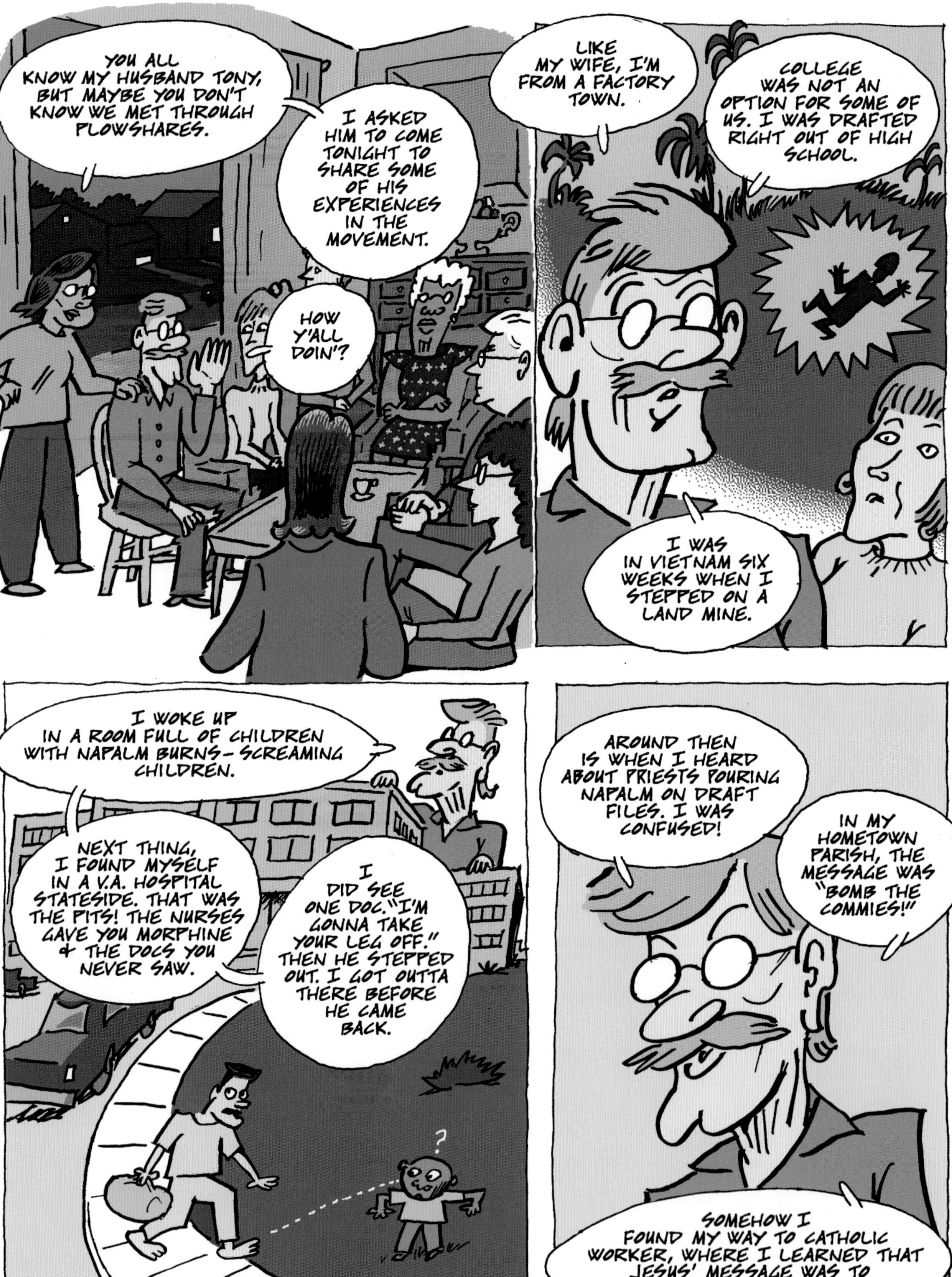

YOU ALL KNOW MY HUSBAND TONY, BUT MAYBE YOU DON'T KNOW WE MET THROUGH PLOWSHARES.
I ASKED HIM TO COME TONIGHT TO SHARE SOME OF HIS EXPERIENCES IN THE MOVEMENT.
HOW Y'ALL DOIN'?
LIKE MY WIFE, I'M FROM A FACTORY TOWN.
COLLEGE WAS NOT AN OPTION FOR SOME OF US. I WAS DRAFTED RIGHT OUT OF HIGH SCHOOL.
I WAS IN VIETNAM SIX WEEKS WHEN I STEPPED ON A LAND MINE.
I WOKE UP IN A ROOM FULL OF CHILDREN WITH NAPALM BURNS–SCREAMING CHILDREN.
NEXT THING, I FOUND MYSELF IN A V.A. HOSPITAL STATESIDE. THAT WAS THE PITS! THE NURSES GAVE YOU MORPHINE & THE DOCS YOU NEVER SAW.
I DID SEE ONE DOC. "I'M GONNA TAKE YOUR LEG OFF." THEN HE STEPPED OUT. I GOT OUTTA THERE BEFORE HE CAME BACK.
?
AROUND THEN IS WHEN I HEARD ABOUT PRIESTS POURING NAPALM ON DRAFT FILES. I WAS CONFUSED!
IN MY HOMETOWN PARISH, THE MESSAGE WAS "BOMB THE COMMIES!"
SOMEHOW I FOUND MY WAY TO CATHOLIC WORKER, WHERE I LEARNED THAT JESUS' MESSAGE WAS TO LOVE ONE ANOTHER.

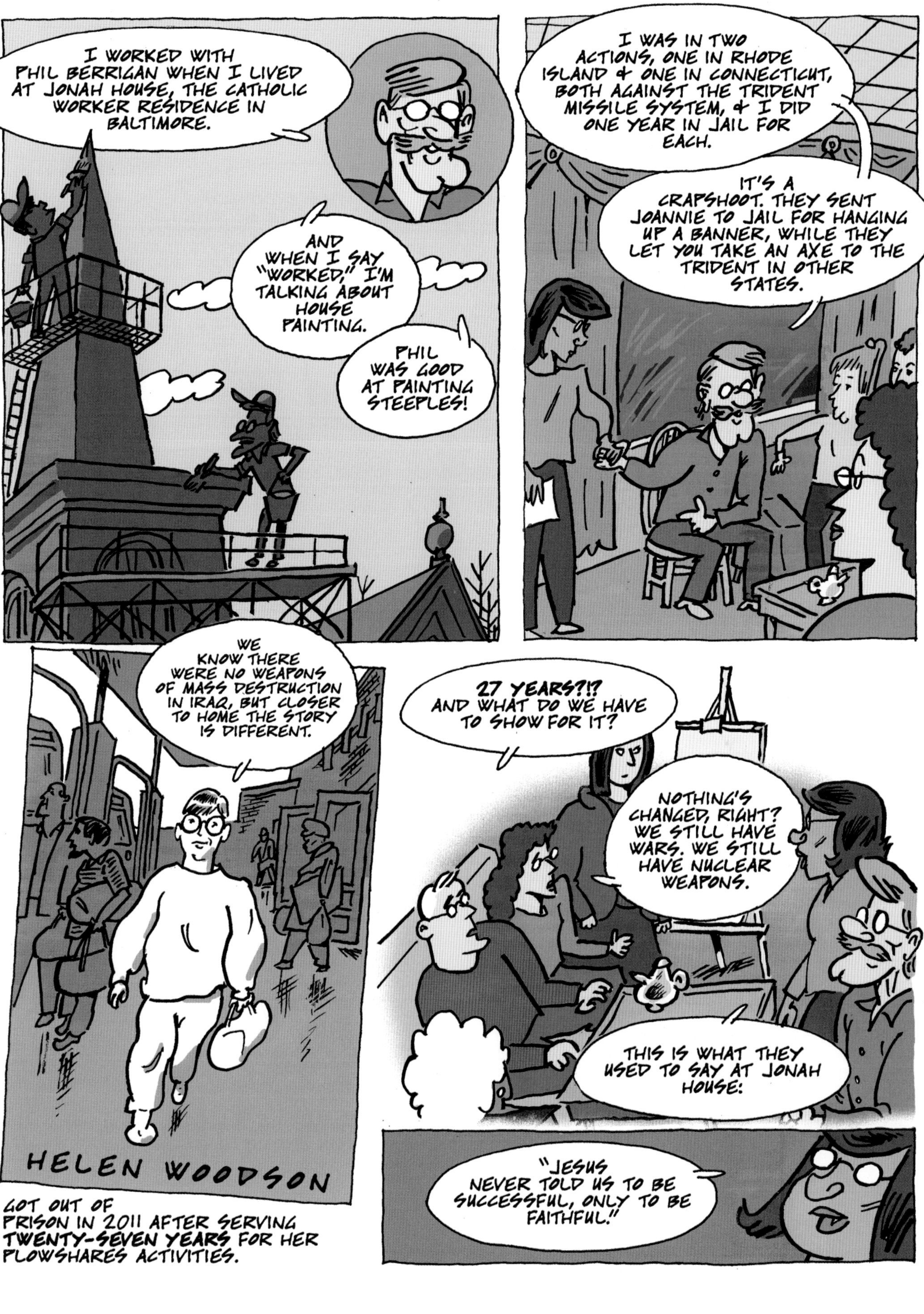
I WORKED WITH PHIL BERRIGAN WHEN I LIVED AT JONAH HOUSE, THE CATHOLIC WORKER RESIDENCE IN BALTIMORE.
AND WHEN I SAY "WORKED," I'M TALKING ABOUT HOUSE PAINTING.
PHIL WAS GOOD AT PAINTING STEEPLES!
I WAS IN TWO ACTIONS, ONE IN RHODE ISLAND & ONE IN CONNECTICUT, BOTH AGAINST THE TRIDENT MISSILE SYSTEM, & I DID ONE YEAR IN JAIL FOR EACH.
IT'S A CRAPSHOOT. THEY SENT JOANNIE TO JAIL FOR HANGING UP A BANNER, WHILE THEY LET YOU TAKE AN AXE TO THE TRIDENT IN OTHER STATES.
WE KNOW THERE WERE NO WEAPONS OF MASS DESTRUCTION IN IRAQ, BUT CLOSER TO HOME THE STORY IS DIFFERENT.
HELEN WOODSON
GOT OUT OF PRISON IN 2011 AFTER SERVING **TWENTY-SEVEN YEARS** FOR HER PLOWSHARES ACTIVITIES.
**27 YEARS?!?** AND WHAT DO WE HAVE TO SHOW FOR IT?
NOTHING'S CHANGED, RIGHT? WE STILL HAVE WARS. WE STILL HAVE NUCLEAR WEAPONS.
THIS IS WHAT THEY USED TO SAY AT JONAH HOUSE:
"JESUS NEVER TOLD US TO BE SUCCESSFUL, ONLY TO BE FAITHFUL."

# HE HAS LIFTED UP THE LOWLY:
## ACCOMPANYING THE POOR & ORGANIZING COMMUNITY

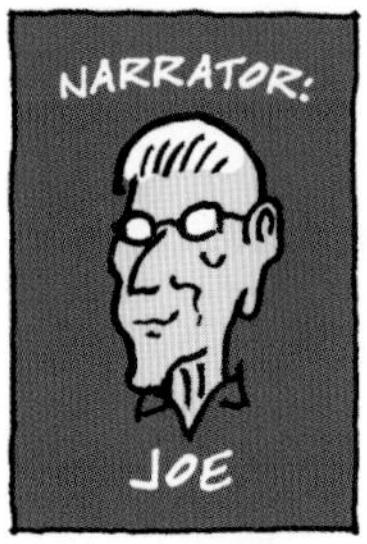
NARRATOR:
JOE

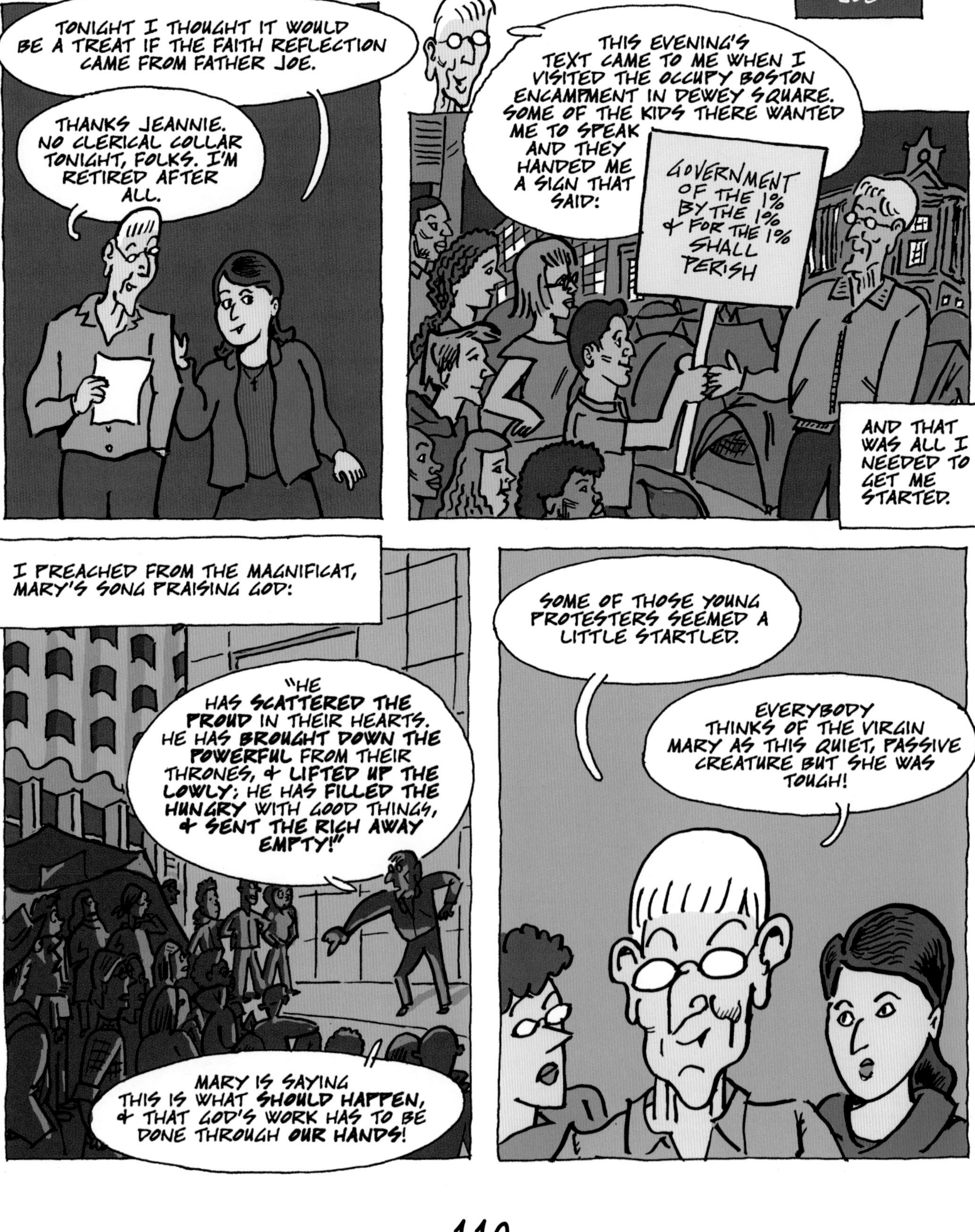
TONIGHT I THOUGHT IT WOULD BE A TREAT IF THE FAITH REFLECTION CAME FROM FATHER JOE.
THANKS JEANNIE. NO CLERICAL COLLAR TONIGHT, FOLKS. I'M RETIRED AFTER ALL.
THIS EVENING'S TEXT CAME TO ME WHEN I VISITED THE OCCUPY BOSTON ENCAMPMENT IN DEWEY SQUARE. SOME OF THE KIDS THERE WANTED ME TO SPEAK AND THEY HANDED ME A SIGN THAT SAID:
GOVERNMENT OF THE 1% BY THE 1% & FOR THE 1% SHALL PERISH
AND THAT WAS ALL I NEEDED TO GET ME STARTED.
I PREACHED FROM THE MAGNIFICAT, MARY'S SONG PRAISING GOD:
"HE HAS SCATTERED THE PROUD IN THEIR HEARTS. HE HAS BROUGHT DOWN THE POWERFUL FROM THEIR THRONES, & LIFTED UP THE LOWLY; HE HAS FILLED THE HUNGRY WITH GOOD THINGS, & SENT THE RICH AWAY EMPTY!"
MARY IS SAYING THIS IS WHAT SHOULD HAPPEN, & THAT GOD'S WORK HAS TO BE DONE THROUGH OUR HANDS!
SOME OF THOSE YOUNG PROTESTERS SEEMED A LITTLE STARTLED.
EVERYBODY THINKS OF THE VIRGIN MARY AS THIS QUIET, PASSIVE CREATURE BUT SHE WAS TOUGH!

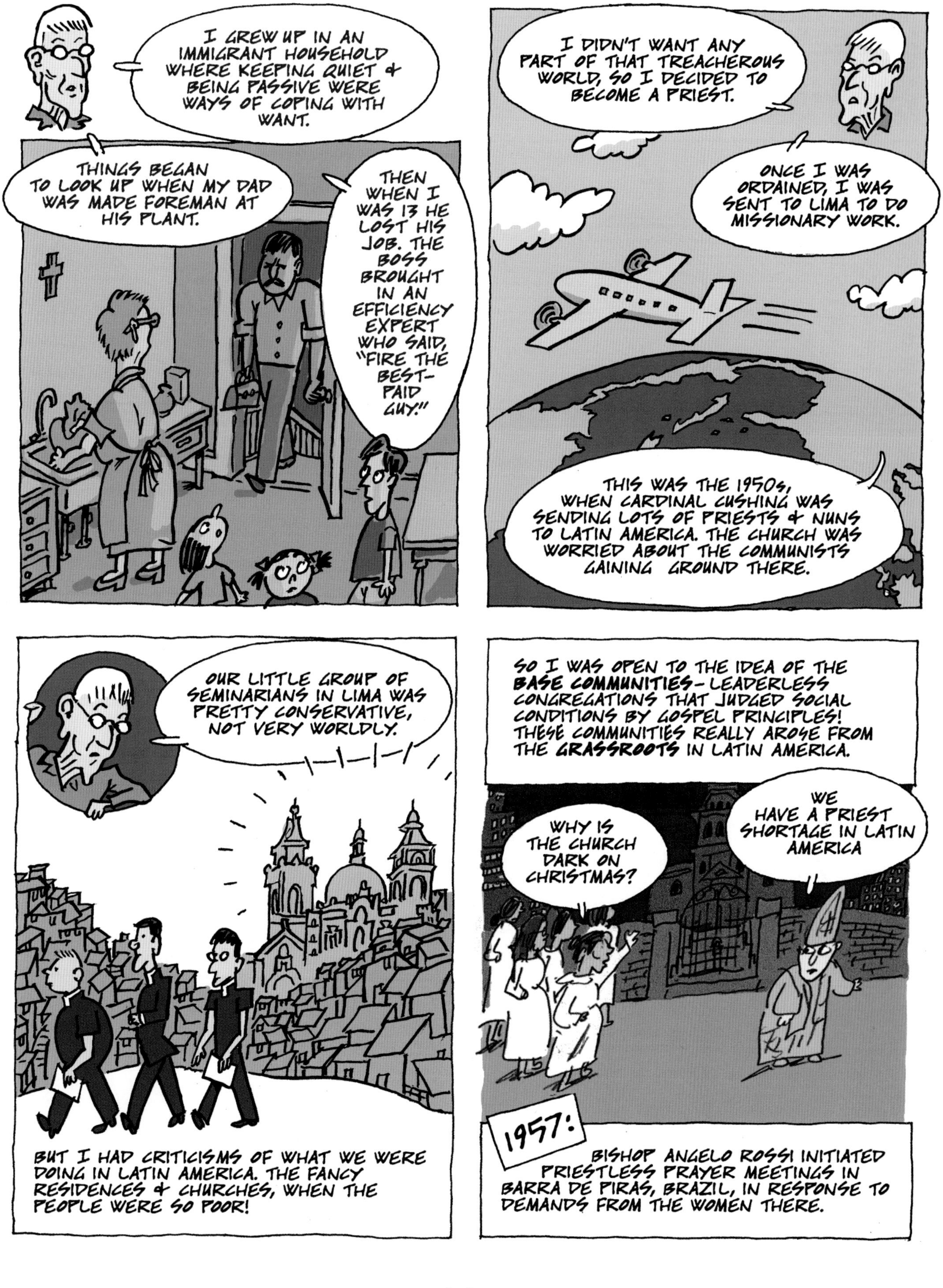

I GREW UP IN AN IMMIGRANT HOUSEHOLD WHERE KEEPING QUIET & BEING PASSIVE WERE WAYS OF COPING WITH WANT.
THINGS BEGAN TO LOOK UP WHEN MY DAD WAS MADE FOREMAN AT HIS PLANT.
THEN WHEN I WAS 13 HE LOST HIS JOB. THE BOSS BROUGHT IN AN EFFICIENCY EXPERT WHO SAID, "FIRE THE BEST-PAID GUY."
I DIDN'T WANT ANY PART OF THAT TREACHEROUS WORLD, SO I DECIDED TO BECOME A PRIEST.
ONCE I WAS ORDAINED, I WAS SENT TO LIMA TO DO MISSIONARY WORK.
THIS WAS THE 1950s, WHEN CARDINAL CUSHING WAS SENDING LOTS OF PRIESTS & NUNS TO LATIN AMERICA. THE CHURCH WAS WORRIED ABOUT THE COMMUNISTS GAINING GROUND THERE.
OUR LITTLE GROUP OF SEMINARIANS IN LIMA WAS PRETTY CONSERVATIVE, NOT VERY WORLDLY.
BUT I HAD CRITICISMS OF WHAT WE WERE DOING IN LATIN AMERICA. THE FANCY RESIDENCES & CHURCHES, WHEN THE PEOPLE WERE SO POOR!
SO I WAS OPEN TO THE IDEA OF THE **BASE COMMUNITIES**– LEADERLESS CONGREGATIONS THAT JUDGED SOCIAL CONDITIONS BY GOSPEL PRINCIPLES! THESE COMMUNITIES REALLY AROSE FROM THE **GRASSROOTS** IN LATIN AMERICA.
WHY IS THE CHURCH DARK ON CHRISTMAS?
WE HAVE A PRIEST SHORTAGE IN LATIN AMERICA
1957:
BISHOP ANGELO ROSSI INITIATED PRIESTLESS PRAYER MEETINGS IN BARRA DE PIRAS, BRAZIL, IN RESPONSE TO DEMANDS FROM THE WOMEN THERE.

THE BASE COMMUNITIES ALSO REFLECTED A RAPID INTEGRATION OF LATIN AMERICA INTO THE GLOBAL ECONOMY: ONE OF THE FIRST ACTIVIST COMMUNITIES AROSE IN SAN MIGUELITO, A POOR SUBURB OF PANAMA CITY WHERE NORTH AMERICA & LATIN AMERICA COLLIDE & INTERSECT.

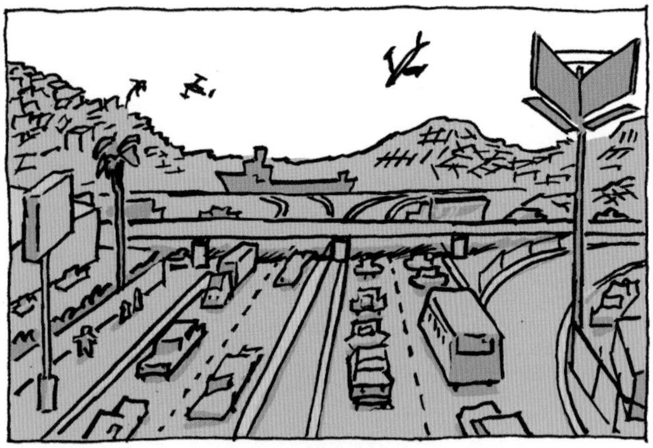

IN SUCH FLUID ENVIRONMENTS, INITIATIVES FROM THE BASE FLOURISHED, WITH THE PROMISE OF SUPPORT FROM A CHURCH IN TRANSITION.

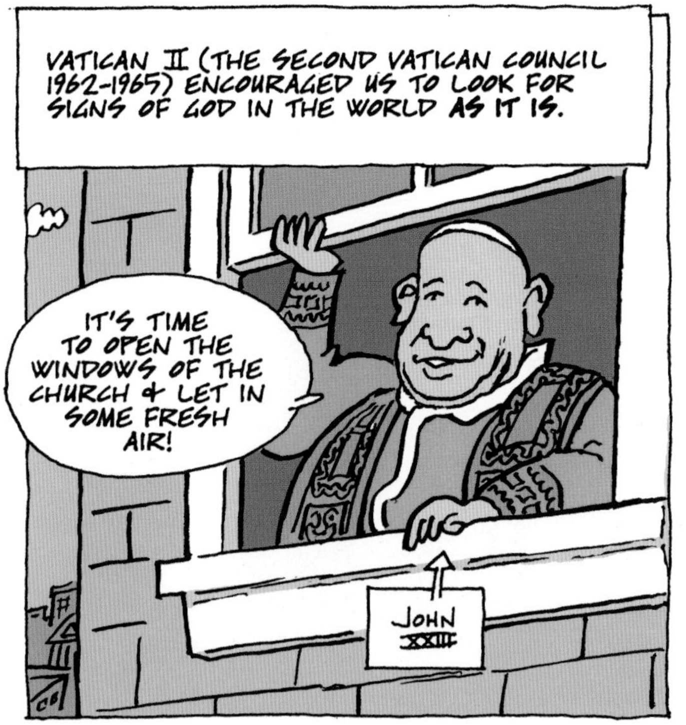
VATICAN II (THE SECOND VATICAN COUNCIL 1962-1965) ENCOURAGED US TO LOOK FOR SIGNS OF GOD IN THE WORLD AS IT IS.
IT'S TIME TO OPEN THE WINDOWS OF THE CHURCH & LET IN SOME FRESH AIR!
JOHN XXIII

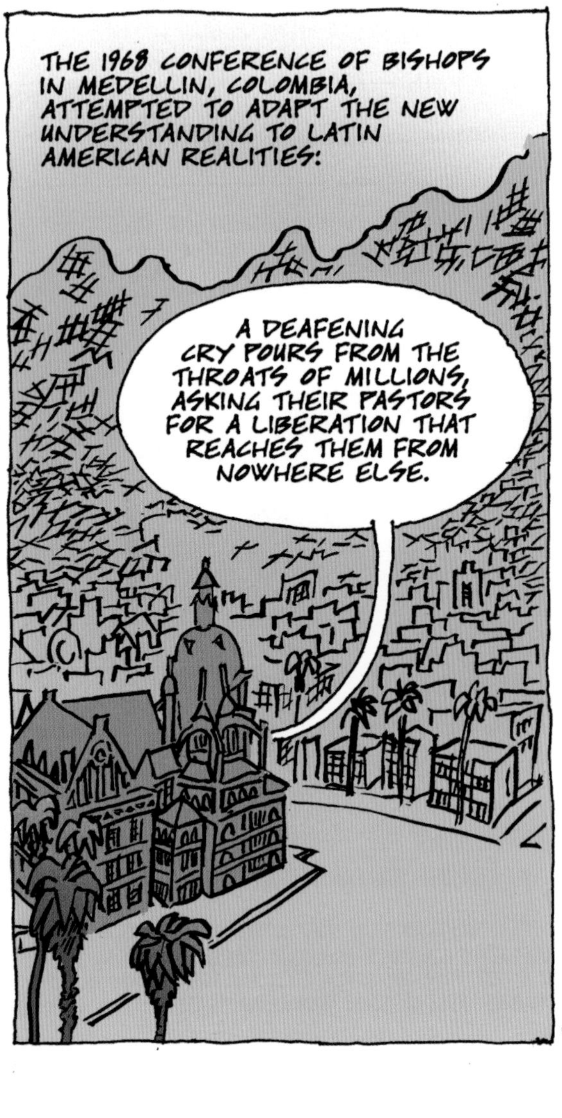
THE 1968 CONFERENCE OF BISHOPS IN MEDELLIN, COLOMBIA, ATTEMPTED TO ADAPT THE NEW UNDERSTANDING TO LATIN AMERICAN REALITIES:
A DEAFENING CRY POURS FROM THE THROATS OF MILLIONS, ASKING THEIR PASTORS FOR A LIBERATION THAT REACHES THEM FROM NOWHERE ELSE.

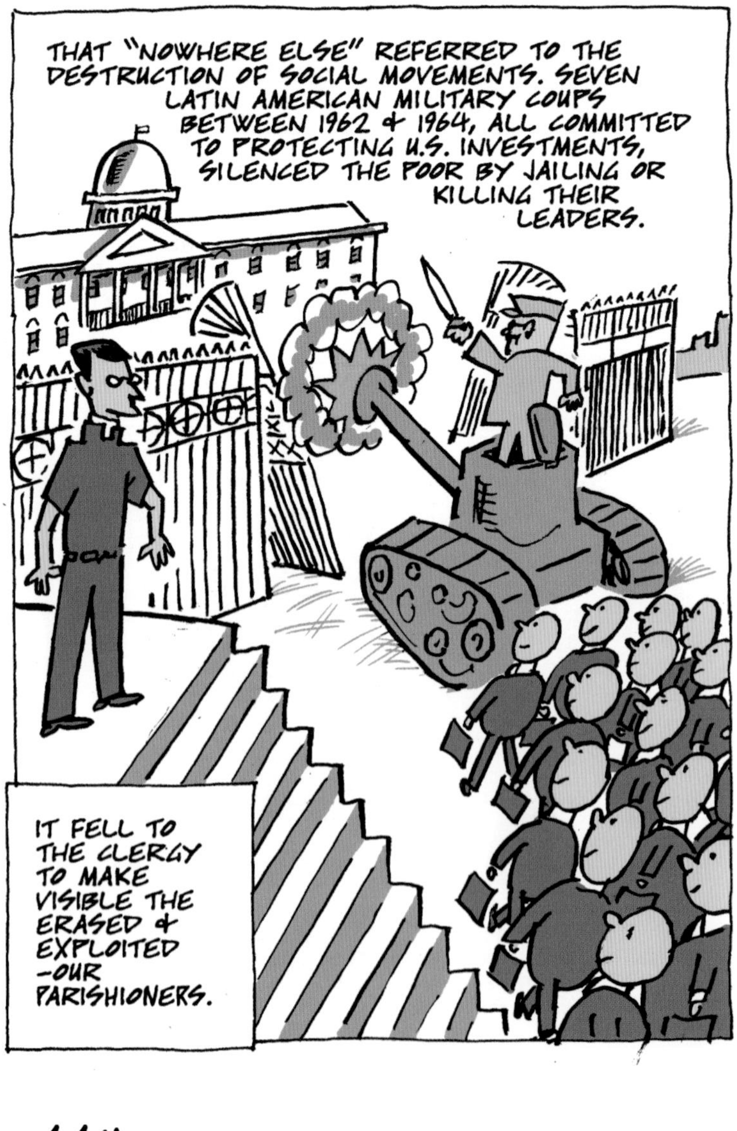
THAT "NOWHERE ELSE" REFERRED TO THE DESTRUCTION OF SOCIAL MOVEMENTS. SEVEN LATIN AMERICAN MILITARY COUPS BETWEEN 1962 & 1964, ALL COMMITTED TO PROTECTING U.S. INVESTMENTS, SILENCED THE POOR BY JAILING OR KILLING THEIR LEADERS.
IT FELL TO THE CLERGY TO MAKE VISIBLE THE ERASED & EXPLOITED -OUR PARISHIONERS.

THIS WAS A BIG CHANGE THAT HAPPENED WHILE I WAS IN LATIN AMERICA. I REMEMBER IN 1964, WHEN I VISITED SOME PRIESTS IN A BARRIO IN CHILE, THEY TOLD ME:

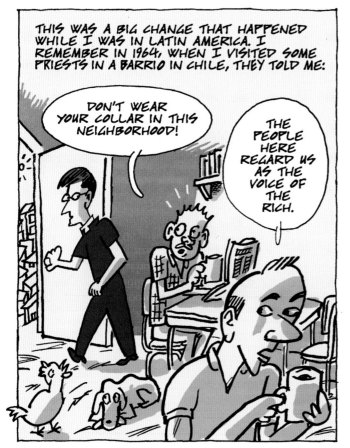

DON'T WEAR YOUR COLLAR IN THIS NEIGHBORHOOD!

THE PEOPLE HERE REGARD US AS THE VOICE OF THE RICH.

BUT IN 1976 SOME OF THESE FELLOWS HELPED SET UP THE "VICARIATE OF SOLIDARITY" TO DEFEND CHILEANS AFTER GENERAL PINOCHET OVERTHREW THE GOVERNMENT & SUPPRESSED ALL THE POPULAR ORGANIZATIONS.

Overnight, the priests have gone from being the enemies of the poor to being their only friends.

BY THIS TIME I WAS TRYING TO START A NEW PARISH IN BOLIVIA'S LARGEST SLUM. EVERY MORNING & EVERY AFTERNOON IN LA PAZ THEY WOULD BURY THE CHILDREN AT A CEMETERY ACROSS FROM MY SHACK.

50% OF BOLIVIAN CHILDREN DIED BEFORE THE AGE OF FIVE.

THE KIND OF MINISTRY I HAD BEEN TAUGHT TO PROVIDE DID NOT INTEREST THESE DESPERATELY POOR PEOPLE. I REALIZED I HAD TO START FROM SCRATCH.

IF I COULD BE PART OF GETTING THEM WHAT THEY NEEDED, I COULD BE TRUSTED.

PART OF MAKING MYSELF USEFUL WAS DOING WHAT I COULD TO DEFEND ACTIVISTS WHO WERE BEING LOCKED UP & TORTURED.

THIS CABRÓN IS A FRIEND OF YOURS? HE WAS HEARD SAYING "DOWN WITH THE GENERALS!"

HE WAS PROBABLY DRUNK.

I HAD TO HIDE MY TRUE FEELINGS OF COURSE. IT WAS A DANGEROUS TIME EVEN FOR CLERGY.

IN EL SALVADOR IN 1980, ARCHBISHOP OSCAR ROMERO CALLED ON GOVERNMENT SOLDIERS IN THE SALVADORAN CIVIL WAR TO REFUSE ANY ORDERS TO SHOOT THEIR "PEASANT BROTHERS."

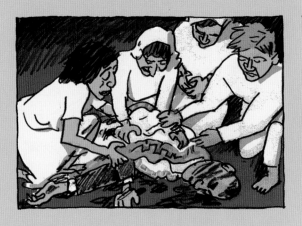

SO THEY KILLED HIM, RIGHT IN THE CATHEDRAL, WHILE HE WAS SAYING MASS.

IN GUATEMALA THAT SAME YEAR, 36 MAYAN PEASANTS WHO HAD OCCUPIED AN EMBASSY TO PROTEST ATTACKS ON THEIR VILLAGES WERE BURNED TO DEATH.

THEIR BISHOP, JUAN GERARDI, ISSUED A REPORT IN 1998, AFTER THE CIVIL WAR ENDED, THAT HELD THE MILITARY RESPONSIBLE FOR THESE & MOST OF THE WAR'S OTHER 20,000 CIVILIAN DEATHS. GERARDI WAS KILLED TWO DAYS LATER.

 THIS WAS NOT A MOVEMENT SEEKING MARTYRDOM. BUT THE JUSTICE COMMITMENT OF THE BASE COMMUNITIES INSPIRED A MURDEROUS RAGE AMONGST THE BENEFICIARIES OF INJUSTICE—THE LATTER-DAY ROMANS, PHARISEES, PUBLICANS, & MONEY-CHANGERS.

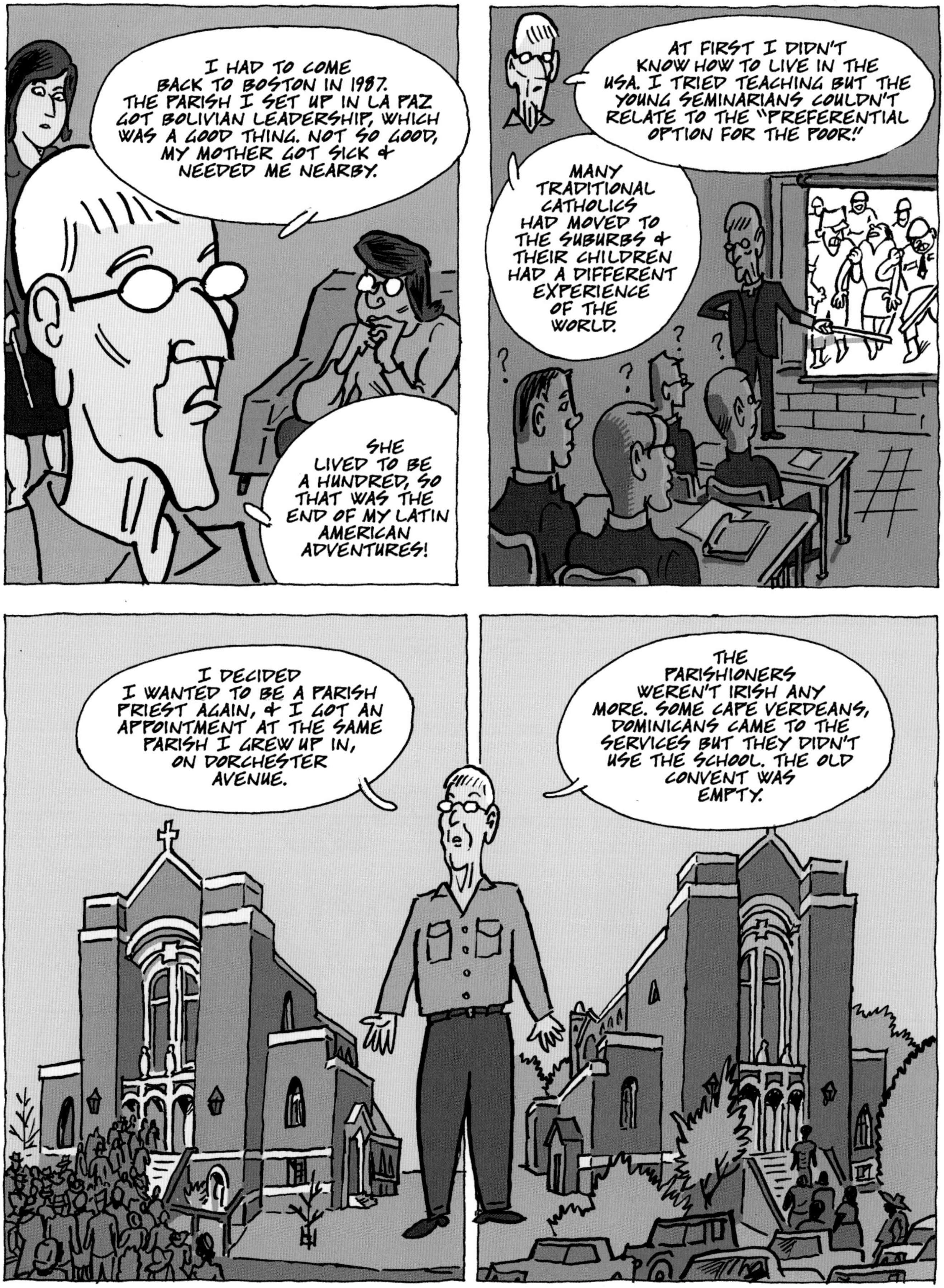
I HAD TO COME BACK TO BOSTON IN 1987. THE PARISH I SET UP IN LA PAZ GOT BOLIVIAN LEADERSHIP, WHICH WAS A GOOD THING. NOT SO GOOD, MY MOTHER GOT SICK & NEEDED ME NEARBY.
SHE LIVED TO BE A HUNDRED, SO THAT WAS THE END OF MY LATIN AMERICAN ADVENTURES!
AT FIRST I DIDN'T KNOW HOW TO LIVE IN THE USA. I TRIED TEACHING BUT THE YOUNG SEMINARIANS COULDN'T RELATE TO THE "PREFERENTIAL OPTION FOR THE POOR!"
MANY TRADITIONAL CATHOLICS HAD MOVED TO THE SUBURBS & THEIR CHILDREN HAD A DIFFERENT EXPERIENCE OF THE WORLD.
I DECIDED I WANTED TO BE A PARISH PRIEST AGAIN, & I GOT AN APPOINTMENT AT THE SAME PARISH I GREW UP IN, ON DORCHESTER AVENUE.
THE PARISHIONERS WEREN'T IRISH ANY MORE. SOME CAPE VERDEANS, DOMINICANS CAME TO THE SERVICES BUT THEY DIDN'T USE THE SCHOOL. THE OLD CONVENT WAS EMPTY.

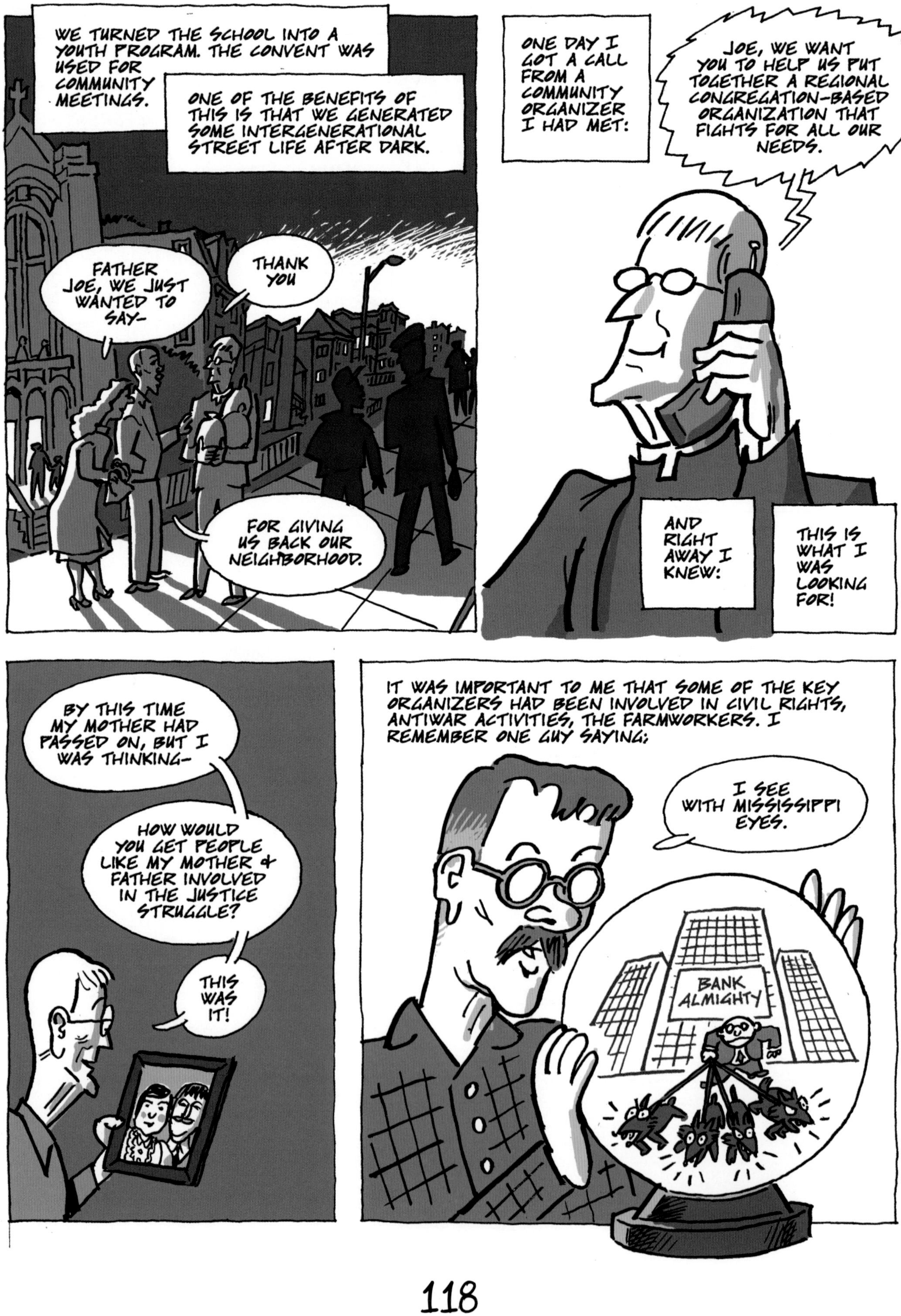
WE TURNED THE SCHOOL INTO A YOUTH PROGRAM. THE CONVENT WAS USED FOR COMMUNITY MEETINGS.
ONE OF THE BENEFITS OF THIS IS THAT WE GENERATED SOME INTERGENERATIONAL STREET LIFE AFTER DARK.
FATHER JOE, WE JUST WANTED TO SAY-
THANK YOU
FOR GIVING US BACK OUR NEIGHBORHOOD.
ONE DAY I GOT A CALL FROM A COMMUNITY ORGANIZER I HAD MET:
JOE, WE WANT YOU TO HELP US PUT TOGETHER A REGIONAL CONGREGATION-BASED ORGANIZATION THAT FIGHTS FOR ALL OUR NEEDS.
AND RIGHT AWAY I KNEW:
THIS IS WHAT I WAS LOOKING FOR!
BY THIS TIME MY MOTHER HAD PASSED ON, BUT I WAS THINKING-
HOW WOULD YOU GET PEOPLE LIKE MY MOTHER & FATHER INVOLVED IN THE JUSTICE STRUGGLE?
THIS WAS IT!
IT WAS IMPORTANT TO ME THAT SOME OF THE KEY ORGANIZERS HAD BEEN INVOLVED IN CIVIL RIGHTS, ANTIWAR ACTIVITIES, THE FARMWORKERS. I REMEMBER ONE GUY SAYING:
I SEE WITH MISSISSIPPI EYES.
BANK ALMIGHTY

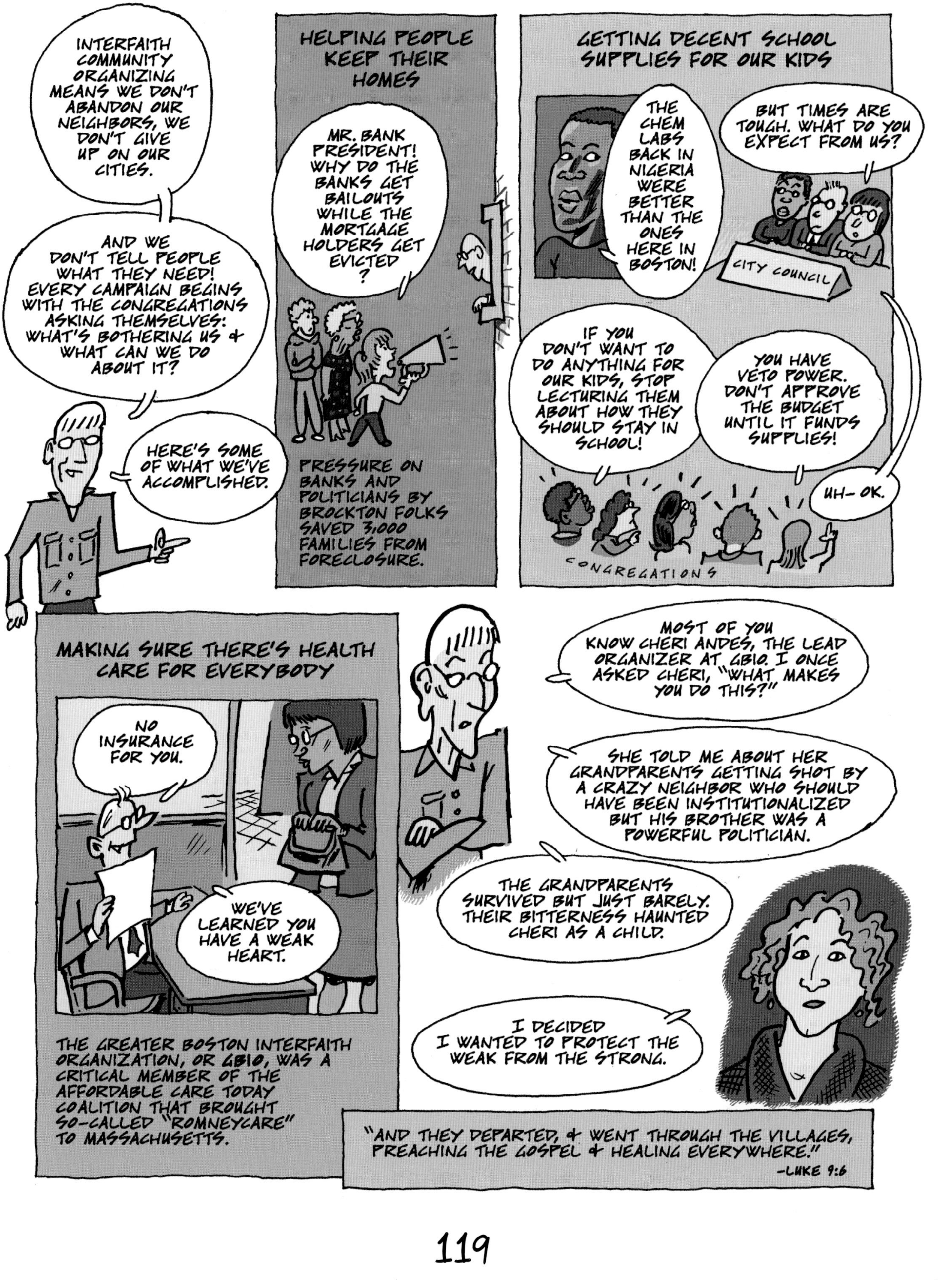
INTERFAITH COMMUNITY ORGANIZING MEANS WE DON'T ABANDON OUR NEIGHBORS, WE DON'T GIVE UP ON OUR CITIES.
AND WE DON'T TELL PEOPLE WHAT THEY NEED! EVERY CAMPAIGN BEGINS WITH THE CONGREGATIONS ASKING THEMSELVES: WHAT'S BOTHERING US & WHAT CAN WE DO ABOUT IT?
HERE'S SOME OF WHAT WE'VE ACCOMPLISHED.
HELPING PEOPLE KEEP THEIR HOMES
MR. BANK PRESIDENT! WHY DO THE BANKS GET BAILOUTS WHILE THE MORTGAGE HOLDERS GET EVICTED?
PRESSURE ON BANKS AND POLITICIANS BY BROCKTON FOLKS SAVED 3,000 FAMILIES FROM FORECLOSURE.
GETTING DECENT SCHOOL SUPPLIES FOR OUR KIDS
THE CHEM LABS BACK IN NIGERIA WERE BETTER THAN THE ONES HERE IN BOSTON!
BUT TIMES ARE TOUGH. WHAT DO YOU EXPECT FROM US?
CITY COUNCIL
IF YOU DON'T WANT TO DO ANYTHING FOR OUR KIDS, STOP LECTURING THEM ABOUT HOW THEY SHOULD STAY IN SCHOOL!
YOU HAVE VETO POWER. DON'T APPROVE THE BUDGET UNTIL IT FUNDS SUPPLIES!
UH- OK.
CONGREGATIONS
MAKING SURE THERE'S HEALTH CARE FOR EVERYBODY
NO INSURANCE FOR YOU.
WE'VE LEARNED YOU HAVE A WEAK HEART.
THE GREATER BOSTON INTERFAITH ORGANIZATION, OR GBIO, WAS A CRITICAL MEMBER OF THE AFFORDABLE CARE TODAY COALITION THAT BROUGHT SO-CALLED "ROMNEYCARE" TO MASSACHUSETTS.
MOST OF YOU KNOW CHERI ANDES, THE LEAD ORGANIZER AT GBIO. I ONCE ASKED CHERI, "WHAT MAKES YOU DO THIS?"
SHE TOLD ME ABOUT HER GRANDPARENTS GETTING SHOT BY A CRAZY NEIGHBOR WHO SHOULD HAVE BEEN INSTITUTIONALIZED BUT HIS BROTHER WAS A POWERFUL POLITICIAN.
THE GRANDPARENTS SURVIVED BUT JUST BARELY. THEIR BITTERNESS HAUNTED CHERI AS A CHILD.
I DECIDED I WANTED TO PROTECT THE WEAK FROM THE STRONG.
"AND THEY DEPARTED, & WENT THROUGH THE VILLAGES, PREACHING THE GOSPEL & HEALING EVERYWHERE."
-LUKE 9:6

# GETTING IN THE WAY:
## PEACEMAKER TEAMS & CONSCIENTIOUS OBJECTORS

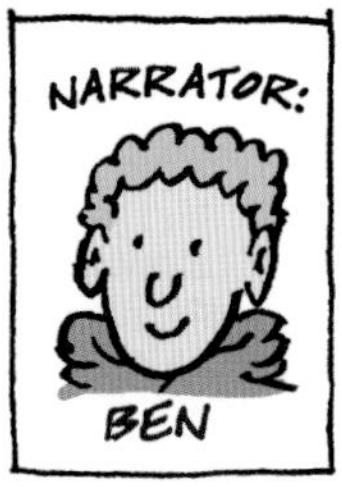
NARRATOR:
BEN

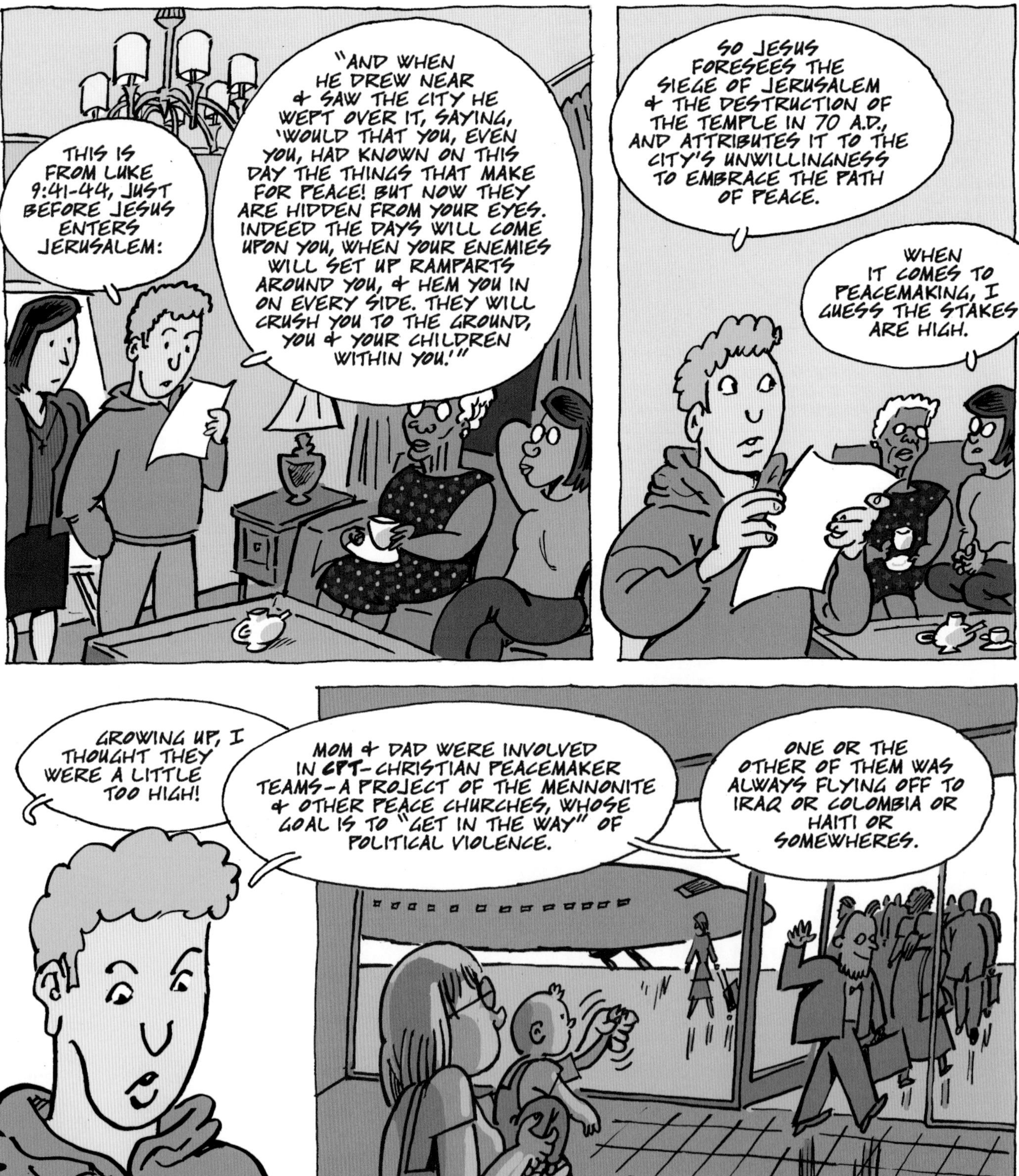
THIS IS FROM LUKE 9:41-44, JUST BEFORE JESUS ENTERS JERUSALEM:
"AND WHEN HE DREW NEAR & SAW THE CITY HE WEPT OVER IT, SAYING, 'WOULD THAT YOU, EVEN YOU, HAD KNOWN ON THIS DAY THE THINGS THAT MAKE FOR PEACE! BUT NOW THEY ARE HIDDEN FROM YOUR EYES. INDEED THE DAYS WILL COME UPON YOU, WHEN YOUR ENEMIES WILL SET UP RAMPARTS AROUND YOU, & HEM YOU IN ON EVERY SIDE. THEY WILL CRUSH YOU TO THE GROUND, YOU & YOUR CHILDREN WITHIN YOU.'"
SO JESUS FORESEES THE SIEGE OF JERUSALEM & THE DESTRUCTION OF THE TEMPLE IN 70 A.D., AND ATTRIBUTES IT TO THE CITY'S UNWILLINGNESS TO EMBRACE THE PATH OF PEACE.
WHEN IT COMES TO PEACEMAKING, I GUESS THE STAKES ARE HIGH.
GROWING UP, I THOUGHT THEY WERE A LITTLE TOO HIGH!
MOM & DAD WERE INVOLVED IN CPT- CHRISTIAN PEACEMAKER TEAMS- A PROJECT OF THE MENNONITE & OTHER PEACE CHURCHES, WHOSE GOAL IS TO "GET IN THE WAY" OF POLITICAL VIOLENCE.
ONE OR THE OTHER OF THEM WAS ALWAYS FLYING OFF TO IRAQ OR COLOMBIA OR HAITI OR SOMEWHERES.

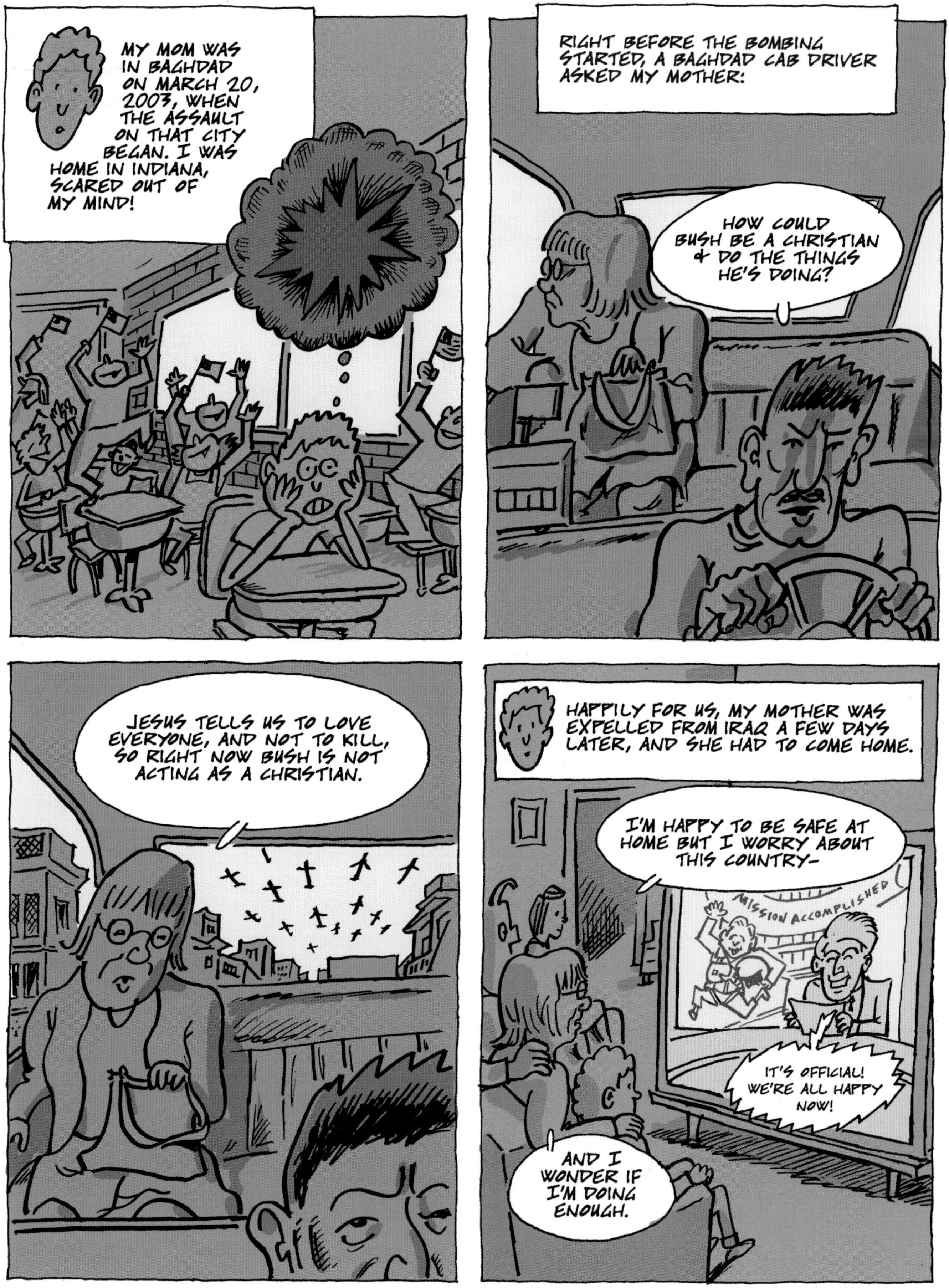
MY MOM WAS IN BAGHDAD ON MARCH 20, 2003, WHEN THE ASSAULT ON THAT CITY BEGAN. I WAS HOME IN INDIANA, SCARED OUT OF MY MIND!
RIGHT BEFORE THE BOMBING STARTED, A BAGHDAD CAB DRIVER ASKED MY MOTHER:
HOW COULD BUSH BE A CHRISTIAN & DO THE THINGS HE'S DOING?
JESUS TELLS US TO LOVE EVERYONE, AND NOT TO KILL, SO RIGHT NOW BUSH IS NOT ACTING AS A CHRISTIAN.
HAPPILY FOR US, MY MOTHER WAS EXPELLED FROM IRAQ A FEW DAYS LATER, AND SHE HAD TO COME HOME.
I'M HAPPY TO BE SAFE AT HOME BUT I WORRY ABOUT THIS COUNTRY-
MISSION ACCOMPLISHED
IT'S OFFICIAL! WE'RE ALL HAPPY NOW!
AND I WONDER IF I'M DOING ENOUGH.

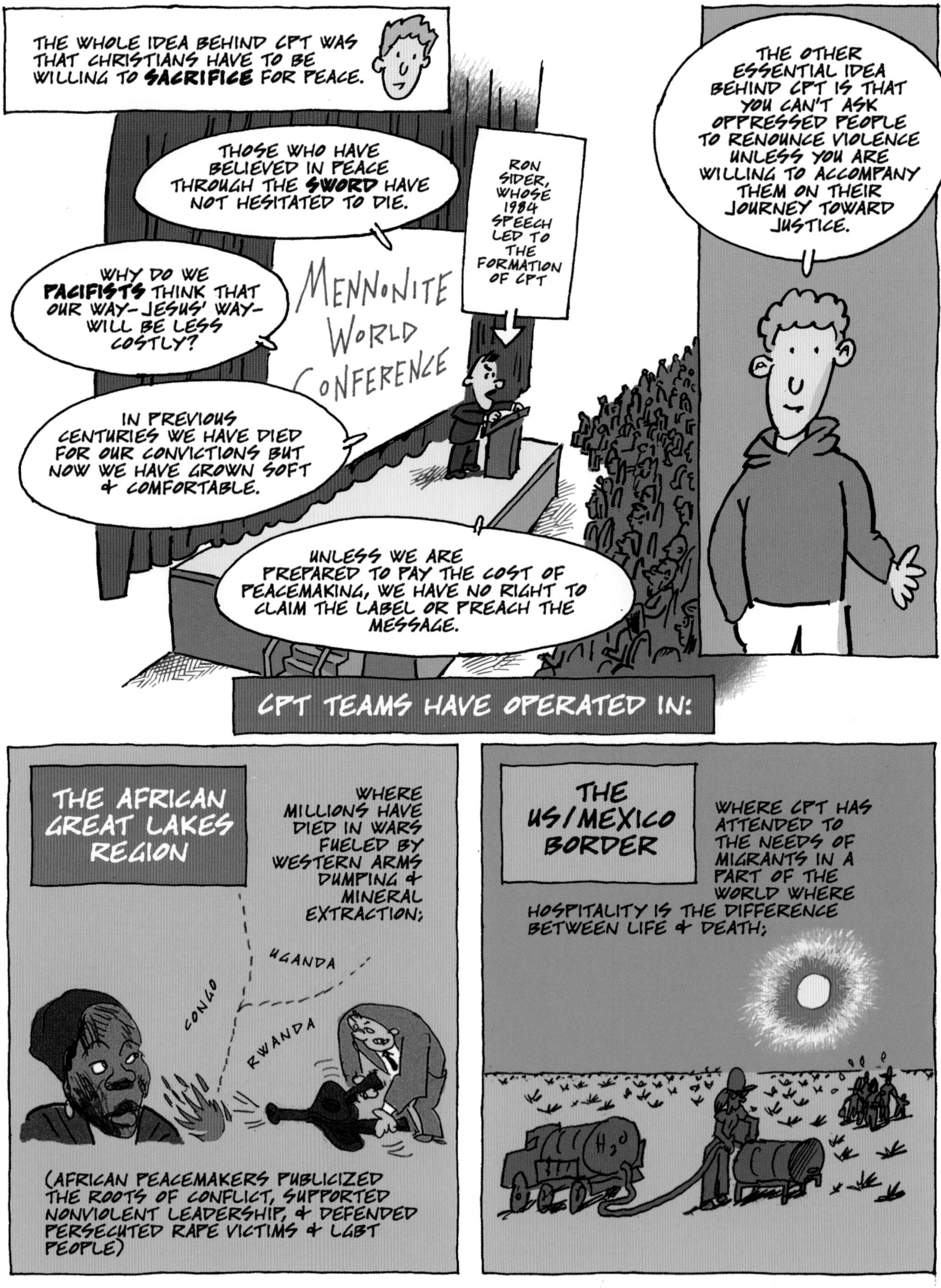
THE WHOLE IDEA BEHIND CPT WAS THAT CHRISTIANS HAVE TO BE WILLING TO SACRIFICE FOR PEACE.
THOSE WHO HAVE BELIEVED IN PEACE THROUGH THE SWORD HAVE NOT HESITATED TO DIE.
RON SIDER, WHOSE 1984 SPEECH LED TO THE FORMATION OF CPT
MENNONITE WORLD CONFERENCE
WHY DO WE PACIFISTS THINK THAT OUR WAY- JESUS' WAY- WILL BE LESS COSTLY?
IN PREVIOUS CENTURIES WE HAVE DIED FOR OUR CONVICTIONS BUT NOW WE HAVE GROWN SOFT & COMFORTABLE.
UNLESS WE ARE PREPARED TO PAY THE COST OF PEACEMAKING, WE HAVE NO RIGHT TO CLAIM THE LABEL OR PREACH THE MESSAGE.
THE OTHER ESSENTIAL IDEA BEHIND CPT IS THAT YOU CAN'T ASK OPPRESSED PEOPLE TO RENOUNCE VIOLENCE UNLESS YOU ARE WILLING TO ACCOMPANY THEM ON THEIR JOURNEY TOWARD JUSTICE.
CPT TEAMS HAVE OPERATED IN:
THE AFRICAN GREAT LAKES REGION
WHERE MILLIONS HAVE DIED IN WARS FUELED BY WESTERN ARMS DUMPING & MINERAL EXTRACTION;
UGANDA
CONGO
RWANDA
(AFRICAN PEACEMAKERS PUBLICIZED THE ROOTS OF CONFLICT, SUPPORTED NONVIOLENT LEADERSHIP, & DEFENDED PERSECUTED RAPE VICTIMS & LGBT PEOPLE)
THE US/MEXICO BORDER
WHERE CPT HAS ATTENDED TO THE NEEDS OF MIGRANTS IN A PART OF THE WORLD WHERE HOSPITALITY IS THE DIFFERENCE BETWEEN LIFE & DEATH;
H₂O

## CPT TEAMS HAVE ALSO OPERATED IN:

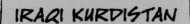

### IRAQI KURDISTAN

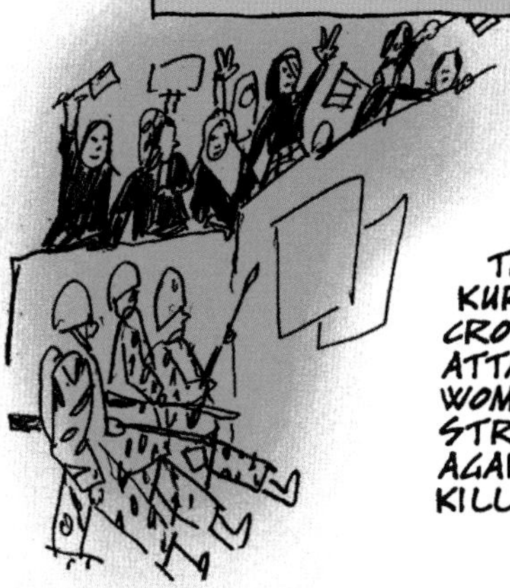

WHERE THE FORMER BAGHDAD TEAM DEFENDS KURDS FACING CROSS-BORDER ATTACKS AND WOMEN STRUGGLING AGAINST HONOR KILLINGS;

### COLOMBIA

WHERE CPT WAS INVITED TO HELP DISPLACED VILLAGERS RETURN TO THEIR ANCESTRAL HOMES DESPITE THREATS FROM PARAMILITARY FORCES CONNECTED TO CORPORATIONS THAT COVET THE LAND;

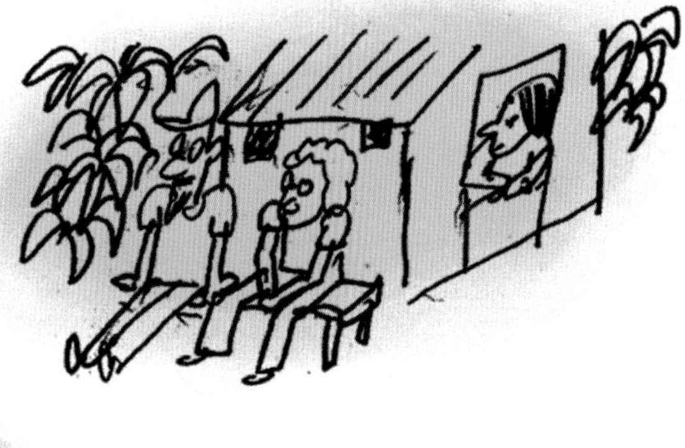

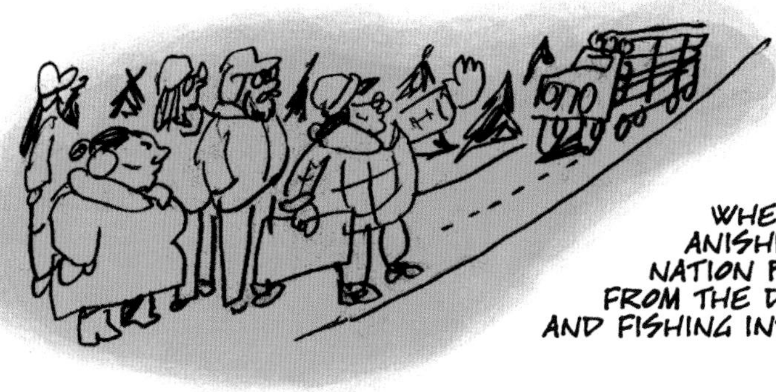

### ABORIGINAL LANDS IN NORTH AMERICA

WHERE CPT WAS INVITED BY ALGONQUIN, ANISHKANABE, LAKOTA, AND OTHER FIRST NATION PEOPLES DEFENDING TRADITIONAL LIFE FROM THE DEPREDATIONS OF LOGGING, MINING, AND FISHING INTERESTS;

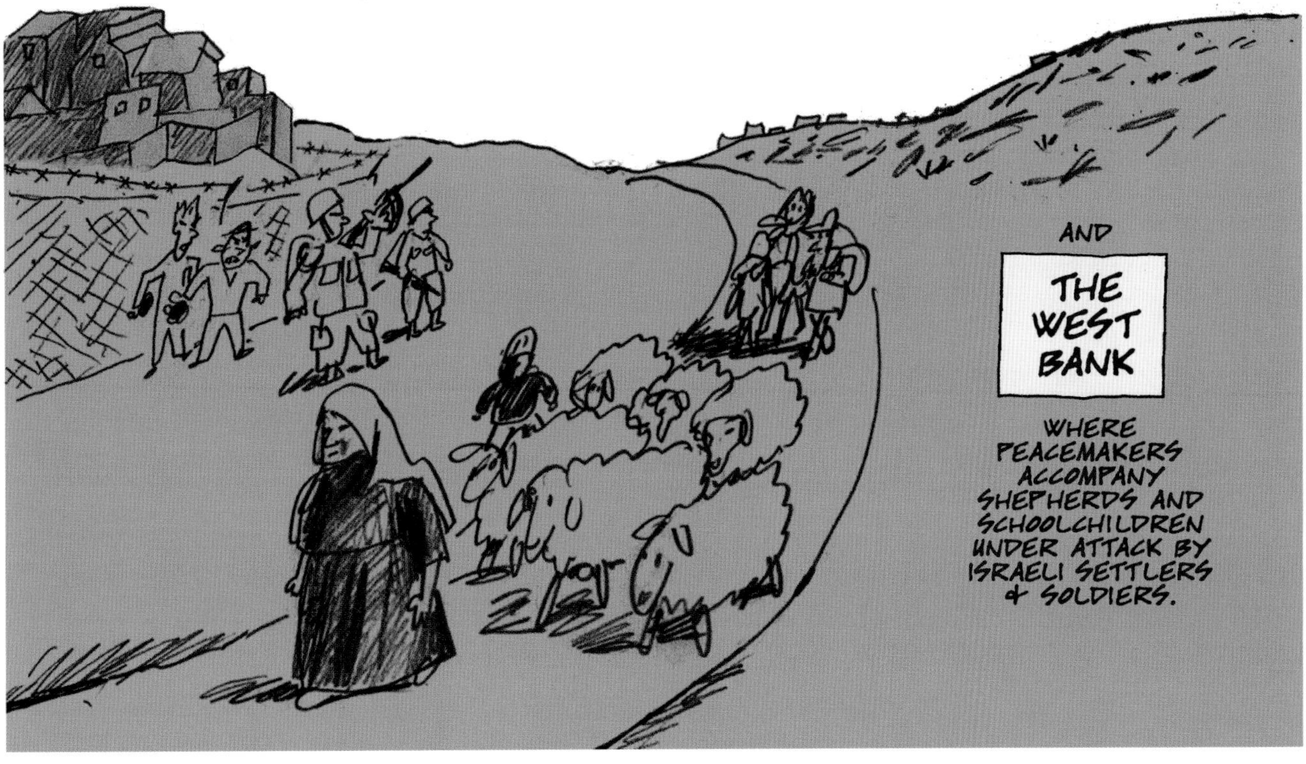
AND
THE WEST BANK
WHERE PEACEMAKERS ACCOMPANY SHEPHERDS AND SCHOOLCHILDREN UNDER ATTACK BY ISRAELI SETTLERS & SOLDIERS.

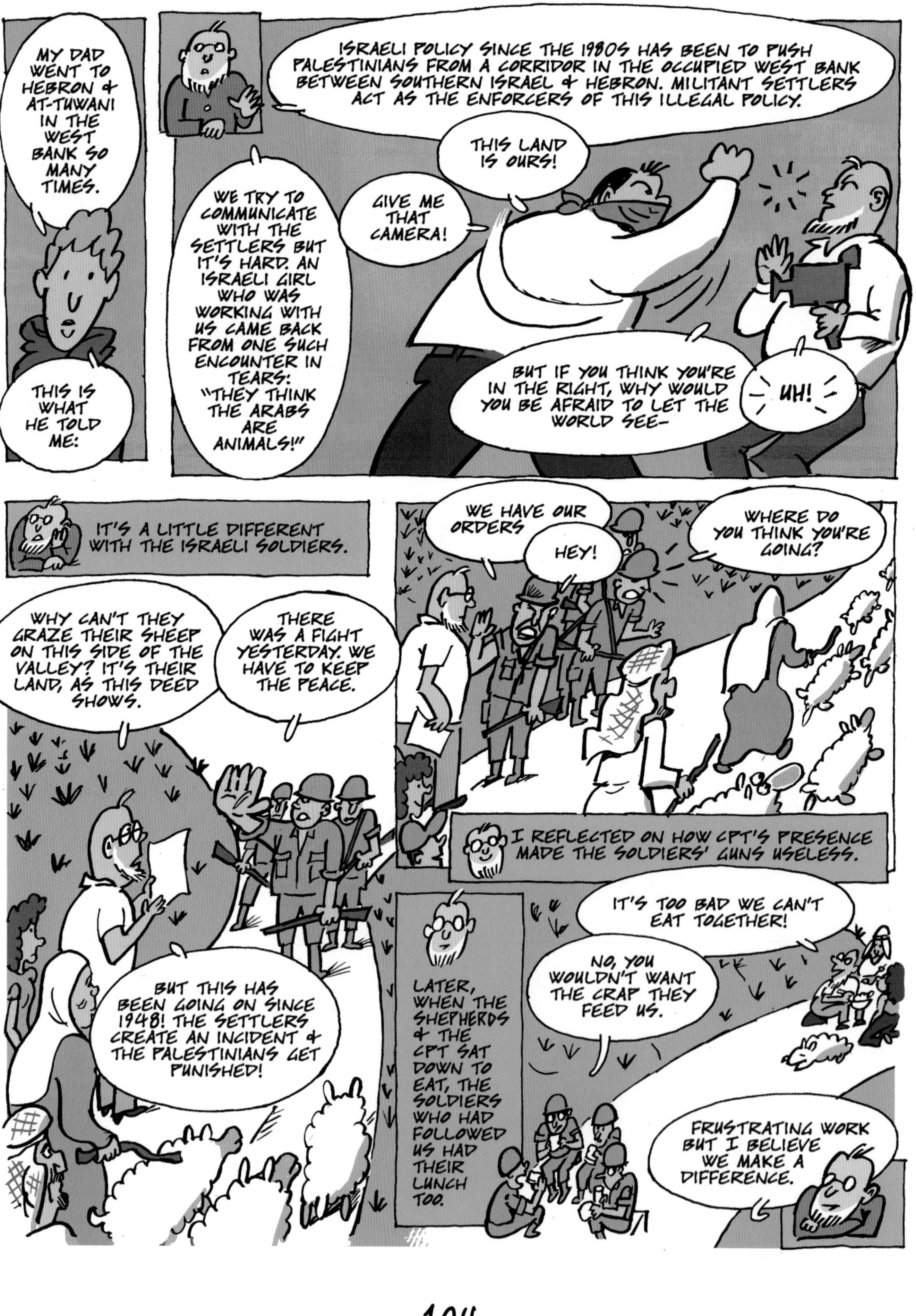
MY DAD WENT TO HEBRON & AT-TUWANI IN THE WEST BANK SO MANY TIMES.
THIS IS WHAT HE TOLD ME:
ISRAELI POLICY SINCE THE 1980S HAS BEEN TO PUSH PALESTINIANS FROM A CORRIDOR IN THE OCCUPIED WEST BANK BETWEEN SOUTHERN ISRAEL & HEBRON. MILITANT SETTLERS ACT AS THE ENFORCERS OF THIS ILLEGAL POLICY.
WE TRY TO COMMUNICATE WITH THE SETTLERS BUT IT'S HARD. AN ISRAELI GIRL WHO WAS WORKING WITH US CAME BACK FROM ONE SUCH ENCOUNTER IN TEARS: "THEY THINK THE ARABS ARE ANIMALS!"
THIS LAND IS OURS!
GIVE ME THAT CAMERA!
BUT IF YOU THINK YOU'RE IN THE RIGHT, WHY WOULD YOU BE AFRAID TO LET THE WORLD SEE-
UH!
IT'S A LITTLE DIFFERENT WITH THE ISRAELI SOLDIERS.
WHY CAN'T THEY GRAZE THEIR SHEEP ON THIS SIDE OF THE VALLEY? IT'S THEIR LAND, AS THIS DEED SHOWS.
THERE WAS A FIGHT YESTERDAY. WE HAVE TO KEEP THE PEACE.
BUT THIS HAS BEEN GOING ON SINCE 1948! THE SETTLERS CREATE AN INCIDENT & THE PALESTINIANS GET PUNISHED!
WE HAVE OUR ORDERS
HEY!
WHERE DO YOU THINK YOU'RE GOING?
I REFLECTED ON HOW CPT'S PRESENCE MADE THE SOLDIERS' GUNS USELESS.
LATER, WHEN THE SHEPHERDS & THE CPT SAT DOWN TO EAT, THE SOLDIERS WHO HAD FOLLOWED US HAD THEIR LUNCH TOO.
IT'S TOO BAD WE CAN'T EAT TOGETHER!
NO, YOU WOULDN'T WANT THE CRAP THEY FEED US.
FRUSTRATING WORK BUT I BELIEVE WE MAKE A DIFFERENCE.

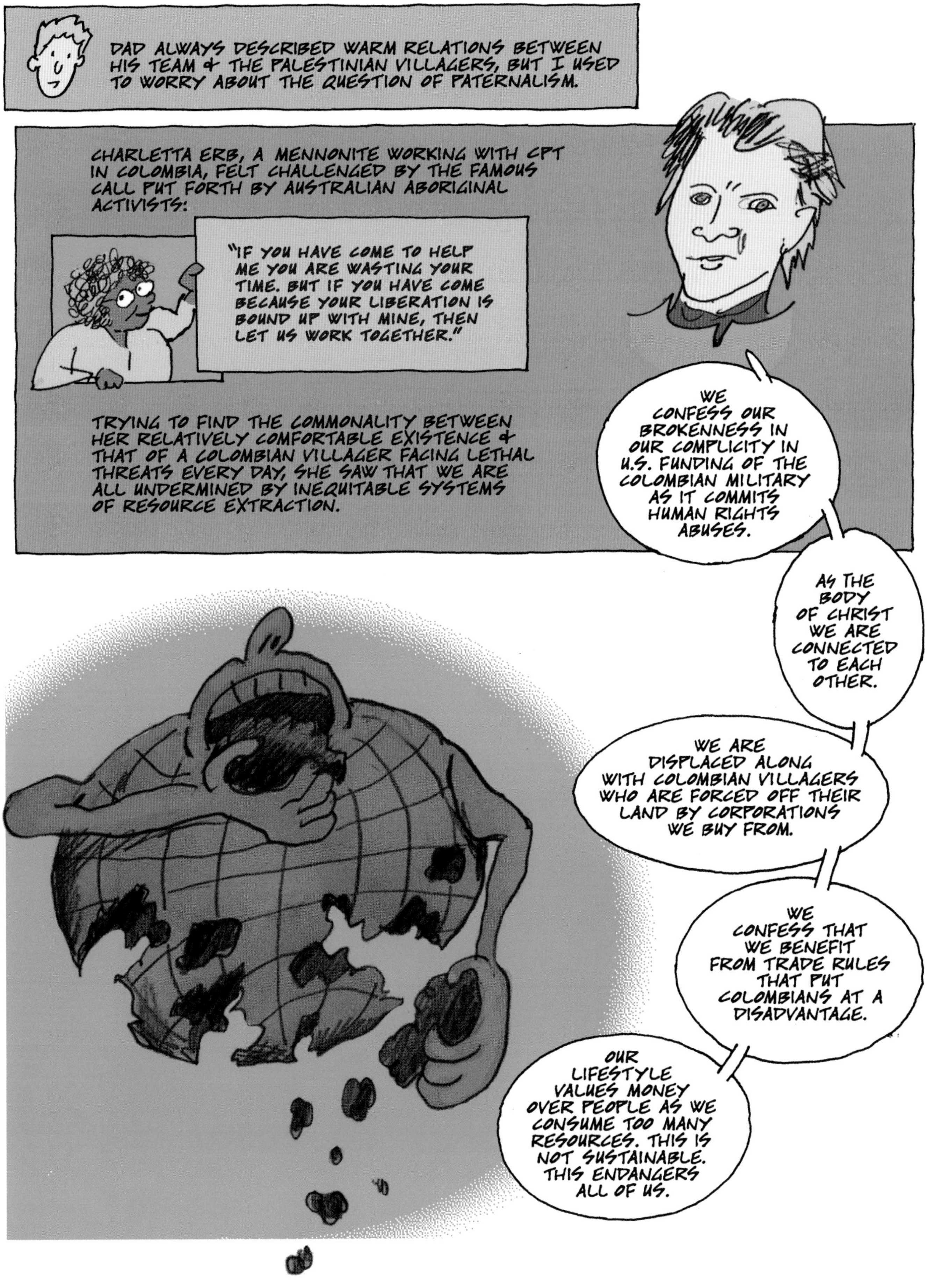
DAD ALWAYS DESCRIBED WARM RELATIONS BETWEEN HIS TEAM & THE PALESTINIAN VILLAGERS, BUT I USED TO WORRY ABOUT THE QUESTION OF PATERNALISM.
CHARLETTA ERB, A MENNONITE WORKING WITH CPT IN COLOMBIA, FELT CHALLENGED BY THE FAMOUS CALL PUT FORTH BY AUSTRALIAN ABORIGINAL ACTIVISTS:
"IF YOU HAVE COME TO HELP ME YOU ARE WASTING YOUR TIME. BUT IF YOU HAVE COME BECAUSE YOUR LIBERATION IS BOUND UP WITH MINE, THEN LET US WORK TOGETHER."
TRYING TO FIND THE COMMONALITY BETWEEN HER RELATIVELY COMFORTABLE EXISTENCE & THAT OF A COLOMBIAN VILLAGER FACING LETHAL THREATS EVERY DAY, SHE SAW THAT WE ARE ALL UNDERMINED BY INEQUITABLE SYSTEMS OF RESOURCE EXTRACTION.
WE CONFESS OUR BROKENNESS IN OUR COMPLICITY IN U.S. FUNDING OF THE COLOMBIAN MILITARY AS IT COMMITS HUMAN RIGHTS ABUSES.
AS THE BODY OF CHRIST WE ARE CONNECTED TO EACH OTHER.
WE ARE DISPLACED ALONG WITH COLOMBIAN VILLAGERS WHO ARE FORCED OFF THEIR LAND BY CORPORATIONS WE BUY FROM.
WE CONFESS THAT WE BENEFIT FROM TRADE RULES THAT PUT COLOMBIANS AT A DISADVANTAGE.
OUR LIFESTYLE VALUES MONEY OVER PEOPLE AS WE CONSUME TOO MANY RESOURCES. THIS IS NOT SUSTAINABLE. THIS ENDANGERS ALL OF US.

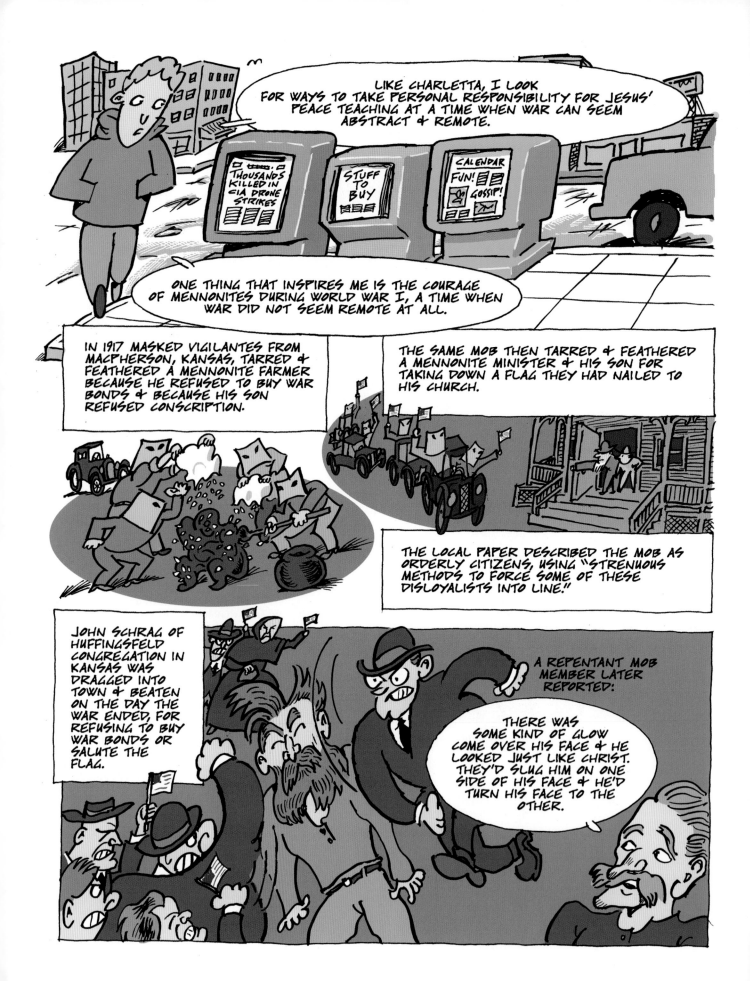

LIKE CHARLETTA, I LOOK FOR WAYS TO TAKE PERSONAL RESPONSIBILITY FOR JESUS' PEACE TEACHING AT A TIME WHEN WAR CAN SEEM ABSTRACT & REMOTE.

THOUSANDS KILLED IN CIA DRONE STRIKES

STUFF TO BUY

CALENDAR FUN! GOSSIP!

ONE THING THAT INSPIRES ME IS THE COURAGE OF MENNONITES DURING WORLD WAR I, A TIME WHEN WAR DID NOT SEEM REMOTE AT ALL.

IN 1917 MASKED VIGILANTES FROM MACPHERSON, KANSAS, TARRED & FEATHERED A MENNONITE FARMER BECAUSE HE REFUSED TO BUY WAR BONDS & BECAUSE HIS SON REFUSED CONSCRIPTION.

THE SAME MOB THEN TARRED & FEATHERED A MENNONITE MINISTER & HIS SON FOR TAKING DOWN A FLAG THEY HAD NAILED TO HIS CHURCH.

THE LOCAL PAPER DESCRIBED THE MOB AS ORDERLY CITIZENS, USING "STRENUOUS METHODS TO FORCE SOME OF THESE DISLOYALISTS INTO LINE."

JOHN SCHRAG OF HUFFINGSFELD CONGREGATION IN KANSAS WAS DRAGGED INTO TOWN & BEATEN ON THE DAY THE WAR ENDED, FOR REFUSING TO BUY WAR BONDS OR SALUTE THE FLAG.

A REPENTANT MOB MEMBER LATER REPORTED:

THERE WAS SOME KIND OF GLOW COME OVER HIS FACE & HE LOOKED JUST LIKE CHRIST. THEY'D SLUG HIM ON ONE SIDE OF HIS FACE & HE'D TURN HIS FACE TO THE OTHER.

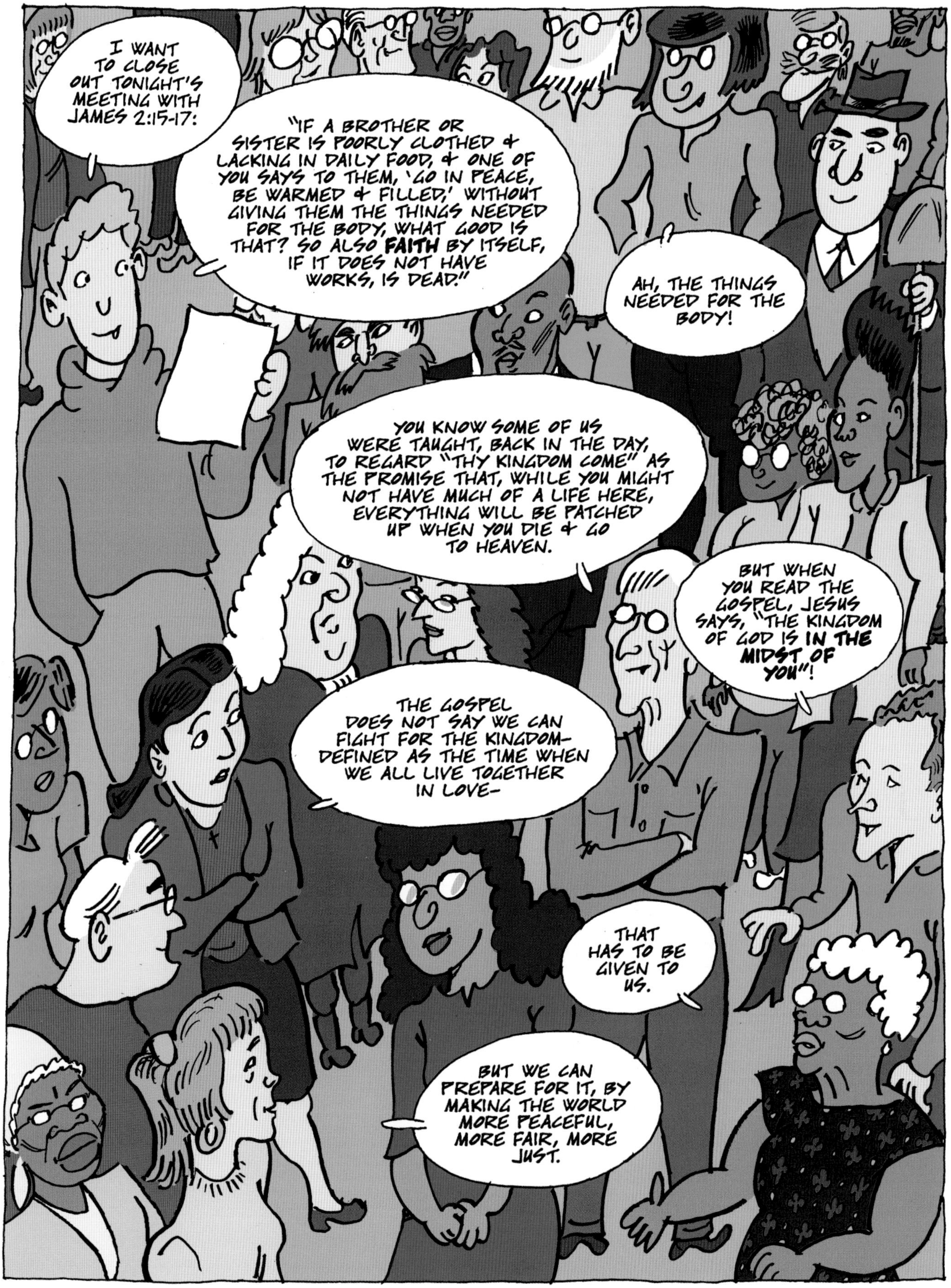
I WANT TO CLOSE OUT TONIGHT'S MEETING WITH JAMES 2:15-17:
"IF A BROTHER OR SISTER IS POORLY CLOTHED & LACKING IN DAILY FOOD, & ONE OF YOU SAYS TO THEM, 'GO IN PEACE, BE WARMED & FILLED,' WITHOUT GIVING THEM THE THINGS NEEDED FOR THE BODY, WHAT GOOD IS THAT? SO ALSO **FAITH** BY ITSELF, IF IT DOES NOT HAVE WORKS, IS DEAD."
AH, THE THINGS NEEDED FOR THE BODY!
YOU KNOW SOME OF US WERE TAUGHT, BACK IN THE DAY, TO REGARD "THY KINGDOM COME" AS THE PROMISE THAT, WHILE YOU MIGHT NOT HAVE MUCH OF A LIFE HERE, EVERYTHING WILL BE PATCHED UP WHEN YOU DIE & GO TO HEAVEN.
BUT WHEN YOU READ THE GOSPEL, JESUS SAYS, "THE KINGDOM OF GOD IS **IN THE MIDST OF YOU**"!
THE GOSPEL DOES NOT SAY WE CAN FIGHT FOR THE KINGDOM- DEFINED AS THE TIME WHEN WE ALL LIVE TOGETHER IN LOVE-
THAT HAS TO BE GIVEN TO US.
BUT WE CAN PREPARE FOR IT, BY MAKING THE WORLD MORE PEACEFUL, MORE FAIR, MORE JUST.
NICK THORKELSON

# CONTRIBUTORS

**PAUL BUHLE**, an officer of a local Christian Youth Fellowship (CYF) in his teenage years, has been active in social movements since that time and has contributed to many publications, including the *Nation*, the *Guardian*, *Journal of American History*, *San Francisco Chronicle*, *Chronicle of Higher Education*, and *Village Voice*. Retired as senior lecturer at Brown University, he has written or edited more than forty books, including biographies of William Appleman Williams and C. L. R. James. His graphic works have included comic art adaptations of work by Studs Terkel and Howard Zinn. He lives in Madison, Wisconsin.

**SABRINA JONES** began creating comics on social justice for the comics anthology *World War 3 Illustrated*. She has worked with Paul Buhle on radical history titles such as *Wobblies!*; *Isadora Duncan: A Graphic Biography*; *Studs Terkel's Working*; *FDR and the New Deal for Beginners*; *Yiddishkeit*; and *Bohemians*. She shed graphic light on justice issues for the Real Cost of Prisons Project and *Race to Incarcerate: A Graphic Retelling*. Sabrina is a member of New York City's Fifteenth Street Meeting of the Religious Society of Friends (Quakers) where she facilitates a Bible study group and volunteers at a homeless shelter.

**GARY DUMM**, a frequent collaborator with the late Harvey Pekar, was the principal artist for *Students for a Democratic Society: a Graphic History* and has contributed to many comic art anthologies including *The Beats*; *Studs Terkel's Working: a Graphic Adaptation*; and *Yiddishkeit*. He is currently working assiduously to complete *A Simple, Ordinary Man*, Scott MacGregor's historical epic concerning race relations, fresh water, and workers' rights in Cleveland, Ohio, circa 1916. His work has also been published in Cleveland newspapers, the *New York Times*, *Entertainment Weekly*, and France's *Le Monde*. His wife and colorist Laura Dumm, a painter and book designer, has added color to many of his comic projects, including some *American Splendor* promotional art. They live in Cleveland, Ohio.

**NICK THORKELSON** is a veteran community activist and comic artist with contributions to many anthologies. *The Underhanded History of the USA* (in collaboration with Jim O'Brien) was a full-length counter-history to mainstream versions. His other work includes *Economic Meltdown Funnies*, *Fortune Cookies*, and *The Comic Strip of Neoliberalism*. Recently he completed a twenty-three-minute animation, *Où est Fleuri Rose?* in collaboration with composer Mark Warhol and animator Amy MacDonald. He lives in Boston, Massachusetts.